AF540222

Multiculturalism in India and Europe

Multiculturalism in India and Europe

Edited by
Rajendra K. Jain

Multiculturalism in India and Europe
Edited by Rajendra K. Jain

ISBN 978-93-5002-279-5

First Published, 2014

Published by
AAKAR BOOKS
28 E Pocket IV, Mayur Vihar Phase I, Delhi 110 091
Phone : 011 2279 5505 Telefax : 011 2279 5641
info@aakarbooks.com; www.aakarbooks.com

Printed at
Saurabh Printers Pvt. Ltd., A 16, Sector IV, Noida

Contents

Contributors

Imtiaz Ahmad was formerly Professor of Political Sociology, School of Social Sciences, Jawaharlal Nehru University, New Delhi.

Divya Balan is a PhD Scholar, Centre for European Studies, School of International Studies, Jawaharlal Nehru University, New Delhi.

Anuradha M. Chenoy is Professor, Centre for Russian and Central Asian Studies, School of International Studies, Jawaharlal Nehru University, New Delhi.

Sara Cosemans holds a postgraduate degree in History from Katholieke Universiteit Leuven, Belgium.

Michael Dusche is currently Fellow at the Centre for Developing Societies, New Delhi. He was formerly Senior Assistant Professor and DAAD Lecturer at the Centre for German Studies, Jawaharlal Nehru University, New Delhi (2000-2005) and Fellow at the Jawaharlal Nehru Institute of Advanced Study, JNU (2009-2010).

Idesbald Goddeeris is Associate Professor, Faculty of Arts, Katholieke Universiteit Leuven, Belgium and Coordinator of Leuven India Focus Chair of the Leuven Centre for Global Governance Studies.

Dipankar Gupta was formerly Professor, Centre for the Study of Social Systems, School of Social Sciences, Jawaharlal Nehru University, New Delhi. He has held several visiting

Professorships and Senior Fellowships in universities in the United States, the United Kingdom and Western Europe.

Rajendra K. Jain is Professor, Centre for European Studies, School of International Studies, Jawaharlal Nehru University, New Delhi and the first and only Jean Monnet Chair in India. He is also Adjunct Professor (Research), Monash European and EU Studies Centre, Monash University, Melbourne. He was formerly Visiting Humboldt Foundation Professor at Constance, Freiburg, Leipzig and Tübingen universities in Germany and Visiting Professor, the Maison des Sciences de l'Homme, Paris, and the Asia-Europe Institute, University of Malaya. He is the author/editor of over 30 books and 100 journal articles/book chapters.

Imre Lázár is Senior Advisor, Department for International Cultural Relations, Ministry of Human Resources, Hungary. He was formerly Director, Hungarian Information Centre, New Delhi.

Bhaswati Sarkar is Assistant Professor, Centre for European Studies, School of International Studies, Jawaharlal Nehru University, New Delhi.

Sheetal Sharma is Assistant Professor, Centre for European Studies, School of International Studies, Jawaharlal Nehru University, New Delhi.

Introduction

Multiculturalism emerged as a response to monocultural policies and practices during colonization. It was "critical of and resistant to the necessarily reductive imperatives of monocultural assimilation".[1] Contemporary literature tends to regard multiculturalism primarily as a political strategy or a policy in practice in various multicultural societies like India, France, Germany, the United Kingdom, and the United States. There is, Will Kymlicka argues, "no universally accepted definition of multiculturalism. The complexity of phenomena of multiculturalism cannot be reduced to just a single policy or principle".[2] There are diverse perspectives and interpretations of the concept and policy of multiculturalism, incorporating political, social, cultural elements in varying combinations. At one end of the spectrum, there are staunch advocates of multiculturalism and on the other, there are critics who regard multiculturalism to be irrelevant and counterproductive. Other perspectives of multiculturalism include those who feel that multicultural policy has been forced upon people. Yet others regard multiculturalism to be at the very root of the process of eroding a sense of belonging that ensures minority attachment and loyalty.[3]

There are, according to Peter McLaren, four types of multiculturalism, viz. conservative multiculturalism, liberal multiculturalism, left liberal multiculturalism, and critical multiculturalism.[4] Conservative multiculturalism seeks to contain cultural diversity and preserve the status quo. It is an ideology of assimilation dominated by racist ideals wherein other ethnic groups and minorities are reduced to mere ''add-ons'' to the dominant culture.[5] Liberal multiculturalism recognizes the existence of inequality between different cultural communities. Its proponents, however, maintain that inequality is more a consequence of the lack of social and educational opportunities rather than cultural differences. To them, equality in society can be achieved by providing equal social, educational and economic opportunities to all individuals rather than giving special rights to minorities.[6]

Left-liberal multiculturalism regards cultural differences as an "essence" that exists independently of history, culture, and power. It tends to disassociate asymmetry from social and historical circumstances and constructions dominated by the majority. Its main emphasis is on the personal, rather than the collective, level.[7]

Criticizing the conservative, liberal, and left-liberal form of multiculturalism, McLaren suggests the adoption of critical-resistance multiculturalism based on both neo-Marxist and post-structuralist ideas.[8] Conservatives and Liberals, according to him, emphasize ''sameness'' whereas the Left-Liberals stress difference. The differences and conflicts emanating from these differences like race, religion, language, class or gender, he argues, are a consequence of larger social struggles over signs and meanings. They are "essentially unstable and shifting and can only be temporarily fixed, depending on how they are articulated within particular discursive and historical struggles".[9] Culture, according to critical multiculturalism, can never be "non-conflictual, harmonious and consensual".[10] Critical multiculturalism, therefore, aims for attaining social justice and equality in a given society.

The preservation of cultural identity and its legitimate recognition is an important challenge in all multi-ethnic societies. A formidable challenge for such societies is how they accommodate cultural differences and to what extent they recognize minority groups and their identities.[11] Each society's response to the challenge of diversity depends on factors like the history of migration to the host country, the cultural gap between two cultures, the political will of the host country, and acceptance by the masses.

This volume begins by presenting a broad overview of the actors and factors that have played an important role in the success and/or failure of multiculturalism in contemporary India and Europe. In the first chapter, Sheetal Sharma argues that the ethno-cultural diversity of India and Europe not only presents interesting patterns of unity amidst diversity, but also poses challenges of the social integration of the "other". While India has been culturally diverse since ages, multiculturalism in Europe is the result of migration. India's relative success in the management of cultural plurality since Independence, she concludes, can be attributed to a combination of political, economic, and socio-cultural forces that have been significant in recognizing and providing legitimacy to cultural diversity. In the European Union, on the other hand, multiculturalism has largely failed as a policy for the management of cultural diversity.

Bhawati Sarkar analyzes why India appears to be more at ease with diversity in spite of all its problems. This, she elaborates, is largely the result of its constitutional vision and the adoption of liberal democratic principles. European states, on the other hand, seem to be struggling. The foundational differences, especially in West European states, were accommodated in the national imagination through citizenship, a civic understanding of the nation, and devolution of power. However, even there it has not gone completely unchallenged as is evident from the cases of Northern Ireland, Scotland, Basque and Catalonia. The current accommodation struggle that European states confront is primarily sourced by diversity that is recent and ongoing as a result of migration. Acceptance of diversity in modern secular Europe, she argues, is possible if it fits in its model of growth and development. In India, on the other hand, diversity is integral to its self-understanding.

In Chapter 3, Sheetal Sharma attempts a sociological exploration of plausible sources of trans-cultural collective bonds between cultures and communities, and how these can be formed, strengthened, and sustained for effective management of cultural diversity in multicultural societies. Drawing on similarities and differences between India and Europe, she examines the discourse and challenges in promoting social integration among culturally diverse groups in multicultural societies. She highlights the nature of conflict generated during interaction of culturally diverse groups and configure forces that might foster social integration in multicultural societies. Promoting integration in socially and culturally diverse societies, Sharma concludes, calls for designing methods of integration which foster a feeling of belongingness to a cohesive social "whole" among people "from below", along with, if not over and above, their specific cultural identities.

The introduction of the term "multiculturalism" in Europe, Michael Dusche argues, marks the passage from immigration perceived only as economic and temporary to a permanent presence of populations. Since the terrorist attacks of New York and Washington on 11 September 2001, multiculturalism was perceived as only perpetuating cultural minority identities, which were perceived as "an obstacle in the way of integration rather than a potential value" in them. Thus, the multiculturalist discourse in France and Germany while staying within the framework of the respective constitutional fundamentals of these two countries is only meant to sensitise the existing constitutional set-up to the needs of the new residents. Egalitarian promises in France, he maintains, risk becoming farcical in the face of prevailing racist tendencies in French society. In the end, it turns out that neither the French republican nor the German communitarian model are "ideal" for dealing with the problems posed by migration into continental Europe. The middle way, he feels, seems to be a notion of inclusion on the basis of a liberally interpreted common legal order. Unlike in France, Dusche maintains, culture was at the basis of the German nation, not republican self-government, for a common culture seemed to be there before popular sovereignty could even be thought of. In terms of the need "to rethink and possibly redefine the relationship between the liberal democratic state and the various religious communities," Dusche argues, "the growing Muslim community offers controversial material for debate since they conform less to the occidentalist view of how religious communities should be organised".[14]

Imtiaz Ahmed maintains that contemporary academic discourse on multiculturalism as a theory of democracy and citizenship has received little attention in India. There has also been no serious attempt, he feels, to theorize the idea of multicultural democracy. The whole discourse, he maintains, has been centred on a single fundamental difference between pluralism and multiculturalism. This approach, he points out, is flawed since it ignored the differences between the societies where multiculturalism evolved as an ideology of the state that guarantee democracy. The fundamental difference is that pluralism is silent on the question of the nature of relationship between different pluralities whereas multiculturalism is concerned with the issue of mutual interrelationships among different sorts of pluralities that existing in modern societies. Multiculturalism is about equality and it raises such questions like whether different pluralities can coexist as equals in both public and private domains. Ahmed offers a concise comparative analysis of the historical roots of plurality in both Europe and India. The prospect of intercultural understanding and participation of the minorities in governance, he concludes, is a crucial requisite for a successful multiculturalism to be established in India as well as Europe.

In the next chapter, Dipankar Gupta provides a critique of the soft secularist stand taken by Indian national leaders on various religious community issues. He defines "soft secularism" as a cultivated disposition which is linked to tolerance, fraternity, enlightened thinking and fellow feeling. But after the Gujarat carnage of 2002, he feels that the importance of hard secularism as the only valid form of secularism for modern times cannot be overestimated. He argues that the sectarians of different faiths not only need each other to demonise, but they often admire each other. That is why "a hard and intolerant secularism should replace soft secularism and the most appropriate secular response when sectarians indulge in violence would be to punish them by observing the due process of law". Cultural differences, he asserts, do not lead to cultural conflicts unless there must be the tacit or active support from the state and the administrative machinery. Gupta also argues that riots do not occur because of structural imperatives or social compulsions. Riots do not just happen, they are created. As a confidence-building measure, he asserts, hard and intolerant secularism should replace soft secularism to stand a chance against sectarians. Only that secularism, he concludes, will work which makes religious passions irrelevant to the political discourse. This can happen when the citizens are at the centre and become more vigilant and alert to give strength to the democratic system.

Idesbald Goddeeris and Sara Cosemans discuss Indian migration to the European continent from a historical perspective and highlight its diversity and the challenges they post for India and Europe. The number of other Indians has also increased dramatically over the last few decades. The diversity of Indian migration to the European continent is so vast in terms of migration process, reasons for migration, the settlement pattern, and their dispersal across Europe. Variety is also visible in the professions executed by Indian migrants and in the ways how individual European countries hosted immigrants. In Europe, Indians also do not only identify with India but also, and increasingly, with their ethnicity, religion, or state. The authors discuss the impact of India's diaspora policy on Indian migrants. The authors conclude that the present trends of migration confirm that migration will not be stopped and the diversity characterizing Indian migration will expand further across the European continent in the future.

Divya Balan discusses how Britain has experimented with various policies since the introduction of a policy of multiculturalism and assimilation in the 1960s. She discusses the changes in British policy in the aftermath of the terrorist attacks of 9/11 and 7/7, which transformed the contours of the contemporary integration debate towards the issues of religion and ethnicity from the traditional focus on race and race relations. As a result, multiculturalism as the official policy was described as a failure and the policy of integration and community cohesion was introduced. The failure to integrate immigrants in British society, she argues, does not necessarily reflect the shortcomings of the policy of multiculturalism, but its poor implementation. The inherent inequality and systemic institutional racism that exists in the Britain, she argues, is the primary barrier to integration rather than the strict adherence of ethnic and cultural identities by immigrant communities. The policy of multiculturalism, she suggests, has to be re-invented in Britain by fostering greater intercultural dialogue and by seeking a broader public consensus and greater commitment on multiculturalism and other immigration-related issues.

In Chapter 9, Imre Lazar examines the evolution and role of cultural policy of the European Union. He discusses the various cultural programmes and actions with the Union. In spite of the growing importance of cultural policy in the EU, he argues, culture and related fields remain in national competence as EU institutions can only take "encouraging measures" at the Community level with no effect on the harmonization of the laws and regulations of the Member States. Lazar then discusses the role of culture in the external relations of the EU. He provides a comprehensive overview of the nature and scope of some major EU-India projects in education, science and culture and describes various cultural activities of the EU in India.

In the concluding chapter, Anuradha M. Chenoy argues that multiculturalism appears as an alternative to cultural nationalism as it can provide the space for the coexistence of multiple groups that make up Indian society. When minority cultures are not sufficiently protected even in liberal democracies, multiculturalism maintains the distinctiveness of minority cultures and provides them with special group rights and privileges. She then poses the question whether multiculturalism can promote gender equality alongside cultural equality. Women, according to the feminist argument of culture, are placed submissive in the gender hierarchies and such norms are placed integral to the culture to which they are embedded to. The threat of cultural nationalism of identifying the Indian nation primarily with the majority Hindu religious community has influences on gender policies. She urges the rejection of the notion of cultural nationalism and the need for substituting it with a model of multiculturalism that would allow a feminist culture. Multiculturalism can only work, Chenoy argues, if it is democratic, allows dissent and pluralism internally and externally, and is engaged with feminist culture that radically alters gender roles. It involves equality of women in public and private spheres and also the choice for them to adopting and adapting to the group cultural rights and also to opt out of those aspects of culture that restrict their individual rights. If multiculturalism accepts these, she concludes, it can be a viable and necessary alternative.

The management and accommodation of cultural diversities and difference has become one of the most discussed issues of global political agendas. Unlike the past, contemporary democratic societies are characterized by diversity resulting in deep social cleavages because of religious prejudice, economic hierarchy, cultural discrimination, inter-group rivalry, and historical animosity. The notion of multiculturalism, thus, has been "a strategy for the politics of management of difference, manifest in the dynamics of political claims and assertiveness of identity by minorities and emerging human rights agenda".[12] In fact, multiculturalism tends to be criticized more for its nature and consequences than being acknowledged as a policy for coping with cultural diversity. Thus, "the quintessential paradox underpinning a multicultural governance: how to create an inclusive and pluralistic governance for living together differently yet equally in ways that makes society safe from difference, yet safe for difference?"[13]

This volume offers useful insights into understanding public philosophies and policies how India and Europe seek to cope with cultural diversity and ethnocultural differences.

I would also like to thank my colleagues of the Centre for European Studies, Jawaharlal Nehru University for their support. Special thanks go to Sheetal Sharma for her helpful comments in the preparation of this volume.

NOTES

1 David T. Goldberg "Introduction: Multicultural Conditions," in David T. Goldberg, ed., *Multicultultularalism. A Critical Reader* (Oxford: Blackwell, 1994), p. 7.
2 Will Kymlicka, *Multicultural Odysseys* (Oxford: Oxford University Press, 2007), pp. 61-88.
3 Augie Fleras, *Politics of Multiculturalism, Multicultural Governance in Comparative Perspective* (New York: Palgrave Macmillan, 2009).
4 Peter McLaren, "White Terror and Oppositional Agency: Towards a Critical Multiculturalism," in Goldberg, n. 1, pp. 45-75.
5 Ibid., p. 37.
6 Ibid., p. 40.
7 Ibid., pp. 40-41.
8 Ibid., p. 42.
9 Ibid., p. 53.
10 Ibid., p. 54.
11 Will Kymlicka, *Multicultural Citizenship* (Oxford: Oxford University Press, 1995), p. 10.
12 Fleras, n. 3, p. 24.
13 Ibid., p. 26.
14 See Chapter Four by Michael Dusche in this volume.

1

Multiculturalism and the Social Structure in India and Europe

Sheetal Sharma

Introduction

Both India and Europe are multicultural societies characterized by linguistic, religious, ethnic, racial, regional, and cultural diversity. Amidst vast ethno-cultural diversity, they exhibit a unique social fabric representing "unity in diversity". However, rooted in their respective histories the nature and content of multiculturalism, the way it is modelled and manifest is quite distinct and both experience cultural conflicts of various types and intensity. This chapter attempts to delineate how India and Europe exhibit specific ways in which diverse cultures have existed throughout centuries in respective societies and how they continue to shape the contours of multiculturalism in its present form. It also analyzes what actors and factors have played an important role in success and/or failure of multiculturalism in both societies in contemporary times.

Multiculturalism is a social situation in which multiple cultures coexist and influence one another. The term "multiculturalism" includes a number of interrelated concepts such as identity, cultural diversity, plurality, distinctiveness, equality, and recognition. It emphasizes the importance of cultural belongingness and legitimizes the desire to retain differences.[1] According to T.K. Oommen:

> Multiculturalism or cultural diversity within polities has existed for a long time, but multiculturalism as a value orientation is of recent origin. Many pre-modern empires were multicultural. Similarly, in the colonial states the cultures of the colonizers and the colonized co-existed. Several socialist states were consciously constructed as multinational states which implied multiculturalism in one or the other way.[2]

Cultural diversity is a characteristic of almost all countries and claims of linguistic, ethnic, religious, and cultural distinctiveness are becoming sharper, deeper and stronger than ever. The resurgence of mutually exclusive cultural identities created an awareness of the urgent need to deal with the issues of social integration and the management of ethnic, religious, linguistic and cultural diversity through policies which promote the participation of minority groups into the mainstream and ensure their access to the resources of society.

Social Structure and Multiculturalism in India

Mapping diversity in India is not easy. With a population of 1.2 billion, India represents an array of linguistic, religious, cultural, and racial diversity. In terms of race, it is estimated that 72 per cent of the population is Indo-Aryan, 25 per cent Dravidian, and 3 per cent are Mongoloid and other. According to the 2011 Census, approximately 80.5 per cent of the population is Hindu, 13.4 per cent Muslim, 2.3 per cent Christian, 1.9 per cent Sikh, 0.8 per cent Buddhist, and 0.4 per cent Jain; another 0.6 per cent belongs to other faiths. The Hindus, the religious community in majority, follows a caste system that is a four-fold classification into *varnas*, viz. Brahmins, Kshatriyas, Vaishyas and Shudras. The *varnas* are further sub-divided into numerous (*jatis*), many of which are often found only in specific areas. Linguistically, Hindi is the official language and spoken by approximately 40.2 per cent of the population. Twenty-two languages are officially recognized by the Constitution. Almost one hundred and fourteen languages[3] that are further categorized into 216 dialects or "mother tongues" spoken by 10,000 or more speakers. An estimated 850 languages are in daily use, and there are more than 1,600 dialects.

The diversity characterizing contemporary India is a consequence of a long historical process spanning over three millennia. Knowing history is important because many races and tribes since time immemorial have shaped Indian culture.[4] *Ab initio*, India is a homeland of diverse communities and represents a "composite" culture. In India, cultural plurality is historically taken for granted. India means plural[5] and/or multicultural. Indian society is a product of gradual and continuous accumulation of cultural elements drawn from myriad sources. Beginning from the ancient period to modern through medieval times, India was invaded and conquered a number of times. Each of these invasions resulted in cultural contacts with the foreigners and each of them made an important and indelible contribution giving rise to a "composite" culture that characterizes Indian diversity. Each ethnic group contributed to the language, literature, art, architecture, food and dress styles. All these influences and cultural traits are so inextricably related that now they cannot be clearly identified in their original form.[6] Cultural diversity manifesting itself in this mode, where there is recognition of identity and its dignity, makes multiculturalism a value that has always been cherished in India.

Unlike the West, the debate around multiculturalism in India has remained ideological and normative, emphasizing multiculturalism as a value orientation. Cultural diversity in India, as stated earlier, is neither a recent phenomenon nor a consequence of the increasing population of immigrants. On the contrary, being a huge country of complementing diversities and imbalances since ancient times, cultural mixing and migration has aided development in modern India. In fact, despite the presence of complex social categories and sub-divisions within divisions, the secret of India's deep and underlying unity amidst cultural diversity lies in the fact that "different social, religious and cultural orders adopted the ways of synthesization and harmonization" between each other.[7] The process of synthesization encompasses a long historical process that has produced an extremely complex society which is an amalgam of four basic dimensions: social stratification, cultural diversity, caste hierarchy, and religious plurality.[8] Although, singly or collectively, these divisions have, at times, resulted in causing discrimination and conflict but India has been resilient to such divisive forces and has been successful in resisting disintegration so far. Its diversity and complexity notwithstanding, the secret of India's unity and integrity is incredible. The answer to this strength is largely a political question, which essentially involves a political recognition of identity, where political institutional arrangements played a significant role in the protection and maintenance of identity.[9] In order to understand the resilient character and strength of India's unity amidst diversity, it is pertinent to identify actors and factors that have played a significant role in creating conditions for survival of multiculturalism in contemporary India. To a large extent, answers to questions of India's unity and integrity can be found in the nature of combination of forces of political, economic, and cultural nationalism, that played an important role is nation-building during the years of the freedom struggle and immediately after Independence.

Although multiculturalism as a fact and reality in India existed since time immemorial, it is interesting to figure out that when and how did the idea of nation became a reality in the minds of the people? How did people belonging to diverse socio-cultural, linguistic affiliations begin to imagine India as a nation and developed a sense of collectivity and belongingness? The sense of "collectivity", as an Indian, emerged partly through the experience of united struggles for freedom. There were also a variety of cultural processes through which nationalism captured the people's imagination. A common history, myths, fiction, folklores, songs, symbols, festivals, values, and practices—all played a part in generating a strong sense of nationalism and people started discovering that something was bonding them together.[10] The management of diversity, however, became critical after Independence. Effective management of diversity was essential in the process of nation-building since diversity no longer remained a social fact, but a challenge that had to be politically addressed. The founders of modern India under the leadership of Jawaharlal Nehru enabled India to acquire a unique multicultural character. It was Nehru's realistic and practical approach towards cultural diversity, respect for traditional social institutions and communities that provided constitutional legitimacy to multiculturalism and facilitated a policy framework that was conducive for sustenance of multiculturalism since 1947. In general, "it was India's anti-colonial nationalist leaders, who swore by the country's multicultural reality and emphasized for the multicultural underpinnings of political institutional arrangements."[11] Nehru particularly, respected India's diversity, cherished its traditional values and found India's "unity in diversity" incredible and fascinating. He remarked:

> The diversity of India is tremendous; it is obvious. It lies on the surface and anybody can see it. It concerns itself with physical appearances as well as with certain mental habits and traits.... Yet, with all these differences, that have retained their peculiar characteristics for hundreds of years, (they) have still more or less the same virtues and failings (that) have been throughout these ages distinctively Indian in character.[12]

Since Independence, the presence of enormous diversity necessitated the adoption of policies in India sought to safeguard the interests of individuals irrespective of socio-cultural, economic, linguistic, ethnic, parochial differences. The constitutional framework adopted by India recognizes differences and diversity, and guarantees equal citizenship, rights, protects linguistic, cultural, religious minorities. Some of the major provisions in the Constitution of India providing equal opportunity and rights for all citizens are as follows:

Article 14: ensures equality before the law and equal protection by the law.

Article 15: prohibits discrimination on the grounds of religion, race, caste, sex and place of birth.

Article 21: No person shall be deprived of his life or personal liberty except through the procedure established by law.

Article 25: ensures freedom of conscience and the right to freely profess, practise and propagate religion.

Article 26: ensures the right to manage religious institutions, religious affairs, subject to public order, morality and health.

Article 29: protects the right of minorities to conserve their language, script or culture.

Article 30: provides for the protection of the interests of minorities by giving them a right to establish and administer educational institutions of their choice. The State is directed not to discriminate against minorities' institutions in granting aid.

Article 350A: directs the State to provide facilities for instruction in the mother tongue at the primary stage of education. Along with the Constitutional provisions, there are a number of other directives that safeguard the religious and cultural practices of monitories in India. Freedom to practise one's faith in everyday life and celebrate religious festivals, are some of the basic freedoms that minorities enjoy along with their counterparts of other major or minority religions.

Besides constitutional provisions, the concern for protecting cultural diversity is reflected in various other initiatives and efforts. The concern is evident dealing with the issue of maintaining cultural distinctiveness of tribes in India. Nehru emphasized that along with the effort of bringing them into the mainstream,

> every care should be taken to retain the individuality of their cultures. People living in these areas should feel that they have perfect freedom to live their own lives according to their wishes. India should signify for them a protecting as well as a liberating force. The policy of the state was not to interfere with tribal affairs but to offer the largest measure of autonomy.[13]

Commenting on the problems of integrating various communities in India, Nehru firmly advocated that do not "treat them by some single formula because they differ greatly among themselves. It seems obviously undesirable to deny them some kind of self-government or autonomy."[14] He cautioned against any attempt at homogenization of various cultural communities.[15] He forewarned the Chief Ministers and stated that "in the efforts of achieving social integration there is a tendency for assimilation (of tribes specifically in this case) into the mainstream culture or homogeneous whole. However, such a step would lead to conflicts between communities"[16] rather than achieving social integration.

Nehru enunciated five basic principles[17] regarding state policy in the Northeast:

1) people should develop along the lines of their own genius and we should avoid imposing anything on them. We should try to encourage in every way their traditional arts and culture;
2) tribal rights in land and forests should be respected;
3) we should try to train and build up a team of their own people to do the work of administration and development;
4) we should not over-administer these areas or overwhelm them with a multiplicity of schemes. We should rather work through and not in rivalry to their social and cultural institutions;
5) we should judge results, not by statistics or the amount of money spent, but by the quality of human character that is evolved.[18]

This demonstrates that going slow on the process of cultural homogenization and the adoption of a democratic approach by policy-makers since 1947 has been the basis of India's unity in diversity.

India was able to sustain multiculturalism because its political foresight incorporated elements of tradition and modernity, diversity and equality as well as respect and dignity in a fine balance. There was a combination of realism and cultural sensitivity in the approach towards the management of diversity. Nevertheless, the founders of modern India were not opposed to assimilation as it was indispensible for the project of nation-building. However, the design for assimilating diverse communities was a rather gradual and voluntary process of adaptation through education and cross-cultural contacts. It was understood that integration cannot be forced upon; and it should happen on its own without any special effort. Thus, providing Statehood on the basis of linguistic category was the most comprehensive and effective method of political recognition of cultural and ethnic identity[19] in India that helped in containing and sustaining the multicultural character of Indian society, weaving it into a harmonious whole.

Thus, there is something living and dynamic about the Indian heritage which shows itself in ways of living and a philosophical attitude to life and its problems. Ancient India was a world in itself, a culture and a civilization which gave shape to all things. Foreign influences poured in and often influenced Indian culture and interestingly, they were harmoniously assimilated and absorbed. Interestingly disruptive tendencies arising because of foreign influence gave rise to an attempt to find a synthesis immediately. Some kind of a dream of unity has occupied the mind of India since the dawn of civilization. That unity was not conceived as something imposed from the outside, a standardization of externals or even of beliefs. It was something deeper and, within its fold, the widest tolerance of belief and custom is practised, every variety acknowledged, and encouraged.[20]

Conflicts in Contemporary India

Though the cultural plurality is constitutionally recognized and guaranteed in India, conflicts persist between individuals and communities of different cultural affiliations manifest in the form of communal violence, tensions, ethnic clashes, etc. Given the significant changes in the socio-economic, political, and cultural landscape of India in the last decade, there is an increase in the number of instances of conflicts rooted in socio-cultural identities. As a result, identity politics has acquired a new (socio-political) meaning which is used in a purely instrumental fashion. Some may and have argued that identity politics has contributed to the democratization of society, but it is also true that it has generated a crisis which may be difficult to handle if it grows out of proportion.

In the (recent) past, there have been instances of conflict and contestation within and in-between communities especially the migrant communities in some areas. The presence of "others" (migrants from a particular region with a different language and set of cultural practices) in a politico-linguistic area has been opposed by certain regional/parochial, and jingoistic political parties. The crux of these issues has been understood/debated by intellectuals, political commentators, and masses as a means to raise political, linguistic and emotional temperament by creating a divide between "indigenous" and "migrants" in order to garner popular votes and consolidate political position at local level. However, being region-specific and temporal in nature, these conflicts have not posed a serious threat to social integration in India so far. Conflicts with immigrant communities emerge when migrants are seen as a threat to economic opportunities of the locals. Otherwise "cultural pluralism in India operates with the belief that living together requires not just respect for other individuals but also some concern for their feelings and sentiments. Unlike the West, the differences over manners of appearance and wearing of religious symbols"[21] in India have never been an issue of contestation. With a few exceptions, the multiplicity of dress, food habits, language, and customs are all sources of bonding rather than division. The manifest differences among culturally diverse groups are, in fact, perceived as aspects of community practice that are left to members and communities to determine themselves, reflecting a concept of the self and tolerance that form the bedrock of India's composite culture.

Multiculturalism in Europe

As compared to India, multiculturalism in Europe is of a slightly different character and is an interesting case exhibiting "unity amidst diversity". Historically, Europe has always been a mixture of Latin, Slavic, Germanic, Uralic, Celtic, Hellenic, Illyrian, Thracian and other cultures. Although Christianity unified Europe but, it is accepted that geographic and cultural differences continued from antiquity into the modern age.[22] Since the twentieth century, immigration transformed the socio-cultural texture of Europe. And more recently immigrants (national, intra-European Union and from third countries) have become one of the major factors bringing social change in contemporary Europe.

Migration to Europe is a part of the phenomenon of international migration[23] inherent in the process of globalization. Some of the most rapid and radical changes in the history of Europe have been brought about by the phenomenon of international migration since the Second World War in general and over the last two decades in particular. After experimenting with socialism for 45 years, the fall of the Berlin Wall brought Central and Eastern Europe back into the continental migration system.[24] Since the 1980s, there has been large scale migration of people from the Third World, especially from Africa and Asia, to Europe in search of better socio-economic prospects and seeking work and/or refuge. Over time, South Europe emerged as an attractive destination for migrants with moderate skills, less education, low human capital and professional capabilities. Western Europe registered the influx of a distinct category of immigrants possessing better education, professional skills and those who can rapidly adapt to modern lifestyles and technologies. With recent enlargements, accompanied by freedom of movement of people the demographic composition of society is changing faster than ever. In fact, migrants are altering the demographic and socio-cultural make-up of Member States' populations, greater than their internal birth rates or death rates. According to Eurostat estimates, the European Union is receiving approximately 2 million migrants every year. In 2006, about 3.5 million people settled in a new country of residence in the European Union, and foreign citizens are 86 per cent of total population of immigrants. The number of non-EU nationals is more than the EU citizens among most of the Member States. Among 3 million non-national immigrants to the EU Member States, more than 1.8 million were not EU citizens.[25] Migration is a growing and is a permanent part of Europe's future. With settling of populations with different national backgrounds, linguistic[26] groups, ethnicities, cultures, religions[27] and values, Europe[28] has become multicultural. And social integration of culturally diverse communities has become a challenge that needs to be addressed immediately.

Although in recent years there has been a slight shift

towards the acceptance of the legitimacy of regional and ethnic (immigrant) minority differences, for many people cultural, ethnic, and racial otherness still continues to be a threat and a challenge.[29] Evidence establishes that immigrants face disadvantages in everyday life, in the areas of legal rights, education, employment, living conditions, justice, health, and civic participation. They remain concentrated in particular regions, in ghettos or in suburbs, and substantial percentage of them remain excluded even after they and their subsequent generations become citizens. Citizens from Member States of the European Union too face barriers to integration outside their own countries within the Union because of diversity within and between the Member States. Public resentment of migrants as the 'other', and fear of 'cultural' difference leads to discrimination, marginalization, and exclusion of migrants in everyday life. More often than not, such instances become sources of tensions between the communities which at times acquire a violent character. Most of the instances of cultural intolerance and friction involving immigrant communities are with Muslims. "The social conflicts involving immigrants, which almost all the member states in the European Union are currently facing in varying degree, represent a direct expression of opposition to a conservative notion of 'we' and a homogeneous and anchored 'national identity'. They are also an intense reaction towards restrictive immigration, citizenship and integration policies and discourses."[30] The rise in support for Far Right political parties in the recent years has also acted as both a cause and a consequence to exploit people's fears and resentments. Hence, a minority of disillusioned and marginalized, and thus alienated, migrants reaffirm their indigenous identity by associating with fundamentalist groups, and get further alienated and segregated from the mainstream. Faced with growing diversity and the rigours of establishing conditions conducive for social integration the question arises as to what forces can hold multicultural Europe together?

Attempts have been made in the past to address the issue of social integration of culturally diverse groups. Numerous policies and recommendations have arisen, and resources have been allocated, at different levels of governance in EU Member States, including the two prominent policies, viz. assimilationist and multiculturalism.

The basic contention of the assimilationist policy is that 'Others' can be accepted as a permanent part of the host society. However, they assume that they will be absorbed as quickly as possible into the mainstream culture. Their differences from the cultural norms of the host community will not be encouraged and may even be suppressed if perceived as a threat to the security and integrity of the state. Multiculturalism, on the other hand, is a democratic policy response for coping with cultural and social diversity in society. As a concept, multiculturalism encompasses three dimensions. First, the demographic dimension involves description of existing linguistic, ethnic, religious diversity within a given society and identifies the social significance of cultural distinctions. Second, multiculturalism as a policy refers to various initiatives and programmes designed in order to manage socio-cultural diversity.[31] Finally, multiculturalism as a value orientation acknowledges the existence of ethnic diversity and ensures the rights of individuals to retain their cultural distinctiveness. Individuals are given access to participation in civic life, and adherence to constitutional principles and commonly shared values prevailing in a given society. Embedded in a ideological-normative framework, it is assumed that multiculturalism enriches the diversity of society in general and reduces complexity and social conflict. Thus, within the multicultural framework differences from the cultural norms of the host community are respected and protected in law and institutions. However, there is a risk that this may in some circumstances lead to separate/segregated development. Major European countries like Germany[32], France[33], and England[34] have pronounced multiculturalism as a failure.

The reasons for the so-called failure of multiculturalism are rooted in inherent ambiguities in the structures, processes, and set of values in European society. The contradictory tendencies of these actors and factors render the project of social integration of immigrants, if not ineffective, at least less effective. Some of these contradictions are discussed below.

First, the European Union is a product of the coming together of sovereign states. Article 151 of the Treaty establishing the European Community relating to culture, does not specify the Community's cultural policy but articulates the hope that it will "contribute to the flowering of the cultures of its member-states" and will "encourage diversity along with promotion of shared values".[35] Thus, culture is not a common European subject and managing cultural diversity becomes a challenge. Multiculturalism in the West has been based on the separation between the cultural and the social sphere. Culture has been perceived as a sphere of plurality creating divisions and must therefore be managed. Hence, multiculturalism and multicultural policies are means for managing cultural diversity arising from large scale immigration within and in-between Member States and from other countries. Multiculturalism in the European context has more to do with management of diversity within existing structures, extension of liberal tolerance rather than the participation of immigrants in social, political and civic affairs.[36]

Second, despite the success of economic and political integration (to some extent), socio-cultural bonds in the European Union seem to be missing. Surveys, reports, and studies show that allegiance to national identity among citizens of the Union is greater than supranational identity. There seems to be a subtle and at times manifest North-South and East-West divide compounded by the presence of a large number of immigrants from different parts of the world. Against the presence of the 'other', the spirit of nationalism becomes more intense and hence the chances of social integration become bleak. This is because

> the ethos of the European Union is qualitatively different from that of its predecessor nation-states, which were invariably wedded to the idea of cultural homogenization. If the major emphasis in the European nation-states was equality of individual citizens, the central tendency of the European Union member-states is to secure and preserve their national equality

> and identity. This being so, an integration lag between the different dimensions—economic, social, political, cultural—is bound to be a persistent feature of the European Union.[37]

In this context, the Europeans need to strengthen a sense of belonging that can perceive and acknowledge diversity while giving allegiance to that which is shared. Seen from within Europe, it is easy enough to perceive differences that separate French from German culture. But viewed from outside, say Japan, those differences will seem less obvious than the similarities between the two. What the new Europe must strive for is to generate a sense of belonging among Europeans (insiders) that retains the Japanese (outsiders) view.[38]

Third, with the multiplicity of languages the differences over cultural issues become sharper.

> The kernel of nation-states in Europe was language. While most of them had one official/national language, in those cases where there were several languages, the dominant one became the official language. But this assimilationist policy is untenable in the case of supra-national entity such as the European Union. Understandably the European Union has a dozen official languages which is a radical departure from the past language policy of member-states.[39]

The chance that Europe will ever become a community of people speaking the same language is remote. Ideally speaking, the plurality of European languages is a characteristic that cannot and should not be eliminated.

Fourth, influenced by factors such as the colonial legacy, historical memories (real as well as imagined), and past historical and political relations with the immigrants' home countries each European country follows different models of societal integration, namely *assimilation, differential integration and exclusion,* and *multiculturalism.* But these models of societal integration reflect ambivalence and incoherence due to diverse interpretation of the concept of social integration. The concept of social integration can be interpreted in three different ways. *First,* it is perceived as an inclusionary goal, implying equal opportunities and rights for all individuals either at local, national or international level and becoming integrated implies guaranteeing and improving life chances for all. *Second,* integration is viewed as dissolution of individual identities and distinctiveness among communities and cultures and an (undesirable) imposition of homogeneity where humanity becomes a "homogeneous whole"[40] without inner variations and differences. *Third,* social integration may simply refer to a way of describing the existing and explaining the established patterns of human relations of given society.[41]

The lack of consensus among theoreticians and policy-makers about how the concept of social integration may/must be defined is reflected in the confusion over the means and the process of social integration. Does social integration mean 1) *assimilation*: being here and the same; 2) *integration*: being here but different; and 3) *enclavement*: being here but separate.[42] To establish clarity on what is meant by concept of integration the report, *Integration of Migrants: Contribution of Local and Regional Authorities*, published by the European Foundation for the Improvement of Living and Working Conditions[43] states:

> The concept of integration is understood as the process of inclusion of migrants in the core institutions, relations and statuses of the receiving society. For the migrants, integration means a process of learning a new culture, acquiring rights, accessing position and status, building personal relations with members of the receiving society and growing to identify with it. For the receiving society, integration means opening up institutions, giving migrants equal opportunities and publicly welcoming their integration into society. The concept differentiates between the dimensions of structural integration, cultural integration, interactive integration and identificational integration.[44]

For long, the ambiguity over the conceptualization of social integration was manifest in lack of consensus over policies, the goals of social integration, and the appropriate strategies to achieve it.

Social Integration of Immigrants in Europe

The integration of immigrants is a multifaceted phenomenon involving various dimensions. Any attempt to generalize about the means, nature, extent and degree of social integration of immigrants is fraught with the danger of oversimplification of a complex phenomenon. The degree and pace of integration may vary depending upon the socio-cultural and economic profile of the immigrants, across generations of immigrants, and also on the programmes, policies and prevailing practices at the host countries. The data reveals quite a contrasting nature of the process and product of social integration of immigrants in Europe. Some studies[45] establish that the first generation of immigrants face discrimination in the host country on the basis of differences between citizenship, language, civic participation, occupation, income, and socio-cultural practices. The second generation may not find difficulties regarding adjustment in the new environment (as they are born there), learning the language, acquiring citizenship, participation in social life, and gaining employment. However, the cultural differences (and associated discrimination) persist in the socio-cultural realm such as differences of religious beliefs and practices, value systems, dress and food habits, and the establishment of trust among various communities. Studies[46] indicate that discrimination, adjustment problems, and unemployment may increase for second generation immigrants. The lack of trust between communities, in fact, acts both as cause and consequence of the problem. At times, social tensions involving immigrants are perceived as a result of economic distress in regions of high migration. Immigrants from mostly less developed areas are generally characterized as docile and less resistant to exploitation. They tend to be more productive, can be paid less, treated discriminately, and are more vulnerable to exploitation as compared to locals. As a result, employers tend to prefer immigrant workers. Immigrants are, therefore, perceived by locals as an economic threat by locals. Socio-economic causes of conflicts are generalized into socio-cultural spheres and immigrants as a group become 'them' with a distinct set of characteristic as against 'us'.

The success of immigrant integration programmes largely depends upon the nature and structure of integration policies of the host countries and willingness to accept the 'otherness of the other'. The lesser the gap between the culture[47] of both communities, the quicker is the integration. Most EU Member States have favourable policies for economic integration evident in a common market, a common currency and the four freedoms of the movement of capital, goods, professionals and workers. However, their attitude towards cultural integration is not only ambiguous, which makes it difficult to attain meaningful cultural integration. The Union has long recognized that integration is a necessary part of a comprehensive immigration and refugee strategy. The primary responsibility for integration of immigrants lies at the national and local levels. However, this has yet to be addressed successfully through coherent integration policies.[48]

The 1999 European Council in Tampere expressed a new willingness to cooperate in developing a comprehensive strategy to address integration under the heading of "fair treatment of third-country nationals". Since the Amsterdam Treaty (1999), the European Union has had a mandate to require Member States to address the issue of discrimination on grounds of race and religion. Directives require Member States to frame laws against racial discrimination in employment, and the movement of goods and services; to establish a statutory body to provide assistance to individual victims; and to ban religious discrimination in employment. In October 2002, the Justice and Home Affairs (JHA) Council urged the European Commission to come forward with proposals for a more comprehensive integration strategy.[49]

In its Communication on "A Common Agenda for Integration, Framework for the Integration of Third-Country Nationals in the European Union" (COM(2005) 389), the European Commission recommended the exchange of information and good practices between regional, local and urban authorities through networks operating at EU level. Other institutions like the European Parliament, the Council of the European Union, the Committee of the Regions, the European Economic and Social Committee and the Council of Europe (Congress of Local and Regional Authorities of Europe) supported exchange and cooperation[50] at the European level where local municipalities and cities can adopt the best practices and learn from each other's experiences in identifying problems confronted in developing socially inclusive strategies pertaining to how to integrate immigrants best, and encourage their participation in society.

In the absence of coherent policies, cooperation among Member States is facilitating an exchange of experiences with, and ideas about, managing migration and the integration of immigrants. The emerging consensus amongst Member States is that they need to manage migration better. They also need to work with the migrant's country of origin on everything from border control to development issues; evolve well-advertised, easy-to-understand schemes for skilled migration; charter a clear and fair route to citizenship for newcomers; and effectively check and curb entry of illegal immigrants. However, efforts to advance these aims at the EU level have not so far been fully developed.[51]

The development of a comprehensive strategy for social integration of immigrants necessitates the use of a multidisciplinary approach and appropriate methodology to generate information and data regarding migration and related aspects, that can address policy needs. The approach requires *a)* detailed profiling of immigrants, *b)* analysis of actors and factors influencing social cohesion and conflict, *c)* identifying, countering, and pacifying divisive forces, *d)* wherever possible and appropriate, the perspectives and insights of immigrants should be included in framing research questions, and *e)* immigrants themselves can be included in research teams, advisory groups, and their point of view can be factored in while framing policy recommendations.

Amongst the factors that influence the design of policies for the social integration of immigrants are the history of a nation, migratory trends, its philosophy and value system, perceptions of the "otherness of the other", and clarity about the concept of integration. Some groups belonging to a particular socio-cultural and religious affiliation are more prone to friction. Not all immigrants in Europe are marginalized or face discrimination. However, Europe as a whole confronts the challenge of integrating the 'other' in one way or the other. In these circumstances, Europe has two choices. "It can seek to deny the processes of cultural heterogeneity and hybridization and allow ethnicity-based antagonisms to grow by imposing an overarching Europeanist ideal of good life."[52] However, given the pace and impact of both globalization and Europeanization, the process of migration and mixing of culture is irreversible. Alternatively, Europe can recognize multiplicity of cultures and follow an approach where the 'other' becomes 'European' through engagement with the 'other', in ways that do not erase tradition and cultural autonomy. "Such an approach necessitates strengthening of European civil society, the establishment of a strong European public sphere, and the creation of a political culture that all Europeans share. While people in the economic field are mostly motivated by their interests, social and political integration needs more than a compromise on interests. Social and political integration touches the level of identity and values."[53] It needs a common self-understanding, a self-understanding that can be found only in "discourses of self understanding".[54] It is up to the Europeans, Amin Ash points out, "to make up their minds which values they want to guide their lives. Most Europeans do not even agree on the fundamental values on which the European Union is based or ought to be based. Until now, the Union has not been able to initiate a discussion about values. What is needed now is a Europe-wide discussion on what we want the European Union to be for all of us and of what visions we have about the future of the European Union."[55]

Conclusion

Equality in a culturally diverse society means cultural pluralism but cultural diversity without equality leads to hegemony. Therefore, for achieving the goal of social integration a society must negotiate between cultural pluralism and cultural hegemony.[56] It must be realized that the "age of cultural purism has ended".[57] As Fernand Braudel, the prominent French historian of civilization, remarked:

> The history of civilizations, in fact, is the history of continual mutual borrowings over many centuries, despite which each civilization has kept its own original character. It must be admitted, however, that now is the first time when one decisive aspect of a particular civilization has been adopted willingly by all the civilizations in the world.[58]

Instead of mourning the loss of an imaginary cultural heritage, we need to articulate "a new definition of culture. This definition will have to be based not on some abstract notions and traits but on a deep sense of social and filial empathy, a sense of reaching out to others, and enriching oneself through the discovery of the other. An ethics of coexistence can nourish a sense of cultural empathy without alienating anyone."[59]

Europeans have undoubtedly been far more successful in the formation, organization and functioning of the Union as compared to regional organizations constituted in other regions of the world. The EU is just half a century old and its major enlargements have happened only in the last fifteen years. In such a short span of time, it is natural to experience problems, challenges and face stumbling blocks. It is not likely to find sustainable solutions to all the problems rather quickly and the European Union would continue to face challenges, insecurities, contrasts, conflicts, and liabilities of newness till it emerges stronger. Before critical scrutiny, the European Union must be given some time to grow, mature, adjust to recent enlargements, and stabilize itself. A young Union, attempting to weave a large number of culturally diverse nations into a cohesive whole is obviously vulnerable to ups and downs.

NOTES

1. Rajeev Bhargava (ed), *Multiculturalism, Liberalism and Democracy* (New Delhi: Oxford University Press, 1999).
2. T.K. Oommen, "Socio-Political Transition in the Indian Republic and the European Union," *European Journal of Social Theory*, 7(4), 2007, pp. 519-537.

3. According to the 2011 Census, 29 languages are spoken by one million or more people.
4. Such as the pre-Aryans, the Indo-Aryans, the Greeks, the Huns, the Turks, and the Mughals.
5. Saumyajit Ray, "Understanding Indian Multiculturalism," in Christopher Sam Raj and Marie McAndrew (eds), *Multiculturalism: Public Policy and Problem Areas in Canada and India* (New Delhi: Manak Publications, 2009), p. 69.
6. R.S. Sharma, *India's Ancient Past* (New Delhi: Oxford University Press, 2008), pp. 1-5.
7. J.C. Johari, *Indian Political System: A Critical Study of the Constitutional Structure and the Emerging Trends of Indian Politics* (New Delhi: Anmol Publications, 1987), second edition.
8. T.K. Oommen, "Futures India: Society, Nation State, Civilization," *Futures* 36, 2004, pp. 745-755.
9. Harihar Bhattacharyya, "Multiculturalism in Contemporary India," in special volume on "Pluralism and Multiculturalism in Colonial and Post-Colonial Societies," *International Journal on Multicultural Societies (IJMS)*, Vol. 5, No. 2, 2003, pp. 148-161.
10. *India and the Contemporary World-II*, Textbook in History for Class X (New Delhi: National Council of Educational Research and Training, 2011), p. 70.
11. Bhattacharyya, n. 9, p.156.
12. Jawaharlal Nehru, *Discovery of India* (Bombay: Asia Publishing House, 1961), pp. 56-62.
13. Jawaharlal Nehru, *Letters to Chief Ministers*, Vol. 1 (Delhi: Oxford University Press, 1986), pp. 151-152. Cited in Bhattacharya, n. 9, pp. 156-157.
14. Jawaharlal Nehru, *Letters to Chief Ministers*, Vol. 2 (New Delhi: Oxford University Press, 1986), p. 364.
15. Advised the Chief Ministers of states in the Northeast in his *Letters to Chief Ministers* in the early 1950s mentioned in Jawaharlal Nehru, *Letters to Chief Ministers*, Vol. 2, n. 14, p. 148. Here Nehru specifically discussed the cultural diversity of territorial units of the country, most notably in the Northeast (characterized by the complex diversity of tribes, religions and non-tribal groups).
16. Nehru, n. 14, p. 148.
17. These are mentioned in the *Foreword* to Verrier Elwin's *A Philosophy for NEFA*, Second edition, published by S. Roy on behalf of the North-East Frontier Agency, 1960.
18. Although these policies are specifically targeting different

communities and groups in the northeast but can be applied in general in any/all other times and spaces, wherever the issue of protection of cultural identity is involved.

19. Bhattacharyya, n. 9, p. 162.
20. Nehru, n. 13, pp. 56-62.
21. Gurpreet Mahajan, "Multiculturalism in the Age of Terror," *Political Studies Review*, Vol. 5, 2007, pp. 332-334.
22. Robert C. Ostergren and Mathias Le Bossé, *The Europeans: A Geography of People, Culture, and Environment* (New York: Guilford Press, 2011), p. 226.
23. According to the predictions made by the United Nations, if current trends continue, the numbers of people migrating worldwide will increase by 40 per cent over the next 40 years.
24. Corrado Bonifazi, Marek Oko'lski, Jeannette Schoorl, Patrick Simon, *International Migration in Europe: New Trends and New Methods of Analysis* (Amsterdam: Amsterdam University Press, 2008).
25. According to official national statistics and Eurostat estimates, at the end of 2006, the total number of non-nationals living in the EU Member States was 29 million, representing 5.8 per cent of the total EU population. More than half of these were citizens of non-EU countries. In absolute terms, the largest number of foreign citizens live in Germany (7.3 million), France (3.6 million), Spain (4.6 million), the United Kingdom (3.7 million) and Italy (2.9 million).
26. German is the most widely spoken language (about 90 million people according to 2006 statistics). French, English and Italian are each the mother tongue of around 60 million EU citizens. Besides the 23 official languages, there are about 150 regional and minority languages, spoken by up to 50 million people.
27. The EU has significant religious diversity, reflecting diverse history and culture. A majority of the population professes Christianity, predominantly Roman Catholicism, Protestantism and Eastern Orthodoxy. See http://www.indexmundi.com/european_union/population.html.
28. Demographically, the European Union is a highly populated, culturally diverse union of 27 Member States. According to estimates of 1 January 2010, the population of the EU was about 501.6 million people.
29. R.D. Grillo, "Transmigration and Cultural Diversity in the Construction of Europe," Revised version of a paper presented to the "Symposium on Cultural Diversity and the Construction

of Europe: Complementarity or Incompatibility?", organized by Fundaci Jaume Bofill and the Universitat Oberta de Catalunya in December 2000 in Barcelona. http://www.europadiversa.org/eng/pdf/ponencia_grillo_ eng.doc.

30. Sergio Carrera, *A Comparison of Integration Programmes in the European Union: Trends and Weaknesses* (Brussels: Centre for European Policy Studies, 2006), pp. 19-20.
31. It was in this usage that "multiculturalism" first gained currency after it was recommended in the 1965 Report of the Royal Commission on Bilingualism and Biculturalism. This Report recommended that multiculturalism replace the bicultural policy based on the British and French Charter groups around whom policies for ethnic diversity in Canadian society had been organized for over a century. See Maren Borkert, et al. (2007), *Local Integration Policies for Migrants in Europe*, European Foundation for the Improvement of Living and Working Conditions (Bamberg: European Forum for Migration Studies, 2007).
32. Angela Merkel said that, an attempt to build a multicultural society has been an "utter failure" the idea of people from different cultural backgrounds living happily "side by side" did not work.
33. Former French Prime Minister Nicholas Sarkozy commented that immigrants must "melt into a single community, which is the national community, if you do not want to accept that, you cannot be welcome in France." It's a failure, Sarkozy said of multiculturalism. The truth is that, in all our democracies, we've been too concerned about the identity of the new arrivals and not enough about the identity of the country receiving them."
34. The British counterpart David Cameron stated that multiculturalism has encouraged "segregated communities" where Islamic extremism can thrive the multicultural policy has failed to promote a sense of common identity centred on values of human rights, democracy, social integration and equality before the law.
35. Banus quoted in Oommen, n. 2, p. 532.
36. Gerard Delanty, *Community: Key Ideas* (New York: Routledge, 2010), p. 72.
37. Oommen, n. 8, pp. 745-755.
38. Anthony Pagden, (ed), *The Idea of Europe*, Woodrow Wilson Center Series (Cambridge: Cambridge University Press, 2002), p. 24.

39. Oommen, n. 2, p. 527.
40. As some theorists assert that, "the revolutionary means of information communication, media, rapid transportation, MNCs/TNCs, are contributing to homogeneity, habits, practices, styles, symbols, language, experiences, aspirations, opportunities, ideas, outlook, choices, lifestyles, consumption patterns, tastes, preferences, and identities are shared globally. Facing powerful forces of globalization societies and cultures are experiencing homogenization and cultural convergence."
41. *Social Integration: Approaches and Issues*, Briefing Paper No. 1, World Summit For Social Development, United Nations Research Institute for Social Development. www.unrisd.org/bp1.pdf
42. Grillo, n. 29.
43. Wolfgang Bosswick and Friedrich Heckmann, *Integration of Migrants: Contribution of Local and Regional Authorities* (European Forum for Migration Studies (EFMS) at the University of Bamberg, Germany: European Foundation for the Improvement of Living and Working Conditions, 2006).
44. Ibid., p. 11.
45. Christine Inglis, *Multiculturalism: New Policy Responses to Diversity*, Policy Paper No. 4, Management of Social Transformations (MOST), 1995. At UNESCO, www.unesco.org/shs/most.
46. Dominique Meurs, Ariane Pailhé and Patrick Simon, "Discrimination Despite Integration: Immigrants and the Second Generation in Education and the Labour Market in France", in Corrado Bonifazi, Marek Oko'lski, Jeannette Schoorl, Patrick Simon, *International Migration in Europe: New Trends and New Methods of Analysis* (Amsterdam: Amsterdam University Press, 2008).
47. This involves both material and non- material aspects of culture. While the material aspect is tangible in nature and is manifest in the form of artifacts, clothing, food, architecture, language, etc., the non- material aspect includes intangible aspects of culture existing in the form of values, norms, beliefs, and practices that are passed on to successive generations and learnt through the process of socialization.
48. Mariya Aleksynska and Yann Algan, *Assimilation and Integration of Immigrants in Europe*, IZA DP No. 5185, Discussion Paper Series (Bonn: Institute for the Study of Labour, 2010).
49. G.P. Freeman, "Immigrant Incorporation in Western

Democracies," *International Migration Review*, 38(3), 2004, pp. 945-969.

50. Bonifazi, Oko´lski, Schoorl, and Simon, n. 24.
51. Hugo Brady, *EU Migration Policy: An A-Z* (London: Centre for European Reform, 2009).
52. Amin Ash, "Multi-Ethnicity and the Idea of Europe," *Theory Culture Society*, 21(2), 2004, pp. 1-24.
53. Susanne Moser, "The Importance of Values for Social and Political Integration in Europe," paper presented at International Congress on Justice and Human Values in Europe, 9-11 May 2007, Karlsruhe.
54. Juergen Habermas quoted in Amin Ash, "Multi-Ethnicity and the Idea of Europe," *Theory Culture Society*, 2004, pp. 1-24.
55. Ash, n. 52. pp. 1-24.
56. T.K. Oommen, "Political Federalism and Cultural Diversity", lecture under the auspices of the Foundation for Community Transformation at the Sri Lanka Foundation Institute, Colombo, 2 April 2006.
57. Ibrahim Kalin, http://blogs.reuters.com/faithworld/2010/11/01/guestview-the-slow-death-of-multiculturalism-in-europe.
58. Fernand Braudel quote by Kalin, Ibrahim (2010), http://blogs.reuters.com/faithworld/2010/11/01/ guestview-the-slow-death-of-multiculturalism-in-europe/
59. Kalin, n. 57.

2

Unity and Diversity: India and Europe

Bhaswati Sarkar

Diversity is a fact of all societies and states and unity is a challenge that all in turn face. The experience and success of striking a balance between them differs from country to country. India is often described as a classic example of a country that has been able to maintain unity of its amazingly diverse social reality. No European country can compare with India in terms of its diversity. However, diversity management and accommodation is perhaps today one of the most serious challenges that confront European states. The model of regional integration of the European Union with its 27 Member States has added a new dimension to how diversity is to be understood and responded to.

Focusing on the Indian and European experience, this chapter attempts to analyze why India in spite of all its problems appears to be more at ease with diversity while European states appear to be struggling? The chapter further argues that the context, nature and approach to diversity in India and Europe is significantly different. However, Europe could do well to learn from the Indian experience in its attempt to strike a balance between unity and diversity.

Diversity in India

India is among the most diverse societies in the world. The people of India are said to have had a continuous civilization since 2500 B.C.E. It has people from all the major religions in the world—Hindus, Muslims, Christians, Sikhs, Buddhists, Jains and Zoroastrians (Parsis). Hindus constitute about 82 per cent of the population, but India also has the second largest population of Muslims in the world, an estimated 149 million. Religious diversity is coupled with enormous linguistic and cultural diversity. India is one of the most linguistically diverse countries in the world. According to the 2001 Indian Census, there are a total of 122 languages and 234 mother tongues. These figures do not report languages spoken by fewer than 10,000 speakers. For instance, in 1961 around 1,652 mother tongues were returned in the Census.[1] There are many ethnic groups and communities living here. The main ethnic groups are Indo-Aryan (72%), Dravidian (25%), Mongoloid and others (3%). The people from northern India belong to the Indo-Aryan group, who are descendants of the Aryans who first entered the subcontinent around 1500 B.C. Those from the northeast of the country are usually from the Mongoloid group and south Indians, especially people from the southern Indian state of Tamil Nadu, are generally of Dravidian origin, probably among the oldest inhabitants of the land. There are also many tribal communities in India known as the Adivasis—the original inhabitants of this ancient country. They fall under the category of Scheduled Tribes. Numerous tribal communities can be found in different regions of India. In the northeast, there are tribes like the Khasis, the Mizos, the Nagas and the Tripuris. Central India has the largest number of tribal groups. There are also tribal communities found in the southern Indian states of Andhra Pradesh, Karnataka, Tamil Nadu and Kerala. The islands off the mainland such as the Andaman and Nicobar and Lakshadweep have their own tribal groups as well. While the national Census does not recognize racial or ethnic groups, it is estimated that there are more than 2,000 ethnic groups in India.[2]

None of the European states can compare with India in terms of its diversity. One must also remember India came out of colonial rule scathed and bruised by the trauma of Partition, insecure and challenged on a number of fronts. Most political analysts of the 1960s and the 1970s had, in fact, predicted the fragmentation of India. The fact that India managed to sustain as a unified country was largely because of its willingness to adapt, accept and recognize its diversity. If the detractors have been proved wrong, it is, as Mahajan argues, primarily because the existing framework of democracy makes room for diversities of various kinds of religious, linguistic and ethnic to coexist in many different ways. The willingness to experiment with different ways of accommodating diversity has enabled the country to remain a strong and unified whole.[3]

The Constitutional Framework: Response to Linguistic, Regional and Religious Diversity

The Indian Constitution has been singularly significant in India's quest to balance unity and diversity. This document gives an insight into how the newly independent state set about to balance the complex issue of unity and diversity.

Settling the Language Issue

The debate surrounding language in the Constituent Assembly and the language policy that was put in place is a case in point. Several years before Independence, Mahatma Gandhi had tirelessly supported Hindustani, which was a combination of Hindi and Urdu and could be written in either Devanagri (a Sanskrit) script or Perso-Arabic script as the best choice for a national language. However, after Partition the focus shifted from Hindustani to Hindi, which was spoken only by Hindus. The Constituent Assembly debates clearly indicate that two groups emerged, one that supported Hindi as a national language because they believed that the use of English was incompatible with India's independence.[4] At that time, they were referred to as "Hindiwallas" and another group who agreed that English should be replaced but believed that Hindi should not be imposed on people as a national language. Granville Austin points out that the language issue was controversial because it was felt to be an important fundamental right. After six weeks of intense debate between the two groups, there was a vote.[5] The vote was tied 77-77.[6]

The Constituent Assembly finally decided that Hindi would be an official language of the Union and not the national language of India because it was seen as an imposition that attempted to erase the cultures of other language speakers. In addition, it was also decided that English would continue as an Associate Official Language for a period of 15 years or until the Parliament would decide otherwise. The Eighth Schedule was included in the Constitution in 1950 and provides formal and constitutional recognition to dominant regional languages in the spheres of administration, education, economy and social status.[7] Initially, the Eighth Schedule listed 14 languages as the official languages of Indian states. Today there are 22.

On the question of linguistic division of states in the tumultuous days following Independence, both Jawaharlal Nehru and Sardar Patel felt that the volatile issue be postponed and other more pressing matters like integration, refugees, and economic reconstruction taken up first. Thus, the Congress began to change its position and adopt the attitude expressed by the Dar Commission, namely, that "Congress stands relieved of all past commitments".[8] The Party's programme for the 1951 elections stated that although the policy of the Congress had been "clearly and unequivocally in favour of the formation of linguistic provinces", still the Congress would stand by the conclusion of the JVP (Jawarharlal Nehru, Vallabhbhai Patel and Pattabhi Sitaramay Committee's) Report that the time was not opportune. However, as the agitation in Andhra Pradesh for a Telugu language state intensified, it became apparent to the Congress Party as well as to the Government of India that the mounting sentiment in favour of linguistic states had to be addressed if order and unity was to be preserved. Shortly thereafter, the Government of India announced that it would set up a commission to examine the linguistic states issue on an all-India basis and recommend a suitable solution. In 1956, the State Reorganization Commission recommended that state boundaries be redrawn to take into account linguistic realities. Eventually, there was general reorganization of states along linguistic lines. Once state reorganization was carried out administratively, virtually all states legislated a single official language.[9]

Opting for Federalism

Independent India opted for federalism as a way of governance. Federalism offers a way for diverse communities to come together and derive the strength of unity while retaining their identity. It is no exaggeration to say that the stability of India as a nation depends critically on the strength and flexibility of its federal structure. Maintaining an appropriate balance between the Centre and the states in a federation is, to quote Buchanan, "like keeping a satellite in place, with centrifugal and centripetal forces keeping each other in check."[10]

India's federal experiment to begin with had a strong unitary bias and a centralizing tendency. The Constitution proclaims that India is a "union of states", rather than a federation, and constitutional features supporting this assertion are numerous. There is a large Concurrent List of powers, and residuary powers lie with the Centre. State Governors are appointed by the Centre, but they must assent to laws passed by State Assemblies. In some instances, the President's assent is required for bills passed by State Assemblies. The Parliament, with a qualifying majority, has the power to redraw the boundaries of the states, to divide them, and to create new ones. The Centre has the power to dismiss an elected state government in certain circumstances and to replace it with what is called "President's rule". Dissatisfaction with this centralized federalism became widespread when in the 1970s the Congress Party weakened, ceased to govern both the states and the Centre and coalition politics emerged. In the late 1980s, a panel appointed to review Centre-state relations (the Sarkaria Commission) recommended that the states be allowed more autonomy. Over a period of time centralized federalism has given way to cooperative and competitive federalism.[11]

Tackling Religious Diversity

Though more than 80 per cent of the population of India are Hindus and religion was the basis of Partition and the formation of Pakistan, India did not declare it as the official or established state religion. On the contrary, the Preamble to the Indian Constitution declares India as a "sovereign, socialist, secular, democratic Republic" committed to treat all communities as equal.[12] Scholars have characterized Indian secularism in a variety of ways. Rajeev Bhargava, for instance, characterizes Indian secularism as one of "principled distance". The State, according to him, neither mindlessly excludes all religions nor is merely neutral towards them.[13] Rajeev Dhavan disaggregates Indian secularism as comprising three components—religious freedom, celebratory neutrality (state assists both financially and otherwise in the celebration of all faiths), and reformatory justice.[14]

The Constituent Assembly debates between 1946-1949 reveal that there was no real consensus on the direction that Indian secularism would take. There were several voices in the Assembly. For instance, B.R. Ambedkar wanted to severely restrict the role of the religion in the public sphere. K.T. Shah demanded that there be an article expressly stating that the Indian state has "no concern with any religion, creed or profession of faith". There were others like K.M. Munshi who said that the State must take into account that India was a nation of people with "deeply religious moorings". Ultimately, the "equal respect" theory where the State respects and tolerates all religions won the day. This was also how Nehru understood secularism. "A secular state is not [an] irreligious state: it only means that we respect and honour all religions giving them freedom to function."[15]

Thus, Article 25 of the Indian Constitution enshrines the individual's right to freedom of religion. It gives all religious communities the right to "profess, propagate and practise" their religion. It is pertinent to note that the right to propagate one's religion was included in deference to the concerns of the minority communities, particularly Muslims and Christians, who maintained that preaching and propagating their faith was an essential part of their religion. The Constitution, at the same time, empowers the State to intervene in Hindu religious institutions. Article 17 requires the State to abolish untouchability one of the most abhorrent practices of

Hinduism. Although equality of citizenship is guaranteed by the Constitution, there are provisions for reservations or affirmative action in elections, educational institutions and government jobs for lower castes and tribes.[16]

While most societies grant individuals the right to religious belief, in India communities enjoy the right to continue with their distinct religious practices. Perhaps the most significant part of this is that in all matters of family, individuals are governed by their community personal laws. Religious communities also have the right to set up their own religious and charitable institutions; they can establish their own educational institutions and these institutions are entitled to financial support from the state. Taken together, these are ways by which public recognition has been granted to different religious communities and space made for them to continue with their way of life. On the symbolic plane, policies pertaining to the declaration of public holidays, permissible dress in educational institutions and public jobs, and the naming of public places also acknowledge and give due recognition to the different communities living in India.[17]

European Diversity

Let us now look at how European states have experienced diversity and responded to it. To begin with one may point out that Europe is taken to be the cradle of 'nation-states'. There are different explanations as to how and why nation states emerged, whether they are primordial or modern but that they emerged following the Treaty of Westphalia is widely accepted. The nation-state as a concept implies homogeneity in so much as it comprises a single linguistic, ethnic and cultural community. Though in reality to a variable extent nation states are heterogeneous the tendency of nation-states is to seek homogeneity. Heterogeneity in nation-states of Europe is both foundational and ongoing. The foundational differences especially in West European states were accommodated in the national imagination through citizenship, a civic understanding of the nation and devolution of power.

In Europe, very few states are federal. Here we take a quick look at UK, Spain, Germany and Belgium. The former two do not have a federal system, the latter do. For the United Kingdom, the Scots, the Irish, the Welsh and the English, who comprise the nation-state, heterogeneity is foundational. The same is the case in respect of the Basques and the Catalans in Spain or the Dutch and the French in the case of Belgium. Despite the distinct identities that comprised Britain, the UK evolved a unitary form of government, which has faced challenges from the constituent units for separation and independence. The conflict in Northern Ireland has been violent and voices for Scottish independence have become increasingly strident. The British Government responded by the devolution of power. A referendum was held in 1997 in Scotland and Wales and a year later in both parts of Ireland. This resulted in the creation of the Scottish Parliament, the National Assembly for Wales and the Northern Ireland Assembly.[18] Having been re-elected in 2011 with an overall parliamentary majority, the Scottish National Party announced on 10 January 2012, that it intended to hold a yes/no referendum, proposing both further devolution, and full independence by the autumn of 2014.[19]

Spain emerged from the Franco regime with a new constitution in 1978. Claims for autonomy by historic communities were settled not by opting for a federation but by creating 17 autonomous units of the administration in which Catalonia and Basque regions were given considerable local autonomy. This has, however, not satisfied their demands. Apart from the violence mounted by ETA (*Euskadi Ta Azkatasuna* or Basque Homeland and Freedom) for an independent land for the Basques, mainstream parties like the Catalan, Convergence for Union, Basque Nationalist Party and the Galician Nationalist Bloc in 1998 signed the Barcelona Declaration demanding that the Spanish state be officially recognized as a multilingual, multicultural and multinational state. These parties argued that despite democracy and a unitary character, Spain has not been able to resolve the national question.[20]

Germany's decision to opt for federalism was based on its

long federal tradition which in turn was an outcome of the attempts to unify a German nation split across a large number of dynastic and republican states. In 1815, there were 39 Laender, 25 in the German Reich of Bismarck. In 1949, postwar Federal Republic of Germany was built on this tradition with 16 Laender combined in a federal state. The Basic Law sets out three types of legislative powers—exclusive powers of the federal level (foreign affairs, defence, citizenship and immigration, post and telecommunications); concurrent powers were both enjoy competence but federal laws prevail (civil and criminal law, employment and aspects of health, welfare, energy, industry, transport and environment policy); and federal framework powers where the legislative framework is set by the centre in which the Laender laws have to fit (education, press, land use and planning) and exclusive powers of the Laender and residual powers to the Laender.

Postwar Germany has developed the structures of cooperative federalism with a high degree of economic and social homogeneity. These concerns are also at play in federal and Laender politics. These structures now are challenged in a united Germany in which economics, politics and society are increasingly differentiated in terms of territory. The assumptions of cooperative federalism of nationwide policy standards, uniformity in living conditions equity and solidarity are now challenged by new territorial politics. For instance, since 1990 Hesse and Bavaria have tried different ways of "rolling back" the federal role in concurrent and framework legislation and boost the policy autonomy of the Laender.[21]

Another federal European country, Belgium, has of late been in the news for the seemingly incompatible claims of the Dutch and the French. It was only in 1993 that Belgium opted for federalism to enable its diverse groups to continue to live side-by-side. It has been argued that Belgium's federalism is unique in two respects. Firstly, it forms part of a process of dissociation and not of association. Secondly, it only has a few federated entities. Linguistic differences have long characterized this country nestled between France, Germany and the Netherlands. Belgium is divided into three linguistic communities: Flanders is home to most of its Dutch speakers, known as Flemish; Wallonia is predominantly French; and there is a small German community at the eastern tip of the country. The capital, Brussels, is a separate, bilingual entity. Language has been a critical determinant in Belgium's evolution and continuance as a federation. The country's parties were divided along linguistic lines in the 1970s and now, little communication much less collaboration occurs, partly as a result of the different ideological backgrounds. Flanders advocates free market policies but at the same time is politically conservative, while Wallonia retains its socialistic leanings.

Belgium has been an independent state since its territories were detached from the Dutch kingdom in 1830, except for its occupation by Germany during the two world wars. It was created as a strongly centralized unitary state that operated almost completely in French. This was unacceptable to the Flemish who saw the country as bilingual and bi-cultural. Pressure from the Flemish Movement brought about the 1898 De Vriendt-Coremans law that created legal equality. Language laws instituted territorial monolingualism in the 1930s and French-speaking elites formed the Walloon Movement which eventually focused on predominantly French Wallonia.[22]

Tensions eventually grew between the two major linguistic groups and attempts were made to defuse them by strengthening territorial monolingualism. Laws passed in 1962-63 created linguistic borders but tensions exist to this day. The running of the federation in Belgium has not been smooth with increasing difficulties in forming governments. In 2007 after election in June it took a record nine months to form a government. Much of the trouble stems from the secessionist impulse by the Flemish Belgians based on the "deep resentment in Flanders that its much healthier economy must subsidize the French-speaking south, where unemployment is double that of the north." In 2010, the Belgian government had collapsed. In December 2011, the government was formed after 18 months. The Belgian government is actually a "Grand Coalition" of almost all the parties in the country, led by the

Socialist Party leader Elio Di Rupo. For eighteen months, the Flemish parties refused to budge on their demand for more autonomy, and the Walloon parties refused to allow the country to be further federalized. Neither side had enough of a majority to form a government on their own, so the only way to form a government was for them to come together in a coalition. Talks remained intractable till, in the end, the markets accomplished what the negotiations could not. Belgium had its credit rating downgraded, with the agencies citing the uncertainties over the political situation and the country's future as the reason following which the negotiators hastily agreed.[23]

However, notwithstanding these challenges that foundational identities pose, Europe's primary struggle today is not with foundational pluralities but with the diversity that is ongoing, a diversity that is the result of immigration particularly with Muslim communities that have come in and settled in different states of Europe. As a result of immigration, European states today are marked by a plurality of cultural identities within a single political structure. Europe's problem with this 'Muslim other' first came to public view over the Muslim community's volatile resistance to the publication of the *Satanic Verses* in the United Kingdom in the 1980s. Recent years have witnessed a series of incidents like the Danish cartoon controversy, the question of the veil and *burqa* in France, the murder of Pim Fortyun and Theo van Gogh, and finally the London and Madrid bombings by Islamic militants. These incidents coupled with the fact that today Islam is the second largest religion in Europe after Christianity makes the question of how European states respond to the presence and demand of the Muslim community more than a matter of mere academic curiosity.

Europe is remarkably democratic in the practice of its values and existing human rights regime, why then does it struggle with accommodating Muslims? Two pillars on which the identity of Europe rests need to be understood to comprehend this struggle. These two pillars are Enlightenment with the logic of modernity at its heart and Christianity. Theorists of Enlightenment in England and France noted the existence of plural culture and civilizations. They also acknowledged the existence of many groups and interests. In fact, the existence of many groups and interests became a sign of democracy in the twentieth century. The presence of one ideology, one political party, and a single electoral candidate was taken as a sign of state coercion. The presence of many such associations, interest groups, and political parties was seen to be the minimum condition of freedom. But many, as Mahajan argues, may be part of the same, facets of the same. Plurality merely suggests the presence of many of the same kind. Diversity, on the other hand, points to the existence of many that are different and heterogeneous. Convinced of the success of the logic of modernity and in keeping with their understanding of plurality, Enlightenment thinkers arranged these cultures hierarchically. The history of mankind, they argued, represented progress from the Dark Ages to the civilized enlightened present. All past and existing cultures were judged by this criterion.[24]

Within Europe, German historians from Johann Gottfried von Herder to Leopold von Ranke did use the idea of cultural diversity to question this judgment of enlightenment. They argued that human history was constituted by discrete and heterogeneous cultures each with its own values, moral and aesthetic norms, political and economic structures. Each culture was complete, 'a whole' with its own centre of happiness. The German historians and philosophers acknowledged the presence of diverse cultures but over time and place not simultaneously coexisting within the boundaries of the nation-state.[25]

Subsequently, in the 1960s multicultural theorists questioned the Enlightenment logic and the understanding of plurality on which the liberal democracies were based. The classical liberal wisdom also advocated indifference to social and cultural identities. It suggested that the law should not take note of the identity of a person. Instead, all individuals as citizens must be treated alike. Identical treatment or equality before the law that signalled the absence of discrimination on grounds of religion, race or gender was regarded as the *sine qua non* of a liberal democracy. Contrary to the liberal view of individuals as atomized individuals, multiculturalists argued that individuals are culturally embedded with strong community links. The logic of the liberal theory, the multiculturalists argued, benefits the majority group and leaves it inadequate to deal with the demand of other minority groups and cultures. This weakness of liberalism was criticized by multiculturalism. Multiculturalists argued that the liberal idea of democracy and universal citizenship had indeed made significant strides to ensure equality and freedom but it had not been able to settle questions of discrimination. One of the major problems with the idea of universal citizenship is that it speaks only of individuals as citizens. It recognizes only one membership, viz. that of the state. Liberalism treats individuals as being divorced from community membership. However, the culture and norms of the majority community sets the norm for the whole society and what is accepted in the public sphere is the culture of the majority.

Concerned with the diversity within the boundaries of the nation-state, the multiculturalists argue that individuals are members of communities which determine their life choices and options and unless different cultural communities are equally recognized in the public sphere the state is far from providing a level playing field. In order to address these inequality issues, the multiculturalists argue for rights like rule-exemptions, financial assistance, symbolic recognition, self–government rights, and special representation rights.

An interesting debate emerges between liberals like Brian Barry and multiculturalists like Bhiku Parekh on the question of rule and exemption and limits of freedom of expression and accessibility of opportunities. For Barry, from an egalitarian liberal standpoint what matters is "equal opportunities, existence of opportunity is and objective state of affairs." Parekh, on the other hand, argues that "opportunity is subject driven" and cultural dispositions which determine whether an individual can make use of the opportunity must be taken into account to create a truly level playing field.[26]

In practice, many European states had till recently moved

towards the multiculturalist position to deal with diversity related to immigrants. In the United Kingdom, for instance, the Labour government under Tony Blair was committed to a vibrant multicultural Britain. The rule-exemption policy was widely used to address the concerns of the Sikhs, the Jews and the Muslim community on questions of dress code, dietary restrictions, and time for prayers. The Muslim demand for state-funded Islamic schools like Church schools was acceded to by the Labour government and currently there are seven state-funded Islamic schools operating.[27]

Until recently, the Netherlands was characterized as the most immigrant friendly country. As early as 1979, the Scientific Council for Government Policy completed a report on "Ethnic Minorities". The Council criticized the notion of temporality underlying government policy which left them socially disadvantaged and culturally isolated. In its 1983 Memorandum, the Dutch government recognized the many ways in which the country had come to acquire a different face after the Second World War. It was therefore felt that it was necessary to create conditions in which minorities have equal opportunities. In 1985, non-national immigrants acquired the right to vote in local elections after five years of residence. During 1992-1997, dual citizenship was allowed. In 1994, the Equal Treatment Act put the Equal Treatment Commission in place to deal with cases of direct and indirect discrimination in employment and education. Groups also received public subsidies for broadcasting, education and other welfare activities.[28] In 2000, Germany opened up its citizenship law for both the principles of *jus sanguinis* and *jus soli* to be considered as grounds for German citizenship. This had a positive impact on many second and third generation Turks who could not till then apply for the same.[29]

But multiculturalism has increasingly been pushed on the backfoot because of some of the incidents already mentioned. The rise of Islamophobia among the general public has been combined with a reexamination of multiculturalism by practitioners of state politics. The UK is emphasizing community cohesion. It has introduced citizenship courses in the school curriculum. In 2011, Prime Minister David Cameron declared at a security conference that multiculturalism had failed. He argued that UK needed a stronger national identity: "We need a lot less of the passive tolerance of recent years and much more active, muscular liberalism."[30]

The Dutch reversal of policy has been characterized by scholars as a "seismic shift". Stringent immigration laws are being put in place to monitor and ensure that the kind of people who wish to be members of Dutch society are aware of its culture and values and are ready to fit in.[31] German Chancellor Angela Merkel has recently said multiculturalism is dead. Others like Thilo Sarazzin have argued that the future of Germany is threatened by the wrong kind of immigration especially from the Muslim countries.[32] Bavaria's Premier Horst Seehofer has declared "immigrants from other cultures" to be detrimental and has called for a halt to immigration "from Turkey and Arab countries".[33] Turkey's membership in the European Union is hotly debated and there is a clear rethink on the part of Member States like Germany, France and Austria on the question of Turkish membership.[34]

The reason it has taken little time to move away from the principles of multiculturalism is because Europe continues to be based on the Enlightenment understanding of differences. This is the reason why Chancellor Merkel raises strong objections when Turkish Prime Minister Erdogan urges Turks not to renounce their culture during his visit to Germany in 2008. Merkel asserts that her understanding of "integration" and that of the Turkish Prime Minister is obviously not the same.[35] While Europe may be willing to listen to and admit that other traditions also embody values that need to be explored. Convinced of the success of the logic of modernity and superiority of its values, Europe wants to see the expansion of this modernity and its values on a universal level. It is thus fundamentally unprepared to accord equal respect or equality to the other cultures and that is precisely why it takes European states no time to abandon multiculturalism as a policy and demand near absolute conformity to majority norms and values.

Comparing India

Indian leaders seriously considered and debated the liberal model. However, in a situation where social and cultural identities had been mobilized, where some communities had received separate representation under British colonial rule, a liberal model with its emphasis on the individual did not provide satisfactory answers. Moreover, though colonial rule ended with the partition of the country and the creation of a separate homeland for the Muslim community a significant number of this community chose to stay back in India There were several anxieties about the future of the Muslims in a Hindu-dominated society. There was also the issue of lower castes—communities that were excluded from the rest of the society and denied access to social and economic benefits in society. Faced with this complex reality, the political leadership adopted a distinctive approach that linked equality for the individual with equality for diverse communities. It began with the understanding that equality for individuals would be meaningless unless different communities within the polity existed as equals. The presence of diverse communities was thus acknowledged. Indeed, the existing cultural diversity was deeply valued. It was felt that respect for the individual requires respect for the diverse beliefs and ways of life that these individuals embody. In other words, the individual could not possibly exist as an equal if the community to which he or she belongs were disadvantaged or marginalized in the public domain. It was, therefore, argued that, while the principle of equality before the law was extremely important, it was not enough. If equality was to be realized in practice, then members of the minority communities should enjoy the liberty to lead a life in accordance with their cultural practices. In concrete terms, this meant that minority religious communities needed religious liberty and protection against the threat of cultural homogenization.[36]

The slogan "Unity in Diversity" articulates the sentiment that India can be a strong and unified country while simultaneously affirming its cultural diversity. Cultural homogeneity was not, in other words, seen as a necessary condition for forging a political identity as a nation state. The commitment to this norm has been put to test at various moments in the country's history, e.g. during the demolition of the Babri Masjid, riots in Gujarat, etc., but the commitment remains. As Ainslie Embree remarked: "Those characteristic factors of Indian society which are patently divisive in themselves, have been integrated in a creative fashion in a genuinely cultural pluralism." Embree goes on to argue that in this plural society groups within the framework of the parent political unit have relatively autonomous existences. The groups are the fundamental fact. They are not enclaves in a larger society but in their totality constitute the larger society. This means that there is no single dominant common way of life, not a common vision of what is good for all.[37] On the contrary, groups have their own lifestyles, dress, food, social behaviour, language, religion, and culture. Such characteristics have been present in Indian civilization throughout history. What was needed was to integrate them by mechanisms that would not deny the essential life of component groups within the plural society.

The other factor which has perhaps added to India's capability of accepting and living with the other has been the temper of the largest religious faith of the country—Hinduism. This is certainly not to argue that Indian identity is derived from Hindu identity. India has been a multi-religious country for a very long time. Even pre-Muslim India had Buddhism and Jainism as dominant religions for hundreds of years. Sikhism originated here. However, the fact also remains that Hinduism has the largest following and its worldviews therefore had some relevance. Hinduism is a pluralist religion. It is tolerant of different doctrines and different philosophical schools, including atheism.

In the modernity of Europe, everything is judged. Everything is measured. Empathy is sorely lacking in modern times. All thoughts are expected to be legitimized through fact and evidence and mathematics and science. But many things in life cannot be explained with logic least of all life, death and God. What happens after death? Who knows? Different cultures have different answers. Each is a subjective truth, each as valid as the other. Each is therefore a myth, a story, a belief. Each has a right to exist. The Hindu tradition acknowledges that there may be many ways to God.[38] Chaturvedi Badrinath argues that the Sanskrit expression "*neti*" in the *Upanishads* needs to be added after every definitive description. He translates *neti* as "it is not this alone" which implies that we can reach a conclusion but we cannot claim them to be absolute and final.[39] Amartya Sen has also observed this tradition in Hinduism to doubt, to counter argue. He points out that the "song of creation" or the "creation hymn" in the authoritative *Vedas* ends in radical doubts:

> Who really knows? Who will here proclaim it? ... the gods came afterwards, with the creation of this universe. Who then knows whence it has arisen?...perhaps it formed itself or perhaps it did not—the one who looks down on it, in the highest heaven, only he knows—or perhaps he does not know.[40]

Sen goes on to argue that the issues of plurality and of choice are immensely relevant to the understanding and analysis of the idea of Indian identity. Both Rabindranath Tagore and Mahatma Gandhi argued for an inclusionary form of Indian identity. They did not deny the presence and contingent importance of other identities and emphasized that therefore the Indian identity could not favour any particular group over others within India.[41]

In India, the domain of equality has been extended to the notion of difference. In Europe, the domain of equality is still very much within the notion of sameness. The domain of difference has not really emerged and has not been accommodated within the notion of equality. Europe has experienced that homogenization and development go together. But they are not sure whether heterogeneity and development can go together.[42] Gandhi once said: "I want the windows of my house to be open to the winds blowing from all corners of the world, but I don't want to be blown off my feet."[43] Mark Tully observes that this could perhaps help Christians to question those of their beliefs that have led them to deny the validity of other faiths and all too often the validity of other Christian traditions than their own. The Christians say

Jesus's words are "I am the way, the truth and the light"; this is an absolute view.[44]

The problem that Europe is encountering today in accommodating diversity especially represented by the followers of Islam is that of one absolutist vision encountering another. The Muslim world operates in the name of Islam. It is homogeneous, it is plural but the imagination is very similar and in that sense it is a Muslim world. Muslims would like the world organized in their fashion just as the West would like to be in its fashion. And that is the point of contention between the two. Those who are champions of Islam are convinced of the model established by the Prophet, equally Europe is very convinced of the model established by modernity from the thirteenth century onwards and the material progress that came through the project of modernity.[45] Historically the two religions had violent encounters. At the height of Islamic expansion, Muslim armies conquered and dominated the Hispanic peninsula (700-1200) and Sicily from 828 to 1300. They had made incursions in Peninsular Italy and parts of France. The new rulers called their Hispanic dominion "Al-Andalus". Christians were described as dogs and pigs—both animals despised in Islam. The Christians in Spain coined their own terms to describe the Muslims in a symmetrical way. The revulsion against all those who were not Christians included the Jews. As the Christians reclaimed their lands and consolidated their rule, Jews and Muslims were expelled from Spain.[46]

These historic encounters should not be troubling secular Europe. But it does both because secularism can be as aggressive and as dogmatic as any absolute religion and because secularism as a natural outcome of modernism stands questioned today. The secularization thesis came under scrutiny in the 1970s. Some pointed out that Europe was the exception not the rule. Europe may have been secularizing but the rest of the world was as religious as ever. Interestingly, Philip Barker also draws attention to the fact that in this Europe where secularism is the norm there are countries that defy the trend—Poland, Ireland and Greece can be easily singled out. Attendance levels are high—70 per cent in Ireland, 80 per cent in Poland, 96 per cent in Greece.[47] Either way as different cultural and religious communities became permanent residents of European societies in the post-Second World War II period they raised critical questions of mutual acceptance of the 'other', of rights which neither Europe's enlightenment logic of modernity nor secularism seem capable of addressing.

Conclusion

In conclusion, one can say that diversity is a challenge for all states and societies. India today is far from a perfect society. It is beset with many problems. Yet it would be hard to deny that its constitutional vision has enabled it to manage and contain the challenges of diversity and forge a sense of unity. In India, liberal democratic principles were adopted innovatively to suit the demands of a diverse society. As Khilnani observes:

> Nehru's idea of Indianness emerged through improvised responses to constrained circumstances: its strength was not its ideological intensity, but its ability to steer towards an Indianess seen as layered, adjustable, imagined, not as a fixed property. While Nehru was attracted by the political and economic examples of the modern West, he was far less taken by its cultural models.[48]

Europe is in a bind. As Stephen Castles remarks: "Failure to make immigrants into citizens undermines a basic principle of parliamentary democracy—that all members of civil society should have rights of political participation—but making them into citizens questions concepts of the nation based on ethnic belonging or cultural homogeneity."[49] In Europe, the homogeneous nation states confronted diversity much later primarily as a result of immigration and the response essentially has been diversity can only be tolerated if they "fit" in the majority framework.

NOTES

1. V.M. Vanishree, "Provision for Linguistic Diversity and Linguistic Minorities in India," at http://www.languageinindia.com/feb2011/vanishreemastersfinal.pdf (accessed on 20 January 2012).

2. http://www.state.gov/r/pa/ei/bgn/3454.htm.
3. Gurpreet Mahajan, "Negotiating Cultural Diversity and Minority Rights in India" http://www.idea.int/publications/dchs/upload/dchs_vol2_sec3_4.pdf (accessed on 18 January 2012).
4. Granville Austin, *The Indian Constitution: Cornerstone of a Nation* (New Delhi: Oxford University Press, 2012), pp. 265-307.
5. Ibid.
6. Ibid.
7. A. Sarangi, *Language and Politics in India,* (New Delhi: Oxford University Press, 2009), p. 27.
8. See David D. Laitin, "Language Policy and Political Strategy in India," *Policy Sciences* Vol. 22, No. 3/4, (1989), pp. 415-436 and Marshall Windmiller, "Linguistic Regionalism in India," *Pacific Affairs,* Vol. 27, No. 4, December 1954), pp. 291-318.
9. Ibid.
10. Amaresh Bagchi, "Rethinking Federalism: Changing Power Relations between the Centre and the States," *Publius,* Vol. 33, No. 4, 2003, pp. 21-42.
11. Ibid.
12. http://india.gov.in/govt/documents/english/coi_part_full.pdf. Incidentally most other states in its neighbourhood affirm a religious identity: Pakistan and Bangladesh are Islamic states; Sri Lanka gives a special status to Buddhism; and Nepal is a Hindu state.
13. Rajeev Bhargava, *Beyond Secularism: The Rights of Religious Minorities* (New Delhi: OUP, 2002).
14. Dhavan Rajeev in Sen Ronojoy, "Legalising Religion: The Indian Supreme Court and Secularism," *Policy Studies* 30, 2007, pp. 1-41.
15. Nehru in Ronojoy, n. 14, p. 5.
16. http://india.gov.in/govt/documents/english/coi_part_full.pdf
17. Gurpreet Mahajan, *Identities and Rights: Aspects of Liberal Democracy in India* (New Delhi: Oxford University Press, 1998).
18. Connie Smith, "Devolution in the UK: Powers and Structures in Scotland, Wales and Northern Ireland," at http://www.clicp.ed.ac.uk/publications/briefings/briefing01.pdf.
19. http://articles.businessinsider.com/2012-01-09/europe/30606610_1_alex-salmond-snp-scotland.
20. Montserrat Guibernau, "Catalonia: A Non-secessionist Nationalism," in Michael Seymour, ed., *The Fate of the Nation State* (Montreal: McGill-Queens University Press, 2004), pp. 234-246.
21. See Charlie Jeffery, "Federalism and Territorial Politics," in

Stephen Padgett, William E. Paterson and Gordon Smith, eds., *Developments in German Politics 3* (New York: Palgrave Macmillan, 2003), pp. 38-59; also see Hartmut Klatt and B. Arthur Gunlicks, "Forty Years of German Federalism: Past Trends and New Developments," *Publius*, Vol. 19, No. 4, Autumn 1989, pp. 185-202.

22. Deschouwer, Kris, *The Politics of Belgium: Governing a Divided Society* (London: Palgrave Macmillan, 2009)
23. See http://en.wikinews.7val.com/wiki/After_9_months,_Belgian_coalition_delivers_government http://gulfstreamblues.blogspot.in/2011/12/after-18-months-belgium-will-have.html
24. Gurpreet Mahajan, *The Multicultural Path: Issues of Diversity and Discrimination in Democracy* (New Delhi: Sage Publications, 2002), pp. 55-56.
25. Ibid.
26. See Christian Joppke and Lukes Steven, eds., *Multicultural Questions* (Oxford: OUP, 1999); Bhikhu Parekh, *Rethinking Multiculturalism: Cultural Diversity and Political Theory* (London: Macmillan, 2000).
27. Nam-Kook Kim, "Redefining Citizenship in the Context of Deliberative Multiculturalism", (n.d.) http://citation.allacademic.com/meta/p_mla_apa_research_citation/0/6/2/9/4/pages62943/p62943-3.php
28. P. Maarten Vink, "Dutch 'Multiculturalism' Beyond the Pillarisation Myth," *Political Studies Review*, vol 5, issue 3, 2007 pp. 337-350. Since 1985, there are publicly subsidized Dutch Muslim Broadcasting Service, 1994 a Hindu one, Islamic and Hindu primary schools, 450 mosques.
29. Veysel Oezcan, "Germany: Immigration in Transition, Migration Information Source, July 2004," http://www.migrationinformation.org/Profiles/display.cfm?ID=235 accessed on 23 September 2011.
30. Claire Worley, "It's not about race. It's about the Community: New Labour and 'Community cohesion'," *Critical Social Policy*, 2005. For Cameroon comments see BBC News UK Politics, 5 February 2011 accessed on 28 April 2011.
31. "Holland's New Greeting for Immigrants 'If it Ain't Dutch, It Ain't Much," *Der Spiegel*, 24 January 2006 http://www.spiegel.de/international/0,1518,397021,00.html (accessed on 14 October 2011).
32. Juergen Habermas, "Leadership and Leitkultur," 28 October 28,

2010 *at* http://www.nytimes.com/2010/10/29/opinion/29Habermas.html?pagewanted=all, accessed on 11 November 2010.
33. Ibid.
34. Second Report of the Independent Commission on Turkey, *Turkey in Europe: Breaking the Vicious Circle,* September 2009.
35. "German Chancellor Rejects Turkish View on Integration," at http://www.dw-world.com/dw/article/0,,3121091,00.htm accessed on 11 April 2009.
36. Gurpreet Mahajan, "Negotiating Cultural Diversity and Minority Rights in India," http://www.idea.int/publications/dchs/upload/dchs_vol2_sec3_4.pdf accessed on 18 January 2012.
37. Ainslie Embree, "India: A Plural Society," *The High School Journal,* Vol. 56, No.1, October 1972, pp.45-53.
38. Devdutt Pattnaik, *7 Secrets from Hindu Calendar Art* (Chennai: Westlannd, 2009).
39. Mark Tully, *India's Unending Journey: Finding Balance in a Time of Change* (London: Snyder, 2007), p. 45.
40. Amartya Sen, *The Argumentative Indian* (London: Penguin Books, 2005), p. 22.
41. Ibid., p. 352.
42. Anwar Alam, in Michael Dusche, *Identity Politics in India and Europe* (New Delhi: Sage, 2010), p. 165.
43. Tully, n. 39, p. 16.
44. Ibid.
45. Alam, n. 42, pp. 162-168.
46. Dusche, n. 44, pp. 162-168.
47. W. Philip Barker, *Religious Nationalism in Modern Europe: If God be for Us* (London: Routledge, 2009), pp. 2-28.
48. Sunil Khilnani, *The Idea of India* (New Delhi: Penguin Books, 2004), p. 167.
49. Stephen Castles, *Ethnicity and Globalization* (London: Sage, 2000), p. 141.

3

Social Integration in Multicultural Societies: A Comparative Study of India and Europe

Sheetal Sharma

Introduction

Multiculturalism celebrates cultural diversity amongst different groups deriving their identity on the basis of caste, race, region, religion, gender, ethnicity, language, etc. Contemporary societies are multicultural and are characterized by extensive cultural diversity. The present state of multiculturalism is a product of combined forces of globalization, (inter)national migration, industrialization, transfer of information, technologies, knowledge, skills, flow of capital, increased human interaction and linkages at multiple levels. Unlike past multiculturalism, contemporary multiculturalism is complex, variegated, intense, wider, deeper, and defiant[1] in nature. In contemporary multicultural societies, we witness contradictory tendencies in operation. We witness both cultural homogenization and diffusion happening as well as resistance to cultural diffusion, assertion of socio-cultural identities, contestation for/against privilege, domination, exploitation, marginalization and exclusion.

Literature and theoretical explanations pertaining to multiculturalism have grown manifold in recent years. Philosophers, social scientists, academicians, and policy-makers have been interested in understanding and exploring the nature and dimensions of multiculturalism. Existing literature primarily relates multiculturalism to political strategy.[2] There is, as Will Kymlicka argues, "no universally accepted definition of '(liberal) multiculturalism'," and any attempt to provide a single definition to encompass its different forms is too vague to be useful. There is a tendency to simplify complexity and reduce multiculturalism to a single principle or dimension.[3] Multiculturalism is not a single principle of policy, but an umbrella of highly group-differentiated approaches; and each of these approaches is multi-dimensional, incorporating economic, political and cultural elements in a variety of ways.[4] Stuart Hall observes:

> Over the years the term 'multiculturalism' has come to refer to a diffuse, indeed maddeningly spongy and imprecise, discursive field: a train of false trails and misleading universals. Even within a single nation there have been contested interpretations of the policies and practices of multiculturalism. Hence it is difficult to formulate a specific corpus of tenets or practices defining multiculturalism.[5]

Conceptualizing multiculturalism further becomes difficult if undertaken comparatively across countries that are (un)officially multicultural in either/both policy and practice such as India, France, Australia, Canada, the United States, Great Britain, Sweden and the Netherlands.

Multiculturalism in Contemporary India and Europe

Both India and Europe are characterized by cultural pluralism and exhibit fascinating patterns of similarities and differences and unity amidst diversity. Presenting a synthesis of tradition and modernity, both are repositories of rich and refined cultural practices fundamental to civilizations. Among others, both are committed to democracy, constitutionalism, guaranteeing freedom, equality, and liberty to individuals and citizens, and the protection of human rights. Amidst vast ethno-cultural diversity, both India and Europe display a unique social fabric representing "unity in diversity". The distinctiveness of their multiculturalism can be described as a harmoniously balanced, at times, a conflicting collage; a complex mosaic of distinctive socio-cultural traits, customs, traditions, and set of values that prescribe peaceful coexistence and respect for a wide range of diversity within the broad framework of equality, liberty, and rule of (secular) law. Cultural heterogeneity and plurality is valued, cherished and respected as a normative ideal by the state and society in general and is so espoused. The existence and operation of cultural pluralism in different social, economic and political institutions is not without its share of contestation often arising out of charges of misappropriation and cornering of (finite) resources by certain groups leading to polarization in society. However, rooted in their respective histories the nature and content of multiculturalism, the way it is manifest and modelled is distinct in both contexts. Tracing historically, India and Europe exhibit specific ways in which diverse cultures have existed through centuries in respective societies and how they continue to shape the contours of multiculturalism in contemporary times.

Cultural Diversity in India

Since the history of first known—the Harappan—civilization in the Indus River Valley (3000 BCE) till the end of British colonial rule in 1947, numerous empires ruled different parts of India. The early empires were the Aryans[6] (2000 BCE), the Mauryan Empire[7] (326 BCE to 200 BCE), and the Gupta Empire[8] (320 CE to 550 CE). The rise of one and the disintegration of the other empire led to a constant restructuring of territorial boundaries and conflicts between kingdoms. From the twelfth century onwards, initially the northern part of India, then the Indo-Gangetic Plains and gradually the whole of northern India was conquered by the Mughals.[9] Every empire left its impression by enriching and assimilating a rich array of people, practices, norms, values, languages, festivals, ideas, and technologies in the culture. The roots of imperialism in India began soon after the Portuguese arrived in 1498 CE. The British Empire consolidated and controlled, over and above inherent religious, linguistic, and cultural diversity, the scattered and fragmented sovereignty of numerous kingdoms weaving them into a unified entity called

India. After independence in 1947, India as a nation state aspired to, is and has (always) been a multicultural society with extensive religious,[10] ethnic,[11] linguistic[12] and cultural diversity. For the people of India, there has always been a common past, memories, achievements, traditions and even failures. In India, plurality is taken for granted historically. With a multiple set of beliefs and practices, there are layers of diversity. For instance, Hindus[13] who constitute the majority of population, are sub-divided into numerous castes.[14]

In this context, Pandit Jawaharlal Nehru observed:

> It is fascinating to find how the Bengalis, the Marathas, the Gujratis, the Tamils, Andhras, the Oriyas, the Assamese, the Canarese, the Malayalis, the Sindhis, the Punjabis, the Pathans, the Kashmiris, the Rajputs and the great central block comprising the Hindustani-speaking people, have retained their peculiar characteristics for hundreds of years, have still more or less the same virtues and failings of which old tradition or record tells us and yet have been throughout these ages distinctively Indian, with the same national heritage and the same set of moral and mental qualities.[15]

Cultural Diversity in Europe

Europe too is multicultural and presents an interesting case of "unity amidst diversity". All Member States of the European Union[16] are plural having a multiplicity of linguistic,[17] cultural, ethnic, religious,[18] and regional diversity. A variety of historical processes and forces[19] have shaped the socio-cultural and political fabric of contemporary EU. From the beginning of the seventeenth century, the most significant source of cultural (not necessarily synonymous with ethnic) diversity in European nation-states has been regional, often a result of conjoining economically, socially, culturally, and ethnically disparate places into single polities, and engaging them in discourse of nationalism based on common language.[20] From the seventeenth century onwards till the Second World War, there was an interplay between various material and intellectual forces[21] in Europe. Since the Second World War, there has been a large-scale movement of people not only across national boundaries within Europe but also massive immigration from developing countries, seeking better socio-economic prospects. According to Eurostat, there were 32.4 million non-nationals in the EU Member States in 2009. They represented 6.5 per cent of the total EU population of which 55 per cent of immigrants were from countries outside the EU.[22] Through migration, "Europe is now home to millions of people from non-European backgrounds, many religious and cultural dispositions, and many networks of attachment based on Diaspora connections and cultural influences from around the world. Europe is as much a site of longings rooted in tradition—regional, national and European—as it is a site of transnational and trans-European attachments."[23]

Multiculturalism is accepted and is a part of public discussion acknowledging cultural pluralism as an inherent fact of contemporary European society. In Western Europe, the use of the term "multiculturalism" entails and acknowledges the permanent presence of immigrant populations and the formulation of policies aimed at subsequent integration of immigrants (minorities) into the mainstream. Though different Member States have approached and adopted a multicultural framework over time but all of them have not necessarily defined and modelled it in a similar way. Variations in models occur on the basis of the structure of the state, their recognition of regional and linguistic diversities, and the presence of minorities.

Multiculturalism was first adopted as an official policy by Sweden in 1975 to deal with the issue of the integration of immigrants. Subsequently, Britain, the Netherlands and the Scandinavian countries also adopted multicultural policies. Some countries have institutionalized pluralism through the creation of regions granting limited power, as in Italy and Spain. Other countries have built the state upon linguistic pluralism, e.g. Belgium and Switzerland, where each of the linguistic and territorial communities have their own institutions. In France, Germany, Great Britain and the Netherlands, the term "multiculturalism" refers to the supposedly communitarian form of organization of the immigrant population around a common nationality or religion (or both) and the accompanying demand for their specific voices in the public sphere.[24]

In recent years, multiculturalism in Europe has been severely criticized and has been pronounced as a failure.[25] Critics of multiculturalism assert that it views cultures and ethnic groups in essentialized and static terms, which strengthens ethnic cleavages and thereby breeds separatism and ghettoization. It is further rejected for its failure to provide a viable and sustainable sense of national unity and cohesion in multi-ethnic societies. After the tragic incidents of 9/11, 7/7, and the Madrid train bombing in 2004, have led to greater scepticism of multiculturalism as a viable model of societal integration.[26]

Conversely, diversity in India is not the result of increasing numbers of immigrants. India, in fact, has been a homeland of diverse communities since ages and its social fabric has always been plural.[27] The presence of such a diverse population has necessitated the adoption of policies aimed at safeguarding the interests of minorities. There has been no official attempt to impose a blanket cultural unity among the culturally diverse groups in India.[28] "As diverse communities coexist within the state, multiculturalism raises the issue of their equality. It asks whether the different entities, constituting the many, are granted an equal status within the polity."[29] The protection of minority interests is one of the principal features of the Constitution of India, which not only recognizes differences and diversity, but guarantees equal citizenship, equal rights, and protects linguistic, cultural, and religious minorities. The various Articles[30] of the Constitution providing rights to the minorities, clearly and firmly acknowledge that India is multi-religious, multi-cultural, multi-lingual and multi-racial. Thus, multiculturalism in India is interwoven in the Constitution and India is multicultural both in policy and practice.

In India, there are visible differences and matters of appearance, such as dress, headgear or wearing of a veil are not major issues of contestation. "Multiculturalism in India operates with the belief that living together requires not just respect for other individuals but also some concern for their feelings and sentiments. This draws upon the particular conception of the self and tolerance. Multiculturalism in India has been characterized by the concept of tolerance and situatedness and also nurtured by it. Tolerance that emanated from a conception of a deeply situated self which invariably provided space for the recognition of cultural diversity; in democratic India it is manifest in freedom to practise one's cultural way of life."[31] As a result, social and public life is infused with expressions of diversity. However, in liberal societies that value individual autonomy the challenges that confront multiculturalism are significantly different. The diversity of cultural forms and practices follows quite easily from the Indian understanding of the self, but it remains a subject of dispute in Europe. Issues such as, should religious symbols (headscarves/turbans/*kadas*) be allowed in schools? Should there be a ban on minarets, surface over and over again in Western democracies on account of their purported conflict with the ideals of individual autonomy and self-defining self.[32]

Although cultural plurality may be politically recognized, and equality among culturally diverse groups may be constitutionally guaranteed by democratic societies, the everyday experience of cultural interaction between individuals and communities having different cultural affiliations are not so harmonious. These encounters often result in violent articulation of cultural intolerance and hegemony. In other words, however highly multiculturalism may be valued by the societies and/or states, there are inevitable and ubiquitous incidents and issues with acceptance or even understanding/recognition of cultural differences.

Conflict in Multicultural Societies

Multicultural societies often witness cultural conflicts, which can occur over any issue such as sharing of resources, power, status, values, ideologies. Culture[33] evolves and gets institutionalized over generations and is difficult to part away with. Bhikhu Parekh delineates three dimensions of cultural reality. *First*, "human beings are culturally embedded... they grow up and live within a culturally structured world and organize their lives and social relations in terms of a culturally derived system of meaning and significance. *Second,* different cultures represent different systems of meaning and visions of a good life. And *third,* every culture is internally plural and reflects a continuing conversation between its different traditions and strands of thought."[34] The problem starts when one group imposes its culture on others based on the idea of cultural superiority. The social reality of contemporary multicultural societies exhibits an uneasy calm between culturally diverse groups as instances of cultural intolerance are on the rise. Turning violent at times, intolerance is manifest in the form of racism, xenophobia, fundamentalism, extremism, communal hatred, tensions, and/or clashes. As a result, the cherished social order and unity is getting fractured. Both India and Europe experience formidable challenges in promoting social integration among a culturally diverse population, promoting social integration, and ensuring and establishing enduring peace and stability. Rooted in their respective history and social structure there is a difference between policy and practice of multiculturalism in India and Europe. Although it is difficult to construct a general framework explaining the specific nature of challenges and conflicts in both the societies yet managing cultural conflict has become a serious challenge for both of them.

There have been unprecedented changes in the socio-economic, political and cultural landscape of India in the last two decades. Contemporary India has become "a site for cultural conflicts rooted in ethnic, caste, and/or parochial identity. The bold assertion of socio-cultural differences and resultant demystification of a unitary identity of 'Indianness' characterize contemporary India... there is resistance emanating from those who proclaim their differences, anguish, and right to their alternative and autonomous identities. One can witness ethnic groups striving for autonomy (Tripura, Assam, Jharkhand), militant politico-religious associations expressing their discontent and searching for a new nation (Jammu and Kashmir), lower castes challenging *Brahminism,* politics of reservation, language, statehood, and women asserting their distinctive voice. No wonder, grand ideologies like 'Hindu civilizational unity' or, 'Indian nationhood' are being questioned."[35]

On the other hand, massive immigration has enhanced the complexity of the socio-cultural texture of contemporary Europe. The recent enlargements of the European Union accompanied by the freedom of movement has compounded the problem of maintaining balance in a rapidly changing socio-cultural and demographic profile. In such a scenario achieving social harmony and integration has become a challenge. Different European countries follow different models of societal integration. In general, one can identify three models of social integration, namely *assimilation, differential integration and exclusion,* and *multiculturalism*. Evolving and responding to changing economic, social and political conditions,[36] these models are influenced by factors such as the colonial legacy, historical memories (real as well as imagined), and political relations with the immigrants' home countries. However, owing to diverse interpretations of the concept of social integration, these models of social integration reflect ambivalence and incoherence. For instance, France and Belgium insist on the assimilation of immigrants and ethnic and religious minorities into the mainstream. On the other hand, Britain, the Netherlands, Luxembourg and the Scandinavian countries, which follow multicultural policies, have accorded public recognition to ethnic and cultural diversity and are far more accommodative of the rights and sensibilities of the religious and cultural minorities.[37]

"Tensions and violence involving immigrants particularly Muslims is the greatest source of societal tensions and violent conflict in contemporary Europe."[38] These conflicts are primarily due to *a)* the social and/or economic disadvantage and discrimination affecting religious minorities and groups, and *b)* terrorist violence inspired by radical ideas (Islamic fundamentalism). While the acts of terror are specific, attract media attention, and are condemned the world over, the discrimination of minorities in everyday life is the major source of social strain.[39] Rooted in cultural differences, these instances are subtle, diffused and often not reported. Such acts of discrimination are a major obstacle to the integration of immigrants and ethnic minorities into mainstream.

The European Union is committed to some form of political multiculturalism. This is evident for instance, from its decision to make respect for minority rights one of the accession criteria for prospective members.[40] However, it is paradoxical that liberal societies which value tolerance and individualism are reluctant to accept individual and collective decisions to endorse a way of life of particular communities.[41] Social conflicts involving minorities and/or immigrants are an "expression of conservative notion of 'we', a homogeneous and anchored 'national identity' giving a sense of belongingness."[42] European societies must "address the crucial issues of the way in which former and current 'migration societies' are significantly shaped by the effects of migration in the long run and of how they learn to be 'multicultural' in the sense that the diversity of their population in ethno-cultural terms challenges the dynamic towards the unity of nation-states."[43]

In recent years, there has been a shift towards greater acceptance of cultural differences. However, for many people religious, ethnic, and "racial" otherness continues to be a challenge and threat.[44]

Promoting Social Integration in Multicultural Societies

Multiculturalism poses a different set of challenges for India and Europe. In varying degrees, both have adopted different legislative, political, socio-economic, normative and ideological frameworks to address the issues and problems arising out of management of cultural diversity and promoting social solidarity. However, balancing the interest of diverse communities is difficult. Since both can neither suppress diversity nor dispense with unity, they need to find ways of reconciling their apparently conflicting demands.[45] A major difficulty in designing programmes and policies for social integration is how to define the concept of "social integration". There is no consensus among theoreticians and policy-makers on how the concept of social integration may/must be conceptualized and brought into practice. In general, "social integration" refers to the principles by which individuals/actors are related to one another in a society.[46] The term can embrace both order and conflict and can be explained in three different ways. Does it mean

a) *assimilation*: (being here and the same) assimilation demands putting down roots and orienting oneself in the dominant culture of the recipient society;
b) *integration*: (being here but different)—here cultural diversity is recognized and accepted in the private sphere and a high degree of assimilation is expected in the public sphere; or
c) *enclavement*: (being here but separate) enclavement demands the acceptance, institutional recognition, and institutionalization of cultural differences in the public sphere; special provision in education, healthcare and welfare, etc., and organization of representation on ethnic/cultural lines.[47]

At times, such distinctions create divisions[48] between the 'in-group' and the 'out-group'. Thus, the lack of consensus over the definition of the term "integration" leads to the formulation of incoherent multicultural policies and practices. The confusion is further intensified when applied to different contexts, i.e. in the public and the private sphere.

The specificity of both the Indian and European experience in promoting social integration in their respective societies limits the possibilities of generalization. Nevertheless, since both are multicultural in their own ways, some of the basic issues and challenges in promoting social integration remain the same. Envisaging and creating a socially inclusive world is a challenge requiring concerted efforts from both the dominant and the marginalized. Some measures can be adopted to ensure a harmonious coexistence of diverse communities in multicultural societies. These principles could be a set of simple non-binding but thoughtful guide against which state and/or society can individually judge and assess their prevalent programmes and policies,[49] and also derive a framework that can be (re)structured as per the nature of the context.

First, social integration calls for changing 'mentalities', of both the minority and majority communities. Social integration and changing mentality is a dynamic, two-way process of 'mutual accommodation' where the stakeholders need to overcome: *a*) the prejudiced notions about the 'other'; and *b*) discriminatory behaviour and practice. The philosophy of 'mutual accommodation' (respecting and granting the 'otherness of the other') must be inculcated in thought and practice equally. Propagating respect for fundamental values of humanity can help in institutionalizing philosophy of 'mutual accommodation'. Since societies cannot be held together by economic interests and political frameworks alone, there is a need to forge trans-cultural bonds that can generate emotional (rather than instrumental) feelings of 'collectivity' and 'relatedness' to humanity. Initiatives like intercultural and cross-cultural interactions, music, literary, food and film festivals, citizens' conclaves, etc. help in transcending mental boundaries drawn around isolated socio-cultural islands. Such measures create emotional bonds between people, promote peace and contentment and envisage a world outside the realm of politics, rational self-interest, hate, terror, and violence.

Respect for 'others' calls for a change in the perceptions and understanding of 'cultures'. Every culture is unique. Evolving over centuries, it provides a sense of belongingness, an image, and an 'identity'.[50] There is nothing problematic with socio-cultural identities as long as they provide a meaning to existence and a sense of belongingness to individuals. However, the problem arises when identities begin to aggressively/violently assert, claim their superiority, and contest for/against relative domination. To restrain these contestations, a change in social discourse is desirable. "What people have in common is more the sense of a common enemy [or evil] than the commitment to a common culture. Instead of promoting the supposedly universal features of one civilization, the requisites for cultural coexistence demand a search for what is common to most civilizations. In a multicultural world, the constructive course is to renounce universalism, accept diversity and seek commonalities. Human society is universal because it is human, particular because it is society. We are similar still we are different. Yet a "thin" minimal morality does derive from the common human condition, and "universal dispositions" are found in all cultures.[51] There is a need to evolve a distinctive way of seeing, and cultivating sensitivity to understand and appreciate differences by broadening our horizon and realizing shared[52] humanity at civilizational level.[53]

Multiculturalism is constitutionally recognized by many societies. But this guarantee is more a political philosophy/ rhetoric. Problems occur when this guarantee is brought in to practice.[54] To overcome these problems, it is necessary to create a political culture and a public sphere that all citizens share. In the realm of economics, people are motivated by interests. Social integration however needs more than a mere compromise on interests. Social integration touches the very identity and values of the people. As Juergen Habermas remarks: "Love or recognition cannot be exchanged for money, one's mother tongue or religious confession cannot be exchanged for job positions. It needs a common self understanding, a self-understanding that can be found only in discourses of self-understanding." Discourses of self-understanding in the public sphere would create social norms and a culture of reciprocity."[55] As and when these set of norms and values emerge, one must theorize about the mechanisms through which they can be diffused in particular social settings and (perhaps) socialize agents. Constructivists have identified two ways, viz. *societal mobilization* and *social learning*. In the former, non-state actors and policy networks are united in their support for norms; they then mobilize and influence decision-making. In the latter, élite decision-makers adopt prescriptions embodied in norms and translate them into policy.[56]

Education too has a potential to play a key role in the process of socialization. (In)formal education has to have more than "a mere formal/academic component. Formal education divorced from moral and philosophical queries is damaging.

Morality does not mean religious education or sermonizing. Secular education should enable us to internalize the moral authority of the collective which transcends the individual and strengthen the process of integration."[57] Multicultural realities can also be understood through trans-cultural (secular) education. "This means capacity to see beyond the horizons of one's own religion, create an accommodative space which is open to other traditions, and generate a sense of a cohesive society. Secular education inculcates spirit of plurality, civility and respect for diverse traditions. Equal respect to all religions...would help us overcome all sorts of sectarianisms and their excessive ritualism,"[58] and thereby create unity amidst diversity. Moreover, programmes and policies for social inclusion should be designed to instil a sense of self-worth and pride in neighbourhoods among the marginalized/excluded groups. Initiatives of sponsored mobility help in building confidence and eliminate the threat of dominant and hegemonic forces. Although it is difficult to see differences without constructing a hierarchical order, which is accentuated by economic inequality, the design of institutional frameworks must incorporate the element of equality rather than hierarchy. For instance, a small change in terminology can bring about a major change in the mindset of the conflicting communities. For instance, instead of using harsh terms like immigrants/ strangers/aliens, one can use soft terms like "new entrants", or working *'with'* the immigrants rather than *'for'* the immigrants. Such changes make multicultural realities welcoming and friendly rather than hostile and/or unwelcoming. It also makes the process of adjustment easier by making 'others' instantly part of the host community. Moreover, while formulating socially inclusive policies and programmes, the state should welcome a spirited dialogue and discussion between policy-makers, academia, the civil society, and stakeholders. Resulting policies will be far more effective in appeal that is likely to promote a feeling of belongingness to a common cultural unit among people 'from below', along with, if not over and above, their specific socio-cultural identities. Moreover, it is quite natural for stakeholders to respect decisions taken through mutual discussion and consensus rather than obeying imposed regulations.

A rigid stand and an inflexible frame of association with socio-cultural identity is vulnerable to conflict and antagonism. As forces of globalization are bound to unite us, it is impossible to live in isolation and retain an exclusive identity amidst rapidly dissolving socio-cultural, economic and political boundaries. Those who perceive 'other' cultures and forces as a threat to their own culture take a rigidly undifferentiated and highly impoverished view of culture. They assume culture to be static whereas cultures are constantly evolving and endlessly porous. It is equally important to realize that all identities are not necessarily desirable. People must be willing to discard those identities which are particularly oppressive, dehumanizing, obsolete, and are impeding to development.[59] Identities are constantly getting (re)created, (re)structured in everyday life. Identity and allegiance to it can be fluid or rigid depending on the context and case in question.

Conclusion

The effectiveness of efforts for the promotion of social integration in multicultural societies depends on a combination of philosophical, theoretical, and practical measures. The essence of such measures must be able to communicate that despite having differences we can work together and constitute a shared public sphere transcending identity barriers. Both India and Europe are, both, adherents of the philosophy and social practice of the ideals of multiculturalism. Living amidst plurality faces contestation and opposition from those who see humanity in the process becoming a 'homogeneous whole'. However, unity does not mean uniformity. Socio-cultural diversity and the forces of social integration mutually complement and supplement each other. They have to strike a fine balance where social integration is achieved not at the cost of exclusion of some or many but social inclusion of all. Along with propagating philosophies, practical steps and initiatives are required to promote ideals of 'social inclusion', 'unity amidst differences', 'assimilation and tolerance' and 'cross-culturalism'. This task is easier to conceptualize than realize in practice. Nevertheless, it is a goal worth striving for.

NOTES

1. Bhiku Parekh, "Unity and Diversity in Multicultural Societies." The paper is an extended version of the lecture delivered at the International Institute for Labour Studies, Geneva, ILO, on 15 November 2004, first published in 2005. http://www.ilo.org/public/english/bureau/inst/download/1parekh.pdf.
2. For instance, on conceptualization of multiculturalism see Charles Taylor, *Multiculturalism and the Politics of Recognition* (Princeton: Princeton University Press, 1992); Will Kymlicka, *Multicultural Citizenship: A Liberal Theory of Minority Rights* (Oxford: Oxford University Press, 1995); Bhikhu Parekh, *Rethinking Multi-culturalism: Cultural Diversity and Political Theory* (Basingstone: Palgrave, 2000); Brian Barry, *Culture and Equality: An Egalitarian Critique of Multiculturalism* (Cambridge: Polity Press, 2001); Tariq Modood, *Multiculturalism*, Cambridge: Polity, 2007); and Anne Phillips, *Multiculturalism without Culture* (Princeton: Princeton University Press, 2007).

   A divergent set of civic programmes might be labelled as 'radical multiculturalism' or 'polycentric multiculturalism' Ella Shohat and Robert Stam, *Unthinking Eurocentrism: Multiculturalism and the Media* (New York: Routledge, 1994); 'insurgent multiculturalism', H.A. Giroux, "Insurgent Multiculturalism and the Promise of Pedagogy", in D.T. Goldberg (ed.) *Multiculturalism: A Critical Reader* (Oxford: Blackwell, 1994), pp. 325–343; 'public space multiculturalism' Steven Vertovec , "Multiculturalism, Culturalism and Public Incorporation," *Ethnic and Racial Studies* 19(1), 1996, pp. 49-69; 'difference multiculturalism', Terence Turner, "Anthropology and Multiculturalism: What is Anthropology that multi-culturalists should be mindful of it?," *Cultural Anthropology* 4, November 1993, pp. 411-429; 'critical multiculturalism', Chicago Cultural Studies Group (1994) in D.T. Goldberg (ed.) *Multi-culturalism: A Critical Reader* (Oxford: Blackwell, 1994), pp. 114-139; 'weak' or 'strong' multiculturalism; R.D. Grillo, "Backlash against Diversity? Identity and Cultural Politics in European Cities" (Oxford: Centre on Migration, Policy and Society [COMPAS] Working Paper WP-05–14, 2005. quoted from Stephen Vertovec and Sussane Wessendorf, *Assessing the*

Backlash, MMG WP 09-04, at www.mmg.mpg.de/working papers.

3. Such as, "protecting endangered cultural traditions", or "validating stigmatized identities", or "repudiating nationalism".
4. Will Kymlicka, *Multicultural Odysseys* (Oxford: Oxford University Press, 2007), pp. 61-88.
5. Stuart Hall, "The Multicultural Question," Papers in Social and Cultural Research no. 4, 2001, Pavis Centre for Social and Cultural Research, The Open University, Milton Keynes, United Kingdom. http://www.open.ac.uk/socialsciences/pavis/papers.php
6. The Aryans brought a new pantheon of anthropomorphic Gods, the Sanskrit language, a multi-tiered social system based on ethnicity and occupation, and religions.
7. The Mauryan emperors had a highly centralized and hierarchical administration.
8. In contrast to the Mauryan Empire, the Guptas maintained a decentralized form of government, using numerous regional and local officials to govern vast territories with an array of local political, economic, and social arrangements. Called the "Classical Age", Gupta authority was religiously legitimized. Multiple components of Hindu culture became crystallized into a more unified system of thought during this period.
9. From the thirteenth century onwards, a large part of north India was ruled by the Mughals. The Mughal empire witnessed its golden period under Akbar, who ruled from 1556 to 1605. However over time, the leadership and administrative capacities of later Mughal rulers faced a setback from inflated, inefficient and corrupt bureaucracies and huge, unwieldy armies.
10. According to estimates, approximately 80.5 per cent of the population is Hindu, 13.4 per cent Muslim, 2.3 per cent Christian, 1.9 per cent Sikh, 0.8 per cent Buddhist, and 0.4 per cent Jain; another 0.6 per cent belongs to other faiths, such as Zoroastrianism and many religions associated with Scheduled Tribes.
11. With only the continent of Africa exceeding the linguistic, cultural, and genetic diversity of India, it is estimated that 72 per cent of the population is Indo-Aryan, 25 per cent Dravidian, and 3 per cent Mongoloid and other. Each of these groups are further subdivided into various—and changing—combinations of language, religion, and, very often, caste. See United States

Library of Congress, Country Profile: India, December 2004, available at: http://www.unhcr.org/refworld/docid/46f913452.html.

12. Hindi is the official language and most widely spoken (approximately 40.2 per cent of population). The 2011 Census listed 216 languages with more than 10,000 native speakers (22 of which are spoken by one million or more persons). An estimated 850 languages are in daily use, and there are more than 1,600 dialects. Twenty-two languages are officially recognized by the Constitution for various political, educational, and other purposes: Assamese, Bengali, Bodo, Dogri, Gujarati, Hindi, Kannada, Kashmiri, Konkani, Maithali, Malayalam, Manipuri, Marathi, Nepali, Oriya, Punjabi, Sanskrit, Santhali, Sindhi, Tamil, Telugu, and Urdu. The other commonly spoken languages are Bengali (8.3%), Telugu (7.9%), Marathi (7.5%), and Tamil (6.3%).
13. The caste system, though being ubiquitous to Hindus, is also prevalent among Muslims, Sikhs, Buddhists, Jains and other religious and ethnic groups with variations in nature and extent.
14. The Hindu caste system is a fourfold classification into *varnas*, viz. Brahmins, Kshatriyas, Vaishyas and Shudras. The *varnas* are further subdivided into numerous (*jatis*), many of which are often found only in specific areas. *Jatis* are characterized by similar hereditary and positions in occupational social hierarchies. About 16 per cent of the total population is classified as Scheduled Castes/*Dalit*; around 8 per cent of the population belongs to one of 461 indigenous groups often called Scheduled Tribes and/or *adivasi*.
15. Jawaharlal Nehru, *Discovery of India* (Bombay: Asia Publishing House, 1961), p. 61.
16. Demographically, the European Union is a highly populated, culturally diverse union of 27 Member States. According to estimates of 1 January 2010, the population of the EU was about 501.6 million people.
17. German is the most widely spoken language (about 90 million people according to 2006 statistics). French, English and Italian are each the mother tongue of around 60 million EU citizens. Besides the 23 official languages, there are about 150 regional and minority languages, spoken by up to 50 million people. However, English is spoken by about one third of EU citizens as their first foreign language, putting it well ahead of German and the others as the most widely used language of the European

Union. German and French are each spoken as a first foreign language by about 10 per cent of the EU population. The emergence of English as a *lingua franca* in the European Union has accelerated over the years. See European Commission, "Europeans and their Languages Survey, 2006," *Special Eurobarometer 243*, Publication: February 2006, at http://ec.europa.eu/public_opinion/archives/ebs/ebs_243_en.pdf.

18. The EU has significant religious diversity, reflecting diverse history and culture. A majority of the population professes Christianity, predominantly Roman Catholicism, Protestantism and Eastern Orthodoxy. Other major religions, Islam and Judaism, are also represented in the EU population. In 2009, the EU had an estimated Muslim population of 23 million, and an estimated Jewish population of over a million. Other significant religions present in EU countries are Buddhism, Sikhism and Hinduism. See http://www.indexmundi.com/european_union/population.html.
19. Philosophical and intellectual ideas of the Renaissance, Enlightenment, the Industrial Revolution, capitalism, the French Revolution, colonialism, and the two world wars.
20. http://www.europadiversa.org/eng/pdf/ponencia_grillo_eng.doc.
21. Important among these forces were new sources of energy, science, technology, territorial acquisition, imperialism, ideological revolution and rise of democracy contingent upon new forms of economic and social organization, the (de)centralization of political controls, governance, welfare state, etc.
22. The largest numbers of foreign citizens live in Germany (7.3 million), France (3.6 million), Spain (4.6 million), the United Kingdom (3.7 million) and Italy (2.9 million).
23. Amin Ash, "Multi-Ethnicity and the Idea of Europe," *Theory Culture Society*, 2004, 21(2), p. 1.
24. Riva Kastoryano (ed), *An Identity for Europe: The Relevance of Multiculturalism in EU Construction* (New York: Palgrave Macmillan, 2008), translated by Susan Emanuel.
25. German Chancellor Angela Merkl, President Sarkozy of France and British Prime Minister David Cameron have openly conceded that multiculturalism has failed.
26. Sergio Carrera, "A Comparison of Integration Programmes in the European Union: Trends and Weaknesses," 2006. Working Paper downloaded from the CEPS website www.ceps.be. http:/

/www.mmg.mpg.de/publications/working-papers/2009/wp-09-04/June.

27. In fact, with so many internal divisions and diversity every community may find itself in a minority.
28. Saumyajit Ray, "Understanding Indian Multiculturalism" in Christopher Sam Raj and Marie McAndrew, eds., *Multiculturalism: Public Policy and Problem Areas in Canada and India* (New Delhi: Manak Publications, 2009), p. 69.
29. Gurpreet Mahajan, "Rethinking Multiculturalism," *Seminar*, No. 484, 1999, p. 61.
30. Article 29(1): right of 'any section of the citizens' to 'conserve' its 'distinct language, script or culture'; Article 29(2): restriction on denial of admission to any citizen, to any educational institution maintained or aided by the State, 'on grounds only of religion, race, caste, language or any of them'; Article 30(1): right of all Religious and Linguistic Minorities to establish and administer educational institutions of their choice; Article 30(2): freedom of Minority-managed educational institutions from discrimination in the matter of receiving aid from the State; Article 347: special provision relating to the language spoken by a section of the population of any State; Article 350 A: provision for facilities for instruction in mother-tongue at primary stage; Article 350 B: provision for a Special Officer for Linguistic Minorities and his duties; Explanation 1 below Article 25 Sikh community's right of 'wearing and carrying of kirpans'. (Source: http://ncm.nic.in/constitutional_prov.html).
31. Gurpreet Mahajan, "Multiculturalism in the Age of Terror," *Political Studies Review*, Vol. 5, 2007, pp. 332-334.
32. Ibid., pp. 331-332.
33. Culture refers to shared symbolic and learned aspects of human society including knowledge, belief, art, morals, law, and customs of particular group, society, or nation. It includes shared language, beliefs, practices, rituals, food habits, dressing styles, symbols, etc. Withstanding its wholeness, we can distinguish between material and non-material aspects of culture; where the former is tangible in nature and is manifest in the form of artifacts, clothing, food, architecture, etc. and the latter includes intangible aspects of culture existing in the form of values, norms, beliefs, and practices that are passed on to successive generations and learnt through the process of socialization.
34. Bhiku Parekh quoted in Raj and McAndrew, n. 28, p. 89.
35. Avijit Pathak, *Modernity, Globalization and Identity: Towards a*

Reflexive Quest (New Delhi: Aakar, 2006), pp. 112-145.

36. In Germany, the term "multiculturalism" has spread since the 1980s. The city of Frankfurt even created a section of "Multicultural Affairs". France too is described as "multiracial", "multicultural", "plural", and "pluri-cultural." This terminology found legitimacy in a political discourse that privileged "the right to difference", accompanied after 1981 by liberalization of the law on foreign associations, which gave legal status to organizations that privileged identities, whether defined as principally social, cultural, secular or religious. In Great Britain, the Commission for Racial Equality promulgated in 1976 the Race Relations Act. The main objectives were to fight against racism, eliminate discrimination, and assure an equality of opportunity and thus establish good relations among different "racial groups". In the Netherlands in the 1980s, a minority policy took the objective of "promoting multiculturalism and the emancipation of ethnic communities". Quoted from www.interactproject.org/.../An_Identity_for_Europe_Introduction_Book_Launch.doc.
37. A.R. Momin, "India as a Model for Multiethnic Europe", *Asia–Europe Journal*, 4, 2006, pp. 523-537.
38. Sergio Carrera and Joanna Parkin, "Towards a Common Policy on Integration in the EU?" in Michael Emerson, *Interculturalism: Europe and its Muslims in Search of Sound Societal Models* (Brussels: Centre for European Policy Studies, 2011), available at www.ceps.eu/ceps/download/5722.
39. *May 2001:* Riots, largely pitting British Bangladeshi and Pakistani youths against White youths, break out in three northern British cities; *May 2002:* Rise (and death) of Pim Fortyn, outspoken Dutch politician who openly castigated Muslim immigration and Muslims' inherent unassimilability; *February 2004: Prospect* magazine editor David Goodhart (2004) publishes "Too Diverse?", an article which controversially suggests that collective attitudes towards welfare are threatened by ethnic diversity. At the same time, the French Parliament votes in favour of a new law to ban the wearing of Islamic headscarves in schools later widely debated; *October-November 2005:* Riots in Paris suburbs and other localities throughout France are depicted as troubles wrought by migrant youths; *October 2006:* Cabinet Minister Jack Straw says he would prefer Muslim women not to wear veils which cover the face. The ensuing debate entails questions as to how much conformity a society should demand

of minorities vs. to what extent they should be allowed to practise values no matter how disagreeable to the majority. Steven Vertovec and Sussane Wessendorf, *Assessing the Backlash*, MMG WP 09-04, pp. 11-12.

40. Will Kymlicka, *Multicultural Odysseys* (Oxford: Oxford University Press, 2007), pp. 37-41.
41. Mahajan, n. 31, pp. 317-336.
42. Carrera, n. 26.
43. Corrado Bonifazi, Marek Oko'lski, Jeannette Schoorl, Patrick Simon, *International Migration in Europe: New Trends and New Methods of Analysis* (Amsterdam: Amsterdam University Press, 2008).
44. R.D. Grillo, "Transmigration and Cultural Diversity in the Construction of Europe," 2007, revised version of a paper presented to the "Symposium on Cultural Diversity and the Construction of Europe: Complementarity or Incompatibility?", organized by Fundaci Jaume Bofill and the Universitat Oberta de Catalunya in December 2000 in Barcelona. Available at http://www.europadiversa.org/eng/pdf/ponencia_grillo_eng.doc.
45. Parekh, n. 1.
46. Gordon Marshall, *A Dictionary of Sociology* (Oxford University Press, 1998); see entry "Social Integration and System Integration".
47. See Grillo, n. 44.
48. Baumann identifies these groups as, a) those who believe in a unified national culture, b) those who trace their culture to their ethnic identity, and c) those who view their religion as their culture.
49. Justice and Home Affairs Council, 2618th Meeting, *Annex: Common Basic Principles on Immigrants' Integration*, 14615/04 (Presse 321), 19 November 2004.
50. Identity either/or on the basis of one's religion, caste, ethnicity, language, region, nationality, gender are socially constructed around defining attributes and are 'given' or mostly 'ascribed' by birth.
51. Samuel P. Huntington, *The Clash of Civilizations and the Remaking of World Order.* (New Delhi: Penguin Books, 1996), p. 318.
52. Diverse in forms but all moral institutions, across civilizations, preach and promote a similar set of values.
53. Pathak, n. 35, pp. 148-161.
54. In Germany, in the "headscarf case" (2003), the Federal Constitutional Court in Karlsruhe found it permissible for female

teachers to wear the headscarf while teaching. Unfortunately, the Court's opinion had only a marginal influence on guaranteeing religious freedom, because ultimately this was a question of the way state governments administer their educational policy. Since Germany's federal structure assigns all aspects of educational policy to the state governments, many states enacted local policies forbidding their teachers from wearing the headscarf despite the court's opinion. The case is quoted from Eric Leise, *Germany Strives to Integrate Immigrants with New Policies*, Migration Policy Institute, Washington DC, http://www.migrationin formation.org/Feature/display).

55. Susanne Moser, "The Importance of Values for Social and Political Integration in Europe," paper presented at International Congress on Justice and Human Values in Europe, Karlsruhe, 9-11 May 2007.
56. Checkel, J. (1999), "Social Construction and Integration", *Journal of European Public Policy*, 6:4, Special Issue, pp. 552-554.
57. Avijit Pathak, *Recalling the Forgotten: Education and Moral Quest* (New Delhi: Aakar, 2009), pp. 21-36.
58. Ibid., pp. 42-43.
59. Pathak, n. 35, p. 150.

4

Discourses on Multiculturalism in Continental Europe

Michael Dusche

Introduction

This chapter looks at the way the North American discourse on multiculturalism has been received in continental Europe, especially in France and Germany. At first glance, the circumstances for a multiculturalist discourse of the traditional republican or liberal state are very different in North America and in the two European countries discussed in this chapter. The North American context, particularly Canada, is marked by conceptions of differential citizenship, territorial autonomy or even national independence, which have hardly any significance in political or academic debates in either France or Germany. Instead, it is generally assumed that immigrants, by choosing their country of destination, have also chosen to conform to the constitutional fundamentals of these countries. Thus the multiculturalist discourse in France and Germany while staying within the framework of the respective constitutional fundamentals of these two countries is only meant to sensitize the existing constitutional set-up to the needs of the new residents. However, as a critical analysis of the North American discourse on multiculturalism reveals, it is less radical and less at odds with established constitutional principles than the first glance may suggest. Thus, multiculturalists like Taylor or communitarians like Walzer, clearly do not wish to be perceived as anti-liberal or anti-republican. Multiculturalism in this reading is an attempt to counter discriminatory tendencies within the individualist liberal framework and it would be wrong to perceive it as a challenge to this framework itself. It is argued that in spite of all appearances to the contrary, the melting pot still prevails over the salad bowl, or, in other words, in spite of much multiculturalist talk about the preservation and institutionalization of cultural difference, the republican model of assimilation still accounts for much of the ability of the US-American society to integrate ever more different strangers into one national super-culture.

In France, the realization of these American state of affairs seems to coincide with the emergence of an almost universal consensus on the need to, maybe redefine, but certainly reemphasize French republicanism in the face of the multiculturalist challenge. At the same time, as discrimination based on identity is rejected, it is maintained that a person is to be granted everything as an individual but nothing as a member of any cultural group. The section on France, however, shows how this egalitarian promises risk becoming farcical in the face of prevailing racist tendencies in the French society. An egalitarian promise not kept and a grievance that cannot be addressed because the object of discrimination is made a taboo-concept in political discourse would indeed be a situation difficult to bear. Nevertheless, it seems far from clear how the multiculturalist alternative would benefit a minority who is internally as dissimilar as every member differs from the majority. The few attempts at forging multiculturalist policies at disadvantaged immigrants have proved futile in the face of the internal disunity of the immigrant community. There is no obvious solution out of this dilemma. The most promising vein seems to be an approach that does not bother so much about ideological questions but pragmatically looks for results.

In the section on the multiculturalist discourse in Germany, emphasis is put on the traditional church-state relations. The traditionally strong Christian churches have carved out for themselves privileges that would be plainly at odds with a republican philosophy of state as we see it in France. Here, the German society retains some of the pre-modern communitarianism that has so much inspired Hegel in his political thinking. Hegel was much averse against Rousseau's idea of an atomised society and despised the idea of a people where individuals form an inorganic mass. In Hegel's conception of a corporate state, persons are represented not as individuals but as members of their respective trades. To the present day, German politics suffers from this corporatist spirit which allows too many associations to come between the individual and the state. A well institutionalized example is the two Christian churches, Protestant and Catholic, which still wield an influence far over the proportion of the individuals whom they represent. Since the inbuilt communitarianism implicit in the German corporate model shares much of the problems regarding the privileging of groups over individuals with some of the multiculturalist positions, multiculturalism has had a more fertile ground to fall back on than in France. The section shows that the most interesting questions regarding the relationship between the state and the immigrant, notably the Muslim, community arises due to the fact that Islam and other religions somehow do not quite fit into the traditional scheme of Church-state relations. This is partly due to the fact that these communities lack the authoritative structures that the churches for instance have developed over the centuries. In the traditional churches, theological as well as political matters were decided by elites and the faithful were expected to follow. This model, having evolved in pre-democratic times, is seen as obsolete today even by many from within the Churches. Outside the Christian sphere, the model becomes completely untenable since in many non-Christian religious communities religious authority has always been diffuse and decentralized. Such a decentralized form of religious practice, however, seems more suitable for a democratic society than the authoritarian structures of the churches. To force such religious communities into the unified framework of a church-like structure would do harm to this diversity and its inherent democratic spirit. It would necessarily lead to privileging some parts of the community over others. Such attempts have been made in France and they are being discussed in Germany as well. So far they have not proved feasible. The lack of authoritative structures in other than the Christian religious communities poses a challenge to the liberal democratic state to redefine its relations with the growing number of religions claiming recognition in Germany.

In the end, it turns out that neither the French republican nor the German communitarian model are ideal for dealing with the problems posed by migration into continental Europe. The middle way seems to be a notion of inclusion on the basis of a liberally interpreted common legal order. This may involve some changes in the corporatist as well as in the republican conception of the state-church relations. Immigrants from non-European cultures can legitimately claim that the nation state and its symbols be rid of any exclusionist elements that they might have acquired over the years while there was no one to challenge this. The impulse behind the multiculturalist objection that the national culture should be made to include people from different cultural backgrounds is legitimate. The nation state cannot legitimately demand assimilation to the particular national culture that it has acquired in a historical process. Legitimately, there cannot be any such thing called 'un-French' or 'un-German'. Whatever French or German national culture may legitimately claim is adherence to its normative background consensus,[1] which is based in each case on similar republican principles of popular sovereignty, liberal principles of individual human rights and democratic principles of justice. To violate these civilizational background assumptions could be called 'un-French' just as well as it could be called 'un-German'. There is nothing culturally specific, i.e. exclusive in these norms. Multiculturalism, as far as it attempts an alternative to the liberal-democratic conception of the state, in particular where it demands group rights on a par with individual rights, has to be rejected. However, what we may accept from the multiculturalist critique is the need to revise our national cultures and to purge them from all particularistic encroachments that have gone unchallenged before we had to deal with pluralism to such an extent as we have to in our present-day multicultural societies. The best principle to govern such a revision, it seems, is the principle of liberality itself: Do not restrict individual liberties where they do not hamper the liberty of another individual. By this rule it would be illegitimate to prevent a Muslim woman from wearing a headscarf for it is by no means clear how this liberty of hers would hamper anybody else's liberty. However, this rule also implies that a Muslim who in the name of religion engages in activities that are directed at the destruction of that same liberal order that allows him to engage in such activities under the constitutional rights of freedom of assembly, freedom of speech, etc. will not be allowed to do so. By the same rule, it would not be permissible to allow parents the liberty of clitoridectomy for it infringes on the right of their daughter to physical integrity and sexual self-determination but it would be wrong not to grant to a Muslim *halal* slaughtering practices for the liberty of religion is not outweighed by the right an animal may have to be killed in a 'humane' way. Human rights and animal rights cannot be placed on the same level. Of course, not all cases are so simple and even the simple cases may give rise to more controversy. But nevertheless, it seems safe to maintain that the principle of liberality provides best guidance for it prevents us from falling into both the republican trap of demanding assimilation where it is unnecessary and the communitarian trap of granting liberties to communities at the expense of individual elementary rights.

European Reception of Multiculturalist Discourse

The term 'multiculturalism' came into wide public use during the early 1980s in the context of public school curriculum reforms in the United States.[2] It was widely popularized as a philosophical concept through Will Kymlicka's book on *Multicultural Citizenship* in 1995. The background of the multiculturalist discourse in Canada is formed by three issues: First, the issue of autochthonous aboriginal people, second, the Anglophone/Francophone multinational setup of the Canadian state and, third, the fact that Canada is the destination of immigrants from all parts of the world. Since Europe hardly has any autochthonous populations with civilizational reference-points highly divergent form the majority civilization, the background of the multiculturalist debate is formed mainly by the issue of immigration, and that mainly from Muslim countries. The discourse on multiculturalism in Europe, therefore, is overwhelmingly a discourse on Islam in Europe. In Europe, the introduction of the term 'multiculturalism' marks the passage from immigration perceived only as economic and temporary to a permanent presence of populations.[3] The discourse on multiculturalism and on Islam in Europe only recently gained momentum due to two factors; first, the terrorist attacks of New York and Washington on 11 September 2001 and, second, the debate on European identity that was catalyzed by the simultaneous negotiations for a constitution of the European Union.

Against this position some bring to bear the universal achievements of modernity such as secularism, the freedom of conscience—which includes the right to profess no religion at all, —independence of the state from religion and a religiously neutral justification for state legitimacy. Increasingly, Muslim scholars take part in these debates. In Great Britain, where anti-discrimination laws in favour of visible minorities are in place, Tariq Modood has criticized that discrimination is not only based on racist attitudes but also on religious prejudice. He has established the fact that discrimination targets especially Muslims and that not for racist but for religious reasons.[4] As another scholar summarizes it:

> In the United Kingdom ... for a long period, the emphasis has ... been put on race ... Also 'general' ethnic categories have been raised, such as Asians—categories that ... underestimate the cultural factor and ignore the religious one".[5]

With Muslim scholars participating in these debates, the debates gain significance also for the Islamic world at large. Without overstating the case, Allievi concedes that "although the European case is peripheral towards the Muslim world ... it is innovative towards the historical situation of the Muslim world."[6] Apparently, "the European Muslim world is living through a process of extremely rapid transformation and it will be of strategic interest to see how the processes of structuring of Muslim communities continues in this crucial phase."[7] In a network analysis of Muslim communities in Europe, Allievi suggests that we are presently witnessing the emergence of new Muslim communities in Europe that differ in important ways from communities as they are traditionally conceived.

> [T]hese networks, although in most cases 'private' ... play their role and are perceived in the public sphere as collective or communitarian in a broad sense ... [The populations involved] enter the European public sphere as a new social actor, with cultural/religious references, which did not previously exist in this same public sphere ... These major changes will ... change our image not only of the Muslim communities in Europe, but of European societies. These changes are possibly also going to affect, through a different comprehension of Islam, the relations of European societies with the 'countries of origin' of the Muslim populations, and in some ways, their idea of Islam; but they will particularly affect some aspects of European Islam, including, in the long ... term, its religious self-definition. Not to mention that they are going to change, in a slow and silent but nonetheless spectacular way, the image and self-image of Europe itself.[8]

Their networks, Allievi argues, produce community between parts of the Muslim world hitherto detached. In many ways, the Muslim 'umma' is more visible in Europe than in the countries of origin, where a believer can practically only find people like himself. More than elsewhere, the internal diversity among Muslims in Europe is clear; certainly more than in the respective countries of origin of the immigrants. The same holds true for the different legal schools of Islam being present in Europe where they mix more easily. Allievi quotes an interviewee born in Africa, but of Yemeni origin, who lives in London and claims:

> I am shafii, but I have to follow the most diffused madhhab here, which is the hanafi one. Personally, as far as the hajj is concerned, I am hanafi, for jihad I am maliki, for the conception of minority I am hanbali.[9]

The quoted case evidences the fact that the migratory *umma* sometimes gives birth to new forms of belief itself. Allievi observes that while European Muslims have to understand themselves as a minority, the implicit theological Muslim self-comprehension is that of a majority, possibly hosting some religious minorities. European Islam, thus, is forced to rework its self-understanding in the light of this situation. According to Allievi, for instance, in Europe the traditional dar al-Islam/dar al-harb dichotomy becomes more and more meaningless for the majority of Muslims.

These internal reworkings of Islam, Allievi suspects, will have an impact on the whole Muslim world. According to Allievi, in future it will not be possible to understand the history and the social evolution of Europe without taking into account its Muslim component. In the same way it will not be possible to understand the history and the social (and even theological) evolution of Islam without taking its European component into account. In the following two chapters, I would like to look at how the pan-European situation is reflected in two of its leading societies, France and Germany.

The Discourse on Multiculturalism in France[10]

According to the French Ministry of the Interior, around 4 million Muslims (8 per cent of the general population) live in France, most of them in and around Paris. Of these, almost three fourth are of Algerian origin; others come from Morocco, Tunisia, and sub-Saharan Africa.[11] In France, unlike in Germany, the nation, officially, has never been understood ethnically. The two dominant traditions of thought—republicanism and nationalism—have focussed either on democracy (equality irrespective of descent, race or religious affiliation) or on an allegiance to a common history in which to share would be a matter of choice, not of descent.[12] Thus, in France, multiculturalism has rarely been a topic taken seriously in academic or political debate. Immigrants had to adapt to the republican idea of the state catering to the individual directly and not allowing intermediaries such as religious or cultural organizations to mediate between the individual and the state. Some French intellectuals fear the tyranny of the majority much less than the tyranny of the minorities.[13] For the defenders of the republican model, negative, as well as positive discrimination is based on the same set of faulty assumptions. There is thus no principled difference between the subjugation of a race or culture in view of its alleged inferiority and the privileging of certain groups of people—say through affirmative action—which is also based on their racial or cultural origin.[14] French intellectuals warn that the concept of multiculturalism, especially in its US-American variant, should not to be taken at face value. The name suggests a radical departure from liberal constitutional principles. In reality, however, multiculturalist policies in the US have largely remained within the limits of liberal constitutionalism. Clearly, priority is given to individual rights above group rights and we are nowhere near multicultural citizenship. Thus, far from serving as a new constitutive principle of US-American policy, multiculturalism only helps the US to advance another step on the old road of liberal pluralism by purging its polity from yet another bias.[15] Multiculturalism, in this reading, is an attempt to counter discriminatory tendencies based on culture. Similar attempts have been made to counter earlier forms of discrimination, i.e. against blacks, Catholic Irish and Italians, Jews, etc.—all of which had been labelled 'un-American' at some point of time.[16] In Raynaud's critical analysis of the US-American discourse on multiculturalism, the republican and assimilationist tendency in US-American 'culture' is still stronger than the import given to multiculturalism. Thus, we can think of school education in Spanish language but treating Spanish as another national language on a par with English still seems far-fetched, not to speak of differential legal practices or multicultural citizenship. Multiculturalism is thus not always what the name suggests: a new openness towards the diversity of national cultures or civilizations or a greater cultural heterogeneity of the American society.[17] Yet others[18] perceive US-American multiculturalism as an attempt to de-emphasize the European heritage domestically in order to accommodate a growing number of non-European Americans into the common egalitarian—and still individualistic—value system, which would be an exercise entirely in the vein of liberal pluralism. Thus, the French discourse seems to de-emphasize multiculturalist ideology, even in the country of its origin, in favour of the republican model that seems to still outweigh the influence of multiculturalism for all practical purposes even in the United States.

The republican model is outlined by Fassin in a somewhat pointed way in that he writes: "Particularities are fine as long as they stay private and do not claim any official legitimation at school or in court: above all, the state must not get involved."[19] Since the mid-1980s, French controversies about problems of immigrant integration and national identity were marked by a vigorous consensus amongst the elites to reject the ideas and practices of multiculturalist policy. The principle political parties, interest groups, decision-makers, and intellectuals basically agreed on a republican model of assimilation as it has been customary in France since the days of the French Revolution. With respect to the Jewish community, French revolutionaries maintained "that Jews should be awarded everything as individuals, but nothing as a group"[20], i.e. there should be no discrimination, but also no privileging, of individuals based on group affiliation, estate, or creed. The conviction that in a democracy the general will (*volonté générale*) will only be distorted by vested interests if associations were to be sanctioned as intermediaries between the citizen and the state dates back to Rousseau's Contract Social and has ever since been a guiding principle in French politics.[21] In the republican model, integration amounts to assimilation into a republican super-culture while competing local, ethnic or religious cultures are relegated into the background and made a private affair of the individuals concerned. If these sub-cultures were to assume a political role, it was feared that this would lead to a fragmentation of the nation and invite foreign intervention in support of the remnants of the *ancien régime*.

The strong republican consensus on inclusion seems to have prevented the agenda of the extreme right which calls for exclusion from citizenship for non-European and non-Christian immigrants. It also seems to have prevented the politics of identity to gain a foothold in France. However, some authors also hold that for some, the republican model serves as an ideological tool to divert attention from the fact that, in practice, French politics does often differentiate along ethnic and religious lines.[22] Failure to recognize this gap between theoretical ideal and practical reality leads to frustration and violence and a sense of despair among immigrant communities in France with the consequence that some turn to the multiculturalist model in hope for some autonomous space where the community as a whole can achieve what is being denied to the individual. In the following, I would like to outline, in a somewhat chronological manner, the achievements and failures of French politics towards integration of immigrant communities.

Like many European countries who witnessed a period of economic growth in the period after the Second World War, France similarly allowed workers to immigrate into the country in the 1960s and early 1970s. In 1975, the immigrant population had almost doubled from 1.77 million in 1954 to 3.44 million.[23] Only in 1974 when the oil crisis struck the economy, the French government stopped the influx of immigrants who were still perceived then as temporary or guest workers. On grounds of their status as guest workers, the French government excluded immigrants from acquiring citizenship and barred their right to form political associations which could voice their demands. However, what the French government eventually did allow for in purview of the immigrants return to their home countries was instruction of their children in their native language, the creation of a National Office for the Promotion of Immigrant Cultures, provisions for TV-Channels in the major immigrant languages, and the establishment of Islamic prayer halls in immigrant hostels and workplaces. These measures were often put in place in cooperation with the governments of the countries of origin of the respective immigrant community.

The election of François Mitterrand as president in May 1981 and the victory of the Socialist Party in the parliamentary elections the following month marked a turning point in the policies of the French government vis-à-vis the immigrant community especially regarding their right to political participation. In October 1981, a law was passed that granted the right to engage in political activities to all associations, no matter which nationality their members held. Immigrants associations had to register with government agencies and received financial support for their work with the thought in mind that thereby the government would obtain interlocutors to consult with in matters concerning the immigrant communities in France. Direct participation in politics being barred for non-citizens, the French government now called on such interlocutors to participate in the framework of consultative structures that were created for politics concerning immigrants. The ensuing question was, who to recognize as a legitimate representative of the various groupings of the immigrant community. Their representatives were divided along various lines. Lack of political experience and a dearth of good leaders who could have integrated the diverse factions and confront the government with a common policy line and agenda seems to be accountable for the ultimate failure of this short experiment in ethno-politics. One of the more successful social movements was Mouvement Beurs which emerged in 1983-1984 as a major anti-racist social movement of mostly young Maghribean immigrants in response to racist infringements on members of their community.

After the failure of these short-lived experiments in multicultural politics and terrified by the Front National and the rising spectre of French ethno-nationalism on the far right of the political spectrum, mainstream politics returned to the righteous path of republicanism. This meant elimination of any policies towards the integration of immigrants that would have been based on ethnic, national or religious identity. Since the republican model rejects the language of identity not only with respect to immigrants but also in view of the Front National who would like the French state to be founded on an ethnically defined French nation, it serves several purposes at the same time. Firstly, it promises integration into an open, ethnically and racially blind republican super-culture, secondly, it clearly demarcates the line not to be crossed for those with a penchant towards Le Pen's xenophobia, and thirdly, it reassures the French of their historical achievement of forging an identity which is not exclusive but principally open for people of all colourand creed. Henceforth, multiculturalism was seen as only perpetuating cultural minority identities, which were perceived as an obstacle in the way of integration rather than a potential value in them. Pierre-André Taguieff went as far as to denounce multiculturalism as embracing ideas that are dangerously close to those of the extreme right.[24]

Far from being only an elite ideology, French republicanism took to the roads in the mid-eighties when SOS-Racisme was founded as a multi-ethnical, multi-national social force to foster solidarity amongst French and immigrant youth against racism. By embracing the republican model of integration through assimilation into the French political super-culture, SOS-Racisme availed itself of an almost ancient and widely accepted trope in French politics. Consequently, SOS-Racisme firmly opposed all attempts at politicizing or officially recognizing ethnic or religious identity while it accepted every right of the individual regardless of its ethnic or religious identity to be accepted as an equal amongst equals.

On the government level, the republican model gave legitimacy to the practice of not preferring representatives of the immigrant community over experts from academia or civil society when it came to consultations regarding issues of integration. In fact, however, the already mentioned lack of acceptable spokespersons from the immigrant communities may have been at the heart of this decision in various policy arenas, the government did deviate from the republican precepts. In spite of the republican model, various elites did give way to the recognition of identities in their dealings with the immigrant communities. Blatt[25] cites two government programmes, France-Plus and the *Conseil de Réflexion sur l'Islam en France* (CORIF), as examples for ethnic-religious politics within an anti-ethnic-religious political framework.

France-Plus was founded in 1985 by North African

immigrants with the support of some socialist counsellors who wanted to promote participation in elections of some 1 to 1.5 million members of the North African community who had obtained French citizenship. Although France-Plus managed to support a couple of hundred successful Maghribean candidates, it turned out that these candidates did not exert any sizable influence on the immigrant population itself. Thus, the ethnic link that was designed to help the immigrant communities through their representatives in government institutions did not work even within these communities themselves. Especially the Beurs candidates who had ventured to represent their communities were ridiculed within these same communities as 'bourgeois' and corrupt. Finally, France-Plus was undermined by internal schisms and financial irregularities so that by the 1992-1995 electoral cycles not a single organization nominated any minority candidates.

When France-Plus failed because of internal disunity, CORIF suffered a similar fate. It was created in 1989 by the Minister of the Interior to help organize and institutionalise relations between the government and the Muslim community in France. CORIF tried to mediate conflicts on 'halal' slaughtering and on the Ramadan calendar but soon got entangled in its competition with the *Mosque de Paris* for the leadership of the Muslim community in France. CORIF proved to be another example for the failure of the government to find a legitimate leadership for the immigrant communities based on ethnic or religious identity in spite of its willingness to compromise on the republican model of integration which would forbid any such ethnically based politics. Since the total embrace of the republican model of integration, the French elites have acted in an incoherent manner with respect to the question of political participation and representation of immigrants.

Recently, there have been new attempts to regulate Islam from above following the model of the Jewish community in France. With the foundation of the Representative Council of Jewish Institutions in France (*Conseil représentatif des institutions juives de France*), a laicist organization of Jews in France had been created. Attempts to create a similar body for Muslims in France failed due to several reasons. Etienne[26] and Dollé[27] mention French Jacobinism and the heterogeneity of the Muslim community in France and its failure to organize itself in a twofold system, *laicist* and religious, as possible reasons as well as governments of respective home countries interfering in the cases of Muslims who have not yet become French citizens, and, lastly, compulsions to harmonize French law with European Union law regarding minority rights.[28]

In spite of the large consensus in favour of an ideological model that rejects any sort of official recognition of ethnic identity, in spite of a powerful nationalistic movement that sees in all affirmation of minority identity a threat against the nation, and in spite of the absence of effective mediators who would have enjoyed recognition and legitimacy vis-à-vis the minority communities, the French political elites persistently recognized and promoted participation in the political process based, at least partially, on identity. Blatt explains this discrepancy by strong independent forces from within France and from without:

> Racist forces from within France tend to entertain and develop an ethnic conscience among minorities in France. Within France, an ethnic awareness is nourished by anti-Muslim and anti-Arabic racism inherited from the colonial era and affecting the way immigrants are treated by employers, landlords, neighbours and, in particular, the police, and also by governmental policies which, in a whole series of domains, implicitly but clearly, treats non-European immigrants differently. From outside the French borders, the global diffusion of 'black' and Arabic culture gives shape and force to an ethnic conscience through music, film, sports, and other vectors and by trans-national movements for the rights of minorities and Islam ... Confronted with the necessity to treat these thorny and explosive questions, the political elites have hence accepted, in an ad hoc and partial fashion, the appearance and recognition of ethnic intermediaries in the political process.[29]

Blatt, holding that there can be no organizational, institutional or ideological basis for a coherent multiculturalist approach, nevertheless maintains that "to pretend that ethnicity does not exist, as the republican model would have it, creates a representational vacuum which leaves immigrant populations and their offspring all the more excluded from the political process and far-off the aim of integration."[30]

From Blatt's analysis, it becomes apparent that identity formations along ethnic and religious lines will persist as long as religious and cultural prejudice and racism persist in the host society. The conclusion to be drawn could be twofold. One possible conclusion would be to secure religious and ethnic minorities an autonomous sphere where they can flourish outside the reach of racism. The other conclusion would be to challenge racism more sincerely. It seems, however, that racial prejudice remains a permanent feature of some parts of the French society. We have seen that republicanism plays a strong integrative role for the French society due to its rootedness in French history, notably the French Revolution. The latter, however, has also embraced the principle of liberality in its Human Rights Declaration of 1789. Article four of that declaration reminds us that "Liberty consists in the freedom to do everything which injures no one else; hence the exercise of the natural rights of each man has no limits except those which assure to the other members of the society the enjoyment of the same rights. These limits can only be determined by law." The main principle of liberality sets limits to the integrative aspirations of republicanism. In the light of the principle of maximal liberty for all, the republican super-culture needs to be as indeterminate as possible. Since assimilation into this super-culture is a necessity for all who want to exercise their right to political participation, the content of that culture must not come into conflict with the liberty of anybody to be (in ethnic, religious or other terms) as he or she likes, and to be part of any culture or religious community s/he desires without risking exclusion from the realm of politics. Thus becoming French cannot mean for the immigrant to have to assimilate into a French ethnic community in all its density.

The Discourse on Multiculturalism in Germany

In Germany, opposition to the notion of multiculturalism was never as marked as in France, for several reasons. One is historical. When enlightenment republicanism was at its peak in France, Germany in the early 19th century was still struggling to become a unified nation that could only then decide on the form of government it wanted to take. The republican notion being a political one and Germany lacking political unity at that time, it was understandable that political unity had to be achieved first before Germans could make up their minds regarding the constitutional form of the ensuing polity. To achieve political unity, German nationalists, following the early romanticist ideas of Johann Gottfried Herder, in the late 18th and the early 19th century resorted to the concept of common culture and language as the basis for political unification. Thus, the terms 'politics' and 'culture' have other connotations in the German political tradition than in the French. Unlike in France, culture was at the basis of the German nation, not republican self-government, for a common culture seemed to be there before popular sovereignty could even be thought of.

Equally for historical reasons, the state and church have never been separated in Germany as they have been in France. To understand the nature of the relationship between the state and religion in Germany, one has to look at the German 'State-Church-Law' (*Staatskirchenrecht*) that regulates the relations between the central and federal states and diverse groups whose members share a common 'world view' (*Weltanschauung*). The German State-Church-Law is perceived by some as the most sophisticated of its sort in all of Europe.[31] For one thing, the definition of 'world view' is the widest conception in Europe of what forms a religious community. If a religious organization fulfils requirements such as assurance of permanence and a certain size and if there is no indication that the organization's principles conflict with the constitution or the European human rights laws, the organization may request that it be granted the status of a corporation under public law. Public law corporation status, among other things, entitles it to levy taxes on its members that the State collects for it and for which the organization pays a fee to the state.

Most religious organizations are registered and treated as non-profit associations and therefore enjoy tax-exempt status. State level authorities review these submissions and routinely grant this status. Organizations must register at a local or municipal court and provide evidence (through their own statutes) that they are a religion and thus contribute socially, spiritually, or materially to society. Among the religious organizations that have been granted public law corporation status are the Protestant and Roman Catholic Church, Judaism, some smaller Christian denominations and, of late, the community of Allevite Muslims. Other Muslim communities in Germany so far do not qualify for this form of public recognition for their reluctance to recognize the right of their members to change or abandon their faith, which conflicts with the constitutionally guaranteed liberty of conscience and relevant Human Rights law on the European Union level.[32] State governments also subsidize various institutions affiliated with public law corporations, such as church-run schools and hospitals. Most public schools offer religious instruction in cooperation with the Protestant and Catholic churches and the Central Council for Jews in Germany (CCJG). A non-religious course in ethics generally is available for students not wishing to participate in confessional instruction. The issue of Islamic education in public schools is becoming topical in several states and at the federal level and chairs of Islamic theology are being established in several German universities. In terms of the need to rethink and possibly redefine the relationship between the liberal democratic state and the various religious communities, the growing Muslim community offers controversial material for debate since they conform less to the occidentalist view of how religious communities should be organized.

NOTES

1. Cf. Habermas' conception of constitutional patriotism.
2. Gregory Jay, "What is Multiculturalism" (Milwaukee: University of Wisconsin, 2002); https://pantherfile.uwm.edu/gjay/www/Multicult/whatismc.pdf
3. cf. Stefano Allievi, "Multiculturalism in Europe", in Proceedings

of the St. Anthony's-Princeton conference on "Muslims in Europe post 9/11", Oxford, 25-26 April 2003, unpublished manuscript.

4. Cf. Tariq Modood, R. Berthoud, J. Lekey, J. Nagroo, P. Smith, S. Virdee, and S. Beishon, *Britain's Ethnic Minorities: Diversity and Disadvantage* (London: Policy Studies Institute, 1997); Tariq Modood and P. Werbner, eds., *The Politics of Multiculturalism in the New Europe: Racism, Identity and Community* (London: Zed Books, 1997); Tariq Modood, "Anti-Essentialism, Multiculturalism and the Recognition of Religious Minorities," *Journal of Political Philosophy*, 6(4), 1998, pp. 378-399.
5. Allievi, n. 3.
6. Ibid.
7. Ibid.
8. Ibid.
9. Ibid.
10. The following section owes much to Blatt's extensive work on the history of immigration politics in France (cf. David Blatt. "Une politique sans ethnicité? Les immigrés en France, entre théorie et pratique," in Hélène Greven-Borde and Jean Tournon, *Les identités en débat: intégration ou multiculturalisme?* (Paris: L'Harmattan 2000), pp. 137-68.
11. cf. Sönke Giard. "Frankreich: Über vier Millionen Muslime suchen ihren Weg," *Das Parlament*, January 2002, pp. 18-25.
12. cf. Joseph Hanimann, "Du sollst keine Götter neben mir haben. Das erste Gebot der Republik: Der Multikulturalismus ist in Frankreich kein Thema mehr," *Frankfurter Allgemeine Zeitung*, 8 July 1993, p. 25.
13. cf. Philippe Raynaud, "De la tyrannie de la majorité à la tyrannie des minorités," *Débat 69*, March-April 1992, pp. 50-59.
14. cf. Éric Fassin, "Du multiculturalisme à la discrimination," *Débat*, November-December 1997, p. 134.
15. cf. Philippe Raynaud, "Multiculturalisme et démocratie," *Débat*, November-December 1997, pp. 152-157.
16. Ibid.
17. Ibid., p. 156.
18. Such as François Furet, "L'Amérique de Clinton II," *Débat 94*, March-April 1997, pp. 3-10.
19. Cf. Didier Fassin, Alain Morice and Catherine Quiminal, eds., *Les lois de l'inhospitalité. La société française à l'épreuve des sans-papiers* (Paris: La Découverte, 1997), p. 135f. See also Denis Lacorne. *La Crise de l'identité américaine. Du melting-pot au multiculturalisme* (Paris: Fayard, 1997); 'Pour un

multiculturalisme modéré.' *Débat* 1997, November-December issue, pp. 159-167. All translations from French or German are mine.

20. cf. Michael Brenner, "Conflict and Coexistence: Jews in Europe under Muslim and Christian Rule," in Satish Saberwal and Mushirul Hasan, eds., *Asserting Religious Identities* (New Delhi: Manohar, 2006).
21. cf. Jean-Jacques Rousseau, *Du contrat social*, ed. by Pierre Burgelin (Paris: Flammarion, 1966), p. 1762.
22. Miriam Feldblum, "Paradoxes of Ethnic Politics: The Case of Franco-Maghrebins in France," *Ethnic and Racial Studies*, 16, 1993, pp. 52-74; Martin Schain, "Policy-Making and Defining Ethnic Minorities: The Case of Immigrants in France," *New Community* 20, 1995, pp. 59-77.
23. Cf. James Hollifield, "Immigration and Republicanism in France: The Hidden Consensus," in Wayne A. Cornelius, et al., eds. *Controlling Immigration: A Global Perspective* (Stanford: Stanford University Press, 1994), pp. 143-77.
24. Cf. Pierre-André Taguieff, *La force du préjugé* (Paris: Éditions La Découverte, 1987).
25. David Blatt, "Une politique sans ethnicité? Les immigrés en France, entre théorie et pratique," in Hélène Greven-Borde and Jean Tournon, *Les identités en débat: intégration ou multiculturalisme?* (Paris: L'Harmattan, 2000), p. 159.
26. Bruno Etienne, "La France multiconfessionnelle face à l'Europe plurielle: le cas statut de l'Islam," *Dialogues Politiques*, April 2002, at www.la-science-politique.com/revue/revue0/ france.htm.
27. Nathalie Dollé, "Qui représentera les musulmans de France?", *Le Monde diplomatique*, January 2002, p. 6.
28. cf. Riva Kastoryano, "Des multiculturalismes en Europe au multiculturalisme européen," *Politique Étrangère*, (1) 2000, pp. 163-178.
29. Ibid., 163f.
30. Ibid., 164.
31. cf. Etienne, n. 26.
32. Ibid.

5

The Multicultural Discourse in India

Imtiaz Ahmad

Pluralism and Multiculturalism

Contemporary academic discourse on multiculturalism in India has been centred on a single salient point, viz. that there is a fundamental difference between pluralism (and one might as its variant include diversity) and multiculturalism.

Pluralism, according to most self-proclaimed theorists on the subject, has characterized societies throughout history, but is silent on the question of the nature of the relationship between the different pluralities. On the other hand, multiculturalism is concerned with the issue of mutual interrelations among the sorts of pluralities what might be found to exist in society. It is concerned with the issue of equality. It asks whether the different pluralities coexist as equals in the public and political arena.

Thus, having nailed itself down to a fundamental difference between pluralism and multiculturalism, the academic discourse on multiculturalism in India bemoans very deeply that multiculturalism as a theory of democracy and citizenship has received little attention. As one theorist notes: "It appears quite paradoxical that in a country, which was among the first few democracies to endorse the principle of equality between groups, there has been no serious attempt to theorize the idea of multicultural democracy."

My own point of departure on this question is that this

mode of formulating the difference between pluralism and multiculturalism is seriously flawed and ignored the difference of the societies where multiculturalism as an ideology of the state and a theory of ensuring democracy evolved. I do not quite deny the relevance of the substantive point that pluralism can be characterized by the presence of diverse groups, communities and cultural orientations or worldviews without being concerned with the nature of the relationship between different cultural pluralities. It is possible that groups or communities may exist within the framework of back-to-back pluralism, that is, within a framework where they exist in relative isolation and independence from one another without coming into interaction only for limited purposes. Or, they may be involved in daily mutual interaction, but their interrelations may be regulated within a framework of dominance and subordination or hierarchical ordering. However, placing undue emphasis upon the difference between pluralism and multiculturalism ignores that historical differences over how societies looked at pluralism and in what ways they have legitimized. It has serious implications for the pragmatic design by which they seek to deal with the question of preservation and sustenance of pluralism within national polities. There is, therefore, no escape from focussing on how these differences have shaped the attitudes of the polities towards both looking at and handling cultural pluralism, religious as well as other, and providing for the preservation of pluralism and diversity in the public-political domain.

Even if we recognize that pluralism has been characteristic of all historical societies (and this point is not denied), at the theoretical as well as empirical level the two kinds of societies that constitute the point of comparison have historically differed in this substantative dimension.

Tradition of Plurality in Europe

The European side of this question will be dealt with in the second chapter of this volume. In order to condense the argument, let me refer to the concept of nationalism as a means of anchoring the argument central to a discussion of the historical evolution of the concept and theory of muiticulturalism. Expressed in the simplest terms, nationalism proclaims a new political ideal, the nation and a new political structure—the nation-state. It postulates that a nation is in need of its own state and that a state is in need of its nation. The demand to provide nations with their yet non-existent own state and the ambitious to provide states with their inexistent nation from then or operated as a mighty weapon to strengthen and to weaken, to make or to unmake new and old states. At least in Europe there existed a bewildering variety of nations: nations without states, self-proclaimed new and self-confident old nations, nations which had constituted themselves and nations which had been defined by others now stood besides or against each other. Often these nations overlapped and sometimes they mutually denied their very existence.

Gellner has argued that the basic unit of the nation is an atomized and autonomous individual and this is arrived at or postulated preceding the destruction of the pre-modem communities, which involves violence. Referring to the formation of the nation in the West, Gellener notes that it is

> a general imposition of high culture on society, where previously low cultures had taken up the lives of the majority... It is the establishment of an anonymous impersonal society, with mutually substitutable atomised individuals, held together above all by a shared culture of this kind, in place of a previous complex culture of local groups, sustained by fold cultures reproduced locally and idiosyncratically by the micro-groups themselves. That is what *really* happens.[1]

This transformation from the 'low culture' to the 'high culture' was not smooth, neither governed by sympathy nor understanding of what was being transformed. Again, to quote Gellener, this transformation was not an awakening of an 'old, latent, dominant force' but

> a period of turbulent readjustment in which neither political boundaries, or cultural ones, or both, were modified, so as to satisfy the new nationalist imperative which now, for the first time, was making itself felt ... (and) this period of transition was bound to be violent and conflict ridden.[2]

It was this specific historical circumstance that fundamentally instituted the specific nature of nationalism in many societies in the West. Thus, nations in the West were sought to be built by destroying the complex structures of local groups and was built on the foundations of atomized individuals. The theoretical formulation, for this was provided by Social Contract philosophers' notion of 'man-in-a-state of nature' and their notion of 'General Will' embodies the idea of nation. Enlightenment's stand towards homogeneity and pluralism points out that Enlightenment rationality is 'instrumental reason' which cannot accept pluralism. Each plurality under pluralism is founded in what Akeel Bilgrami has called 'internal reason'. However, the reason that is advocated by Enlightenment thinkers (with momentary exceptions in Hegel) is not 'internal reason' but 'instrumental reason', which per se rejects pluralism which thrives on cultural differences. Thus, within the social contract theory, there is no place envisaged for pluralism; their overriding normativity is bereft of the description of plural institutions. All three social contract theorists have positively rejected natural communities and intermediate natural institutions. Indeed, as Ebenstein noted:

> Hobbes is vehemently opposed to division of powers or mixed government... (and) to keep the authority of the state strong, Hobbes advises the sovereign not to allow the growth of groups and institutions that intervene between state and individual.

Thus, the notion of rationalism in the political philosophy of social contract theorists is not empirical and without empiricism in politics, democracy is not possible. Even when they talked about democracy, their notion of democracy eventually subscribes majoritarianism.

My limited reading of European history confirms a more cautious interpretation of the historical roots of plurality in Europe. The transition from a unified Latin Christian tradition to a modern Europe of secularized, multi-confessional states was not synonymous with the rise of tolerance and the triumph of pluralism. Instead, this transition, which mainly took place between the late fifteenth and the early nineteenth century was more often than not accompanied by intolerance, persecution, and religious wars. The ambivalent dialectics of tolerance and intolerance, conformity and plurality become especially evident when we focus on what historians call the early modern period, that is the three centuries from the Protestant Reformation of the early sixteenth to the French Revolution of the late eighteenth century. At the beginning of the early modern era, a hitherto unified Latin Christian church broke apart, and the sixteenth and seventeenth centuries were characterized by the institutionalization of rivalling Christian churches in a process that has been labelled 'confessionalization'.

From the eleventh to the early sixteenth century, secular and ecclesiastical authorities in Europe asserted the unity of the Latin Christian Church and used the powers at their disposal to subdue heretical groups. There was a general agreement among late medieval theologians and jurists that heresy—the abandonment of the Church's teachings—constituted a worse crime than Heathenism, for religious dissent was constructed as rebellion against the political and social order. The establishment of the inquisition in the early thirteenth century was the strongest manifestation of the Church's determination to enforce religious conformity. What is important to stress here is that the new Protestant churches —like the old Roman Catholic Church—were fundamentally intolerant. Luther, Calvin and their followers initially demanded toleration for themselves, but their belief in the absolute authority of the Bible, their conviction that their interpretation of Scripture was the correct one, and their self-perception as instruments and executors of divine will led them to advocate the persecution of 'heretics'. The attitude of Protestant reformers towards the Jews also hardened once they realized that the Jews were unwilling to accept the Gospel message, which the Reformation had now restored to its original purity and true meaning.

The emergence of pluralism is often linked to the process of secularization, broadly conceived as the abandonment of transcendent religious orientations by individuals, social groups, and whole societies. For Max Weber, secularization meant the 'disenchantment of the world', the replacement of religious dogma and metaphysical worldviews by non-confessional rational principles. According to modern sociological definitions, the concept of secularization implies that religion as a fundamental, all-encompassing worldview for most people has been replaced by other primary identifications (such as nationalism), while the churches have become specific functional institutions or 'sub-systems' in modern societies. In this strict sense, secularization and the growth of plurality were indeed intimately linked. Only when modern states ceased to define themselves as confessional, when the state's purposes were separated from transcendent religious purposes did religious toleration and pluralism become possible. If the concept of secularization is broadened into a general explanatory concept for all the major rationalizing and modernizing tendencies in Europe over the past three centuries, its relationship to the growth of pluralism appears less clear-cut. Hartmut Lehmann has recently emphasized that the secularization of modern Europe was hardly a linear process. Instead, a number of Protestant and Catholic religious movements have sought to counter the secularizing and rationalizing tendencies in modern European societies. The study of these movements has led Lehmann to suggest that the concept of secularization should be supplemented by the notion of 're-Christianization', which may well be an on-going process. Parts of Eastern Europe experienced a period of 're-Christianization' following the collapse of the Communist regimes in 1989-1991, and after the terrorist attacks on New York City and Washington, D.C. on 11 September 2001, the Christian churches in Europe were suddenly reported to be filled with people again. While there is reason to doubt that this was more than a short-lived phenomenon, it nevertheless indicates that the Christian faith, continues to remain an important orientation for a great number of Europeans—if only in times of crisis.

I have trespassed into this brief discussion of the tradition of plurality in Europe with two purposes in mind. First, I want to reinforce that there is a basic distinction on this question between Europe and India. While Europe, which was historically diverse and plural, underwent a process of establishment of homogeneous nation-states. However, within the special context of India, pluralism and diversity remained a dominant feature of the society until recent times and are today the central concern of the debates concerning multicultural states. Even colonial rule, which was in one sense a remarkable source of homogenization of society and culture, reinforced this concern through reinforcing the already existing cultural pluralism through the instrumentalities of the decennial censuses and the process of legislation whose aim was in the initial stages was to create communities and groups. Second, I wish to make the point that multicultural discourse in India remains centred on the question of pluralism and diversity of cultures as well as the recognition of these diversities in public and political domains. Echoes of distinctive social identities, aspirations for autonomous states, if not for sovereign national status, and exclusive and inclusive claims to territories characterized as homelands are heard today in the former Soviet Union, Eastern Europe, West Asia, Africa and Canada. However, nowhere are they being articulated as powerfully as in South Asia. Nor have such assertions, aspirations and claims as severely strained the social fabric as in India. This makes a consideration of the Indian situation particularly relevant.

Politics of Identity in India

Let us turn now to a consideration of the politics of identity in India. Indian society historically fostered and perpetuated a complex and shifting weave of multiple identities among the diverse people of the subcontinent. Before the advent of Western colonialism these multiple identities were accommodated, if not wholly assimilated, within loose political arrangements. A considerable body of historical scholarship has shown that sovereign authority vested in a centralized state system coexisted with innumerable identities at regional and local levels. The British not only managed to impose colonial control in India, but also initiated a process of recasting Indian social identities. Undoubtedly, such recasting occurred within largely autonomous cultural settings, and colonial initiatives were more successful in creating political categories out of local identifications and affiliations, regional, linguistic or religious, than fashioning the mental world of the people. Even so, the diversity of social and cultural identities that had historically characterized Indian society was swamped by the commanding power of the colonial state. The situation was further complicated by the rise of nationalism in a situation where there were many linguistic and cultural identities.

Put in the simplest terms, nationalism proclaimed a new political ideal, the nation and the nation state. Confusion over the form that the nation state should assume was bound to arise because two mutually incompatible concepts of defining the nation were by this time well-entrenched and both concepts gave inconclusive or contradictory answers when they were confronted not with the generalized question 'What is the nation?', but with the specific and politically ticklish question, 'Who is the nation?'. These mutually exclusive concepts of the nation were the ideal of the democratic and open nation and the ideal of a closed and 'ethnic' nation. Although both concepts normally exist in all modernizing societies and are difficult to disentangle in political practice, they are analytically distinct and should be distinguished if one has to understand the nature, form and consequences of nationalism in the case of a society where identities have historically remained diffused and complex.

The concept of an open and democratic nation arose first. It was influenced by liberalism and is necessarily linked to the basic concepts of a liberal civil society, the rule of law and a democratic government. This open and democratic nation comprises, or at least is supposed to comprise, in any given historical context, all those individuals which have lived together under a common social framework and which, as a result of political reforms have acquired the right of democratic self-determination. It is thus the memory of having lived together, whether as one single entity or separately, the existence of a democratic constitution and the constant practice of self-government which imparts to diverse individuals and groups a common national identity. Such a nation is not only democratic. It is also open. Its individuals are not defined by a common social substance, a singular and exclusive identity, but through a common political relationship.

With this ideal of the open and democratic nation contrasts the closed 'ethnic' nation. This nation is not defined through a political, legal or democratic relationship among its vastly different indifferent individuals and communities, each with its own distinct identity. It is defined through a common biological, religious, cultural, social or 'ethnic' bond, which overrides the various differences among its members, individuals as well as communities. This bond is derived from a common descent, religion, culture, language or history and creates an 'ethnic' identity and 'ethnic' nation. Commonalities of descent, religion, culture, language and history are no longer seen as separate or incidental or autonomous elements of society. They are instead seen as external manifestations or indicators of an ageless and unique primordial community. The 'ethnic' nation is also a closed nation: it is defined by a common substance or social and cultural traits which signify a common descent. Outsiders are either excluded in principle or they have to be completely assimilated.

The three assumptions that underlie this concept of the nation have been briefly summarised as follows:

1. Mankind by nature and historical evaluation divided into different and definable 'people' communities. These groups have the moral obligation and right to preserve and cultivate their specific identity.
2. The defence and development of a specific identity is only possible inside their own state. This state has in most circumstances to be fought for and this collective and heroic undertaking implies the transformation of the respective ethnic group from an objective entity into a self-conscious community.
3. It is through this transformation of a people that the ultimate self-realization of a nation's culture and destiny will be achieved.

These two originally separate concepts of nation and processes of nation-building have by now—through a global process of colonization and decolonization, of increasing modernization and democratization—have entered the arenas of political competition and ideological debate. In these arenas, proponents of both concepts try to monopolize the term 'nation' and they try to deny this title and ideal to their respective opponents. A liberal and nation state is seen as utopian. An ethnic nation and nation state are seen as dangerous and fascist. In this battle for semantic monopoly, the partisans of an 'ethnic' nation state are often the most insistent. Having withdrawn from a liberal conception of society, they proceed to 'expatriate' their opponents from political debate and start to describe them as 'anti-national'. Ethnic nationalism advances the claim of one nation, its own against others. It thus discovers and exacerbates arbitrary divisions and acts as an aggressive and intolerant force. It necessarily sets off a chain reaction of counterclaims and of further attempts of 'ethnic' nation-building. Widespread 'ethnic' conflicts, 'ethnic violence' and 'ethnic civil war' such as the ones we are a witness to in India today, are thus the consequences of 'ethnic' nationalism. To the extent that the liberal concept of nation and nation state serves 'ethnic' nationalism as a catalyst, as a camouflage, or an instrument, it is easy to overlook the fact that these ethnic conflicts and nationalism do not result from the logic and structure of the liberal nation and nation state. They arise from the cultural context and political constellations which have emerged proportionate to the spread of modernization and democratization.

Since Independence, India has been pursuing the ideal of a nation building based on secularism. Indeed, the process of modernization in India has always had as its focus on the reduction of barriers between religions, languages and castes (or tribes) by establishing a secular state and ultimately a unified nation. However, a marginal retracing of Indian history reveals that it was colonial rule that brought Western-type modernization to India and 'invented' the currently accepted view of Indian society as clearly segmented by social barriers.

For example, the separation between Muslims and Hindus, based on religious differences, the separation of tribes from Hindus, resulting from the Western illusion of the 'noble savage', and anti-Hindu ruling power were all impositions foisted by colonial rule.

Communalism in India shows that achievement of the ideal of constructing a secular nation state modelled on the modern Western concept of the civil society has been hindered by realities. Communalism (understood broadly and not merely as religious conflict between Hindus and Muslims) continues to be given a tautological explanation in terms of conflict between religious, linguistic or caste communities or explained reductively as a conflict among secular interests under the cloak of religion, language and caste. As a matter of fact, it is not the ignorant but the highly educated Indians who acquire modern mentality that supports communalism, To truly understand communalism, then, one must go beyond the present interpretations that view it as a conflict of interests between religious groups and assess it from a historical perspective as reflecting the limitations of modern thinking which has dominated since colonial times. It is only from such a perspective that one can adequately clarify the implications of communalism as evidence of contradictions inherent in the process of modernization and identify clues to resolving the problem.

Communalism is caused by the repression of 'daily-life viewpoint' by the dominance of a 'transcendental viewpoint' inherent in modern thinking. In modern society, which emphasizes reason, a rationally objective view tends to repress the irrational subjective view. As Kenichi Mishima, a Japanese scholar, has argued, "post-traditional society, which reveals the danger of reason, requires a proper balance between reason and *the other of reason*".[3] Today, with the collapse of the Cold War structure, the ideal of modernization that is secularism based on reason has also weakened. This has resulted in the current phenomenon of communalism as the liberation of the energy potential of non-reason. This problem is not unique to India, but common throughout the world. It must be understood in the context of the deadlock of modernization, namely, worldwide resurgence of religions, which surfaced with the end of the Cold War. Paradoxically, both secularism under which reason governs religions, and communalism, which liberates non-reason in the form of resurgence of religions, are two sides of the same coin of the modern age. Both are born from modernity and are striving within the limits of modern thinking.

Nonetheless, this strife between secularism and communalism can be regarded as a fluctuating process in the pursuit of a balance between reason and *the other of reason*, namely, as groping for a post-modern *episteme*. The emergence of a new version of communalism since the 1990s can be attributed to economic liberalization that realized the spread of consumerism and the development of the new media, particularly television. During the 1990s, televisions began spreading rapidly reaching into rural villages and low-income households. The spread of TV enormously changed the informational environment of Indian society. The drastic effect of the spread of TVs on society is the realization of nation-wide unification of information. Even before the spread of TVs, the print media existed in Indian society. Nonetheless, the TV, which represents visual images instead of letters, found it much easier to access people throughout the country regardless of social class. As a result, TVs enabled the public to more thoroughly live by sharing the same information.

Transmitting live images real time, TV has permitted local viewers to see things from national and even global standpoints. The public therefore began to have two types of information: direct information obtained through first-hand experiences and information transmitted by TVs comprising images and knowledge but no first-hand experiences. The former constitute the 'bottom up' information from 'daily-life viewpoints', whereas the latter constitute 'the top-down' information scene from a 'transcendental viewpoint'. Obtaining such a 'transcendental viewpoint' is one of the crucial consequences of modernization. The spread of TVs not only accelerated this effort, but also produced a number of magical effects.

Since TV images, despite the incident taking place in a distant place, appear to be as 'real' as those seen in first hand experiences, the 'real' images occasionally confuse viewers by blurring boundaries between 'daily-life viewpoints' and 'transcendental viewpoints'. This magic of encompassing of 'daily-life viewpoints' by 'transcendental viewpoints' works for the generation of the phenomenon of communalism through two processes: the 'magic of categorization' and an increase of warm consumer effects by a middle class syndrome.

To explain the 'magic of categorization', one can refer to any local community in a distant part of the country. To the local people, Ayodhya was a place that had no relation to their daily lives. However, when television broadcasts transmitted scenes of the destroyed Babri Masjid, Ayodhya was no longer an irrelevant place at least in the domain of imagination. As a result, the incident, which was interpreted as communalism between Hindus and Muslims, began to cast a dark shadow over local communities in which both Hindus and Muslims shared a common culture. This meant that local people in every part of India shared the same visual information, which reflected their incorporation into a 'transcendental viewpoint'. In this regard, it is worth pointing out that TVs spread modern thinking, allowing viewers to see their actual daily life from a 'transcendental viewpoint' and the popularization of such a 'transcendental viewpoint' supports the development of majoritarian Hindu communalism. In other words, Indian society has now developed to a stage where the 'magic of categorization' is effective.

What is here referred to as the 'magic of categorization' refers to an effect of categorization from a 'transcendental viewpoint', that is, a strong sense of ties and affinity that has been cultivated by the automatic assumption that any individuals belonging to one category are siblings and share a common identity. For instance, any individual once categorized as Hindu immediately develops a strong affinity to others who similarly describe themselves including strangers living in remote places. Through this 'magic of categorization', this individual feels total sympathy for all Hindus, but on the contrary feels little sympathy for Muslims as enemies. It can be called magic because 'daily-life viewpoints' from which a person regards someone he has never met as a stranger is repressed by the sympathy generated by a 'transcendental viewpoint'. Thus, the situation of communalism involves the 'magic of categorization' since other persons are always categorized into either friends or foes in an inflexible manner regardless of individual differences within each category. This repression of the 'daily-life viewpoint' by 'transcendental viewpoints' has been intensified by the rapid development of new media and market logic. On the one hand, this intensified repression as a result of modern thinking, threatens the dominance of reason and strongly requires a proper balance between reason and *the other of reason*. On the other hand, people's minds are confined by modern thinking, which is typically manifested as the 'magic of categorization'. Thus, the contradiction in modern thinking between the resistance to *the other of reason* and 'magic of categorization' has produced an improper and surrogate solution of communalism.

The best way to attenuate communalism is to stay away from its trap. However, if the ordinary people are aware of and stay away from the trap, the problem concerning the balance between reason and *the other or reason* still remains unsolved. To cope with this problem, we must change our worldview that categorizes objects and people in a uniform view. In other words, we must get rid of the one-dimensional, inflexible state of identities, which emphasize consistency. Gandhi probably had this in mind when, at the height of communal frenzy in Noakhali soon after Partition, he said: "You say Hindus are killing Muslims and Muslims are killing Hindus. I am a Hindu, but I am also a Muslim, a Christian and a Sikh. You are all also all of them."

One significant dilemma has characterized attitudes towards the right to equality from the beginning. On the one hand, it has meant that all citizens have the same rights and no citizen has rights that others do not have. On the other hand, it has meant that an absolute right to equality is meaningless unless citizens are truly equal. Where inequality is pervasive or likely to *be* so, an absolute right to equality is meaningless unless conditions are created for that equality to be real. This dilemma has been at the core of most legal controversies during the past fifty years that the Republic has been in existence. It has become most contentious today.

It would seem that, in order to understand the contentiousness and depth of feeling about the right to equality, we must understand the nature of the polity established by our national Constitution. Human beings have shown an almost amazing ability to deal with and accept diverse political and legal systems when the general right guaranteed under these systems are known in advance. 'Known in advance' means that the social, political, economic and civil rights by which people are to live are established and known well before they are applied to concrete situations. This 'advance knowledge' may occur through tradition, through acceptance overtime, through a recognized historical event, or through common agreement at a rime certain in history. It may be contrasted with the arbitrary exercise of power that responds only to the will of the person or official exercising that power or the wish of a political majority at a given time to change the framework of established rights. The Indian Constitution, and the polity it created, represents the historical creation of a system of rights.

The degree to which a country has recognized rights and a minimum of arbitrary decision-making is the degree to which we call the government of that country legitimate or illegitimate. The conceptual framework of 'legitimacy' *is* generally not one of degree. Average citizens view governments as either legitimate or illegitimate, not somewhere on a continuum. For this reason, once any significant minority of the population considers the government illegitimate, a serious line has been crossed, and the government risks destruction. Legitimacy is, thus, a fragile thing.

Much of the controversy involving the right to equality is generally because significant numbers of people think that this right has been, or should be, altered in violation of the intentions of the framers of the Constitution. This is seen as cheating by one faction. Those opposing that faction's views feel that this violates the fundamental principle of democracy that the Will of the Majority shall prevail. To the extent this controversy involves a fundamental critique of the right to equality enshrined in the Constitution, it is very important to society.

After all, what is a constitution? It is only a method by which powers may be used within limits. If the executive, legislature or judiciary can alter or abridge the rights and constitutional guarantees to citizens, then the constitution is no more than a relatively old piece of paper. And, without a constitution, one has a very different political system. Here one is not referring to the written constitution, but to the real one. This is the one carved into the hearts of citizens. This real constitution is a set of deeply held values and principles enjoying willing acceptance of all citizens. It functions, restrains and controls what government does. Without constitutional values, principles and rules, the system becomes arbitrary, the tool of faction and personality, and a threat to every person within its power. Such were the Nazi and Soviet states.

Unprincipled decision-making, whether by the executive, the legislature or the judiciary, if accepted, spells the end of any real constitution. This is so because, if a constitution does not mean what the people who wrote and ratified it meant by it, then it means nothing at all. It then becomes a tool rather than a barrier to tyranny. Policy then becomes the province of power, not law or reason. This brings us to the question, what are rights?

Rights are integral to the existence of a constitution. Without them it cannot operate. They are much like antibodies that circulate through the blood stream. They protect the integrity of the rules that make up the constitution, giving to people a tool to challenge actions that violate the rules of the constitution. They provide guidelines for executive action, they set limits to legislation and offer the judiciary a device for overturning decisions made by the political or democratic branches of government. However, when distortions, whose origins we are only beginning to understand, affect biological antibodies, those antibodies can turn on the human body wreaking all manner of harm from allergies to death. Likewise, when rights are created to achieve political goals, they can become carriers of tyranny and arbitrary power, rather than the primary defence of equality or liberty.

Not only is such possible, but also that it is a very real problem in the current rights oriented jurisprudence and public discourse. Empirically, rights are claims that someone else must recognize. If one has a right to a piece of land, then another person cannot do anything with that land inconsistent with rights to it. If one has a right to vote, the government may not prevent that person from voting. Constitutional rights make perfect sense when they are understood as claims against the government. Historically, and one could argue logically, this leads to all rights being negative. Rights are negative claims. But if constitutional rights are interpreted positively, all manner of illogic occurs, as well as potential threats to equality and liberty. For then we will end up arguing that rights, like the rabbit in the magician's hat, things that can be materialized by mere will. We will argue that rights are just a manifestation of the will of the legislature or the democratic majority as adopted in a written document.

If rights are nothing but expressions of political will, then they may be created or destroyed by the political actions of the society. Thus, the long-term security for rights is the political process. Further, if there is nothing to a right but positive law, that is, the will of the society as expressed through the law-making process, any deep attachment to rights, or even descriptions of rights as fundamental, should be replaced with a candid recognition that rights are nothing but one era's fancy. However, this is not the view the vast majority of our citizens hold. They value, honour and almost idolize rights. This implies that rights, or some of what we call rights, are not just statements of political will. Rights, real rights, the fundamental rights found in our Constitution, come not from political compromise, but from the core of human nature. Fundamental rights are an aspect of what it means to be human. A society that does not embody them in its system of government and law is not a good society. Fundamental rights exist independent of whether governments or current majorities recognize or honour them. Whether based in purely secular philosophies or in deeply held religious views, a belief in the objective reality of certain fundamental rights has significant consequences for the way in which we think about law and government.

Right of Equality

Let me, with this as background, turn to the right to equality enshrined in the Constitution. The Preamble to the Constitution resolved to secure to all Indians social, economic and political justice and provide equality of status and opportunity. Towards this end, Article 15 prohibits discrimination on grounds of religion, race, caste or any other such grounds, and Article 16(2) lays down that no person can be discriminated against in the matter of public employment on grounds of race, religion and caste. Nonetheless, the Framers of our Constitution were aware that the greatest dilemma of human society is that the government has necessary functions because humans are not angels. Yet, it is precisely those non-angelic humans who are the only way that governments can be staffed. Thus, while government was placed under the obligation to ensure equality of all citizens, it could be presumed that certain cultural and linguistic minorities might have a different experience of political practices.

Accordingly, specific protections were provided by way of fundamental rights to ensure that the right to equality was not denied to such communities. Article 29(1) laid down that any section of citizens having a distinct language, script or culture of its own shall have the fundamental right to conserve the same. This means that if there is a cultural minority which wishes to preserve its own language or culture the state shall not by law impose upon it any culture or language belonging to the majority in that region. Again, the promotion of Hindi as the national language or introduction of compulsory primary education cannot be used as a device to take away the linguistic safeguard of a minority community as guaranteed under Articles 29 and 30. Thus, while Article 29(2) rules out discrimination in state educational institutions and ensures that there is no discrimination against any citizen on grounds of religion, language race or caste, Article 30(1) provides that all minorities, whether based on religion or language, shall have the fundamental right establish educational institutions of their choice and Article 30(2) guarantees that the state shall not in granting aid to educational institutions discriminate against any educational institution on the ground that it is under the management of a minority, whether based on religion or language.

Even though the word 'minorities' forms part of popular political discourse in India, its precise connotation is far from satisfactory. It is used to denote those non-Hindu religious communities whose members are for one reason or another inclined to assert their distinctiveness in relation to Hindus. Thus, Muslims, Christians, Sikhs, Parsis and Jews are commonly described as minorities in India.

This narrowing down of the connotation of the word 'minorities' is both misleading and unfortunate. For one thing, it projects and essentializes Hindus as a closely-knit and homogeneous community. This is factually not true. Second, it treats religious difference to be the only basis for defining a minority community. Minorities are not based on religious differences alone. They are based on social disadvantage and deprivation. Even if the application of the word 'minorities' to the religious communities carries the connotation that they are in some ways socially and politically disadvantaged, arbitrarily restricting it to religious minorities ignores the fundamental nature of Indian society.

Indian society is essentially a segmentary society. This means that the boundaries of social communities are neither fixed nor permanent. Every social community unites itself against others and at the same time becomes segmented into smaller social communities. Furthermore, inequities exist in this society at every level of segmentation of a community. A social community considered advantaged in relation to other similar social communities may contain within it two sub-communities one of which may be more advantaged than the other. Perhaps, the case of the Brahmins in North India would serve to illustrate this point. They are recognized to be an extremely advantaged group by virtue of their caste standing, hold over land and access to higher education and administration. However, this advantaged position of the Brahmins obtains in relation to other castes and communities. Within the Brahmin social community, the Saryupari Brahmins are disadvantaged in relation to the Kanyakubja Brahmins. The situation in respect of such segmentation and distribution of social and political advantages is not particularly different among other social communities whether or not they are recognized as minorities.

In other words, it is problematic in the Indian context to speak of some social communities as minorities and to contrast them with the majority as an essentialized social category or to assume that the minorities are any more disadvantaged and deprived than some communities within an essentialized majority community. Everyone in Indian society is in one sense or the other disadvantaged as the claim of the Brahmins in South India that they should be granted reservation amply demonstrates. Perhaps, the only difference is in the degree, scale and intensity of the disadvantage and deprivation they can be said to suffer and reflect.

Since inequity and social and political deprivation is all pervading within Indian society, it seems that we can classify social communities at any level of social organization into two broad categories. The first category will be of those social communities which are undoubtedly deprived but whose disadvantage and deprivation is less than other social communities. The other category will be of those social communities whose deprivation and social disadvantage is absolute. They are disadvantaged in relation to all other social communities and are advantaged in relation to none.

It may be asked how and on what criteria is one to determine whether a social community is to be classified as relatively deprived or absolutely deprived. Fortunately, this is not an insurmountable difficulty. It will be conceded that access to political power, the degree of social homogeneity and the absence or otherwise of internal economic and social differentiation within the community and the intensity of social and political disabilities to which a social community has been exposed are fairly reliable indices of social and political deprivation and disadvantage and can serve as a basis for distinguishing communities along the absolutely deprived-relatively deprived axis. The position of each community in terms of these three indices is already known and is a principal determinant of the position they occupy in the contemporary society.

Proceeding on the basis of this broadened perspective, five distinct categories of minorities can be said to exist in India. They are:

1. Religious communities towards whom social attitudes range from benign tolerance to open hostility as a result of which they are both marked off as separate and distinct and are discriminated against, although the degree of discrimination practised against them or the threat of social violence to which they may be periodically exposed, particularly if they raise political demands for the preservation of their distinct cultural identity, varies proportionately to the intensity of social prejudice against them. Muslims, Christians, Parsis and Jews are examples of this category of minorities.
2. Communities sharing a common religious tradition or having been historically treated as belonging to a common religious tradition towards whom social attitudes are generally characterized by common identification and acceptance, but when their members seek to assert their distinct identity or begin to claim separate social, cultural and political rights, social attitudes tend towards open hostility and political oppression. Sikhs, the Scheduled Castes and tribal communities, particularly in north-eastern India, constitute examples of this category of minorities.
3. Communities sharing a common social and economic standing and exposed to a common hostility and discrimination at the hand of the larger society end up becoming the target of the counterpart group when its

members are seen as cutting into the advantaged position of the other group or when both the groups are simultaneously seeking to claim limited social and economic resources. Communities of tribals who have existed in close proximity over long periods and shared common deprivation suddenly marking off one group as an enemy, (as happened recently) in Assam where Bodos perpetrated violence against the Santhals, constitute examples of this category of minorities.

4. Communities of refugees and migrants, driven out of their home countries by conditions of political turmoil or economic compulsions, who take refuge in India. Chakmas, Buddhists from Bangladesh, Sri Lankan Tamils, Nepalis and distressed Bangladeshi migrants in different parts of the country are examples of this category of minorities. Even though social attitudes and the hostility and violence to which they may be exposed varies greatly according to their social identity and the degree of economic and political threat they pose to others in a particular region, they share a common fate and suffer similar disabilities and can be said to constitute a distinct category of minorities.
5. Communities whose languages are not recognized and listed under the Eighth Schedule of the Constitution, whose language is listed under the Eighth Schedule, but facilities for their use in education and administration are not provided on account of discriminatory state policies, or whose language was co-opted under Hindi on account of the Hindu undertones of the nationalist movement and the effort to create Hindi as a *lingua franca* of north Indian Hindus even if many of them are older than Hindi and possess their distinct literatures. Communities of speakers of tribal languages such as Santhali and Mundari, speakers of Urdu, Braj, Khariboli and Maithli as well as speakers of a recognized language who currently reside in an area where facilities do not exist for the use of their language in education and administration, such as speakers of Telugu in Kannada-

speaking areas are examples of this category of minorities.

The Indian discourse on minorities was overshadowed by the historical experience of Partition. It did not view minorities from the perspective of social and economic equality, but defined them within the parameters of the discourse of communalism versus secularism and nationalism versus separatism. Because of this, prevailing political realities influenced the decision as to which groups were to be designated as minorities. The Sub-Committee on Fundamental Rights admitted with much candour that 'it is difficult to expect that a country like India where most persons are communally minded those in authority will give equal treatment to those who do not belong to their community'. Thus, in the Report on the Advisory Committee on Minorities, Muslims, Scheduled Castes and Indian Christians were considered to be minorities. Parsis and Sikhs were designated as minorities much later, as late as the latter part of the 1980s. At present, the officially designated minorities in India are Muslims, Christians, Parsis, Buddhists and Sikhs.[4]

There is a widespread misconception that the Indian Constitution confers a series of special rights on the minority communities. However, the debates and discussions in the Constituent Assembly reveal how the safeguards for the minorities, which included separate representation, were eliminated in the name of an unalloyed, pure-nationalism. The only right specifically provided for the minorities in the Indian Constitution is the one relating to their right to establish and run educational institutions of their choice. Even this right was, however, so ambiguously formulated that educational institutions run by minorities could not reserve seats for students of their own community. It was as late as 1991 that the Supreme Court of India in the St. Stephen's case ruled that the right to regulate admissions to maintain the minority character of an institution was "a necessary concomitant right which flows from the right to establish and administer educational institutions under Article 30(1)".

It is important at this point to take note of some features of the discourse on minority rights in the West. The question of group rights or collective rights has come up in the West at a time when communities have more or less disintegrated and community life has all but disappeared. Secondly, it has arisen in a situation where the basic rights of citizenship have been extended to communities that were previously excluded from it and therefore the current Western discourse is more concerned about the cultural rights of minorities. Finally, it has been born out of the experiences of immigrant groups and indigenous peoples and their discrimination and vulnerability in the face of fhe homogenizing political system and culture of Western liberal democracies.

The Indian context is different. While the British provided for community-based representation for purposes of *realpolitik*, the post-colonial Indian Constitution did not grant special rights to minorities with a view to ensuring representation of diverse interests and as aspects of democratic citizenship in a secular and plural polity. On the contrary, given the background of the partition of the subcontinent, the Indian Constitution made a subtle but basic distinction between the cultural rights of religious minorities and political group rights of communities which were socially discriminated through forced segregation or physical isolation. Thus, the Scheduled Castes and Scheduled Tribes were given representation in the political sphere and protected in the economic sphere, while minorities were only granted the right to protect their religion, language and culture and establish and administer educational institutions.

The structure of democracy, as it has been enshrined in the Indian Constitution, rests on the proposition that the Will of the Majority shall prevail. In accordance with this doctrine, we have developed elaborate electoral procedures which are designed to select candidates who represent majority opinion. These elected representatives then sit on all kinds of committees where once again it is assumed that the correct decision will be reached by discovering majority opinion on the basis of one man one vote. Throughout our political system it is taken for granted that for the time being anyway, any elected majority has a perfectly legitimate right to discriminate against its minority opponents in any way it chooses.

Now this belief that majority opinion is 'right' cannot be justified by any process of rational calculation. It is simply maintained as a religious dogma. However, as soon as one comes to think about this matter at all deeply, it becomes quite obvious that government by majority can never be fair. The convention of parliamentary democracy may be tolerable, but no one can reasonably suppose that it is fair or just that the minority should have no share in political decision-making whenever the majority is opposed to it. Clearly, their distinct cultural and religious identities, particularly when combined with the fact that they are likely to be marginalized to a lesser or greater extent by the majority, would seem to ensure that minorities do have a different experience of political institutions and practices from that of the majority. Thus, institutions and practices formed without the input of minority perspectives might well impose burdens on them which are invisible to the majority.

It was for this reason that the leadership in the period following Independence took special efforts to ensure that, though the Indian Constitution did not contain any provision for representation and participation of minorities in politics and governance, they were represented in decision-making forums. This was partly ensured through ensuring nomination of members of minority communities to elective offices and partly through their promotion to positions of power and authority in government Whether this did in fact ensure that the minorities were able to affect political decisions remains an open question, this political practice did give to the minorities a sense of representation and participation in decision-making processes.

Clearly, the disadvantaged position of the minorities in a plural society is maintained by legitimized traditions of discrimination and suppression of rights. One might add that devaluing the culture of the minorities and denying them access to basic assets and resources is part of an integral whole in the project of constructing national hegemonies, and often the struggle to preserve cultural identities on the part of the minorities of various kinds is a weapon to articulate the basic aspirations for equality and dignity in all spheres. Communities are marginalized because a small but dominant minority controls the national resources. In fact, it is a new minority of modern and modernizing elites which exercises hegemony over national life and seeks to advantage minorities not by devaluing their culture alone but also by denying them equal opportunity and access to national resources. The project of constructing a national hegemony can lead to the pernicious use of majority sentiments for political gains while effectively denying minorities representation and participation in governance, thus promoting what has been termed 'majoritarianism'.

The project to constructing national hegemony affects minorities in two ways. First, it builds into the state at every level a bias against the minorities. Second, this bias is reinforced by the challenge from the minorities. This bias works in both subtle and blatant ways. Among the subtle ways, the bias works is on the question of the personal law of the minorities. From the time of the constitutional directive for a uniform civil code superseding all personal laws, there has been a relentless legal and extra-legal pressure to do away with personal laws. This has been done subtly by raising equity considerations although the same equity considerations are ignored when it comes to laws that govern Hindus, such as the law on the Hindu undivided family. This kind of bias works even more subtly in employment in government. Minimal representation of at least some minority communities in this sector is well established. Among the blatant ways this bias works is best demonstrated by the fact that a very high percentage of the detenus under the Terrorist and Disruptive Activities Act were at one time members of minority communities. It is equally demonstrated by an alarming rise in rioting and massacre of members of minority communities, particularly Muslims, Sikhs and Christians, in civil strife. More than a thousand people including women and children were killed during the Bombay riots. Such killings in other states would add up to several thousand. Sikhs were massacred in thousands in 1984. More recently, Christian missionaries as well as ordinary Christians in places as far removed as Orissa and Gujarat have been special targets of attack and intimidation. What is alarming about such violence and massacres is the direct participation of the administration and security forces.

Whether or not there is on the part of the majority an actual intention to exclude the minorities from politics and governance, or to refuse to address their complaints whether real or imaginary, the simple fact that the experience of the minorities is markedly different from that of the minority means that, without some measures assuring that the perspective of the minority groups is reflected in public discourse, it is very likely to be overlooked and so the minority interests are unlikely to be met. Furthermore, whether or not the majority possesses a clear understanding of the interests of the minorities, relations of trust between the two are weak and the minorities tend to be the subject of prejudicial or bigoted attitudes on the part of the majority. This sufficiently underscores the requirement that in any democratic political order some measures should exist to ensure the representation and participation of minorities in governance or at least to guarantee that the perspective of the minorities is not excluded from the political discourse even if constitutional provisions rule out positive discrimination in their favour in legislatures and administration.

One relevant question in this context is whether in a democratic polity, the representation of the minorities should necessarily be measured against the number of members it has in the legislative forums or in the administration. It is possible that others enjoying the support and confidence of a particular minority group will act as representatives on its behalf. For example, for twenty years after Independence, Jawaharlal Nehru was a powerful spokesperson of Muslim interests even though the number of Muslims in the legislature in those days was considerably higher.

Subsequently, Indira Gandhi and, particularly after the

Ayodhya crisis surfaced in Uttar Pradesh, Mulayam Singh had been active spokespersons of Muslim interests. Even if we concede that there is no single individual today who can claim to represent Muslim interests, the point remains that the argument that in a democratic polity only its own members can represent interests is tenuous so long as some bonds of trust exist between members of the majority and minority groups. Consequently, the question worth asking is: how strong are the foundations of trust between the majority and minority political leaders?

The answer to this question in the contemporary political context is likely to vary depending upon which particular minority community one is considering. As far as Muslims and Christian minorities are concerned, at least till about a decade ago there appear to have been some foundations of trust between the majority and these minority communities. Muslim and Christian community members regularly approached legislators and administrators from the majority community with requests and advice. They were active in seeking accommodation from local government bodies, particularly in the field of education, and even met with significant, if not total, success. This willingness to pursue political change through normal political channels and established institutions suggests that, although their claims may not have been satisfied, they did not feel that they could trust officials to attend to their requests with seriousness and some degree of responsiveness.

The Ayodhya episode in the case of Muslims and the rise of atrocities against Christians, both closely related with the rise of a strong right-wing Hindu ideological tendency, usually characterized as Hindutva, and the remarkable convergence that has developed between the representatives of this tendency and the state, seems to have changed this significantly. After the Ayodhya episode, Muslims felt that the members of the majority were not willing even to listen open-mindedly to the reasons for their outrage, let alone respond to it. The language of Muslim grievance shifted from one of requests to one of indifference, and some Muslims actually felt grateful for the episode because it mobilized a formerly quite passive Muslim populace. In the wake of the anti-Muslim and anti-Christian sentiments that have surfaced during the recent years, their capacity to trust the members of the majority to take their concerns seriously and to address them equitably has been seriously damaged.

Of course, the question remains whether the majority's response is itself unreasonable, whether they are right not to entertain much discussion of the reasons against the sense of loss of trust on the part of Muslims and Christians (or Sikhs after the riots of 1984). A loss of trust which results from groups having placed themselves out of the boundaries of a possible shared public culture might not impose an obligation of the majority to reach out to them in the name of equality contrasts to the case of groups which are excluded by the actions of the majority itself. The question of who is to blame for the heightened alienation of any minority group from the majority is undoubtedly unresolvable to either group's satisfaction, but that does not make it irrelevant to reflections on the extent and form of consideration that the majority might owe to the minorities in a democratic polity.

In a broad and general sense, minorities are prone to feeling challenged in democratic governance founded on the principle of majority rule. Even during the high point of the Nehru era, when the state took several steps to remove discriminations and ameliorate the conditions under which minorities lived, the minorities felt a sense of insecurity and discrimination. What has changed substantially today is that the national commitment to require that the distinctive concerns of the minorities, or at least some minorities, be accommodated in public policy, has weakened. This has given rise among at least some minority groups to the feeling which Martin Luther King, Jr. articulated in the context of the Negroes in the United States:

> When the architects of our republic wrote the magnificent words of the Constitution and the Declaration of Independence, they were signing a promissory note to which every American was to fall heir. This note was a promise that all men would be

> guaranteed the inalienable rights of life, liberty, and the pursuit of happiness... . It is obvious today that America has defaulted on this promissory note insofar as her citizens of colour are concerned. Instead of honouring this sacred obligation, America has given the Negro people a bad check which has come back marked 'insufficient funds'.[5]

There would seem, then, to be a mutual obligation to locate modes of discourse which leave open the possibility on intercultural understanding and ensure participation of the minorities in governance.

NOTES

1. Ernest Gellner, *Nations and Nationalism* (Ithaca, N.Y.: Cornell University Press, 1983), p. 57.
2. Ibid., p. 40.
3. Cited in Imtiaz Ahmad, "Has Communalism Changed? – II," *The Hindu*, 13 April 2002.
4. Government of India, Ministry of Welfare, Notification, 23 October 1993.
5. Speech by Martin Luther King, Jr. delivered on the steps at the Lincoln Memorial, Washington, D.C., 28 August 1963.

6

For a New Secularism: Citizen Rights or Community Protection

Dipankar Gupta

I

Before one begins a discussion on "secularism", it is important to be clear on what this term is supposed to entail. Usually, secularism is linked to tolerance, fraternity, and to the joining of hearts and minds irrespective of faith and denomination. This is a soft version of secularism, and predictably, it can never stand up in the face of a determined ethnic strike. It is also generally believed that secularism is a cultivated disposition and that the "correct" education makes a person secular. This point of view is in harmony with the soft secularism that was just alluded to. In such renditions, secularism stands also for enlightened thinking and fellow feeling, but nowhere is the whip being cracked. It is all very voluntary and based on goodwill.

What needs to be borne in mind is that in the true liberal democratic tradition, from the time of John Locke's *Letters on Tolerance*, it was made clear that religion can only function within boundaries set by the state, and on no account could the church, and by extension, any religious denomination, resort to force.[1] That was strictly forbidden and it would invite the severest of punishment as the state alone had the power to use force. This then helps us clarify another popular view that surrounds most discussions on secularism. It is generally believed that in a secular society the state and the church are kept separate, implying that each has its own zone of relevance. What is lost out in such interpretations regarding the modern relationship between the state and the church is that the church is actually subordinate to the state, and that it is the state that keeps the church in check.

So if there is a burst of religious fervour, the government must see to it that it stays within the bounds established by law. The Indian Constitution in Article 30 makes clear that the right of religious denominations to manage their own affairs, freedom cannot be at the expense of disturbing the peace. The only freedom that is unfettered is embodied in Article 25 that gives citizens the freedom of conscience. So when sectarians break the law, the secular response ought to be very simple. Punish them for their wrong-doings by observing the due process of the law. This is true secularism, and not tolerance, kindness and brotherly love. Indeed, there is very little scope for discussion on matters like these. When people are killed, or their property looted, and their futures destroyed, ignorance of the law cannot be considered to be an extenuating factor. One does not have to be told that to kill, maim and loot are criminal activities. There is indeed a limit to tolerance!

Secularism draws its strength from democratic principles of citizenship. It has little to do with religious notions that God made us all equal, or that we are all children of God. God, indeed, has not made us equal, and we do not want to be related to one another. Yet, this makes no difference to the modern conception of liberalism which cedes no quarter to those who have no respect for other citizens' right to life and property. I may not know my neighbour, I may even have little appreciation for other cultures and other ways of life, but I just cannot attack them on that account and hope to get away with it. Secularism will not stand for it, will not even discuss it. Therefore, secularism is not overly bothered about what goes on in the hearts of people so long as they stay well within the bounds of the law that enshrines the rights of citizens.

II

After the Gujarat carnage of 2002, the importance of hard secularism as the only valid form of secularism for modern times, cannot be overestimated. Quite clearly the government of Gujarat was complicit in the killings of Muslims after the Godhra incident. Instead of pulling the Chief Minister out of his chair, the Prime Minister suggested a variety of confidence-building measures to the errant Chief Minister. He was asked to construct homes for those affected, find them jobs, give them armed escorts, get businesses to contribute to their relief and rehabilitation, and so on. Not once was it mentioned that the Government of India would use all its powers to punish the guilty—and that this also included Narendra Modi.

Unfortunately, the demand to punish the guilty is not on the agenda of the opposition either. All they want is the removal of the Chief Minister. This is really political gamesmanship. Of course, Narendra Modi ought to go, but if he sinks alone and is not weighted down by those other criminals who killed, burnt, maimed and looted then he might emerge as a political martyr. To bring credibility to Mr. Modi's ouster, he needs to be punished along with all those who are actually red in tooth and claw. This includes those who torched the railway coaches in Godhra as well as those who stalked and killed Muslims in Ahmedabad, and elsewhere in Gujarat.

This is not the first time that a government is directly implicated in fomenting and leading communal riots in the country. The 1984 killings of Sikhs is a cruel predecessor of what happened recently in Gujarat. The way that the civil liberties groups mobilized in 1984 was however quite remarkable. Instead of doing social science and discovering caste and class antagonisms behind the killings, the Peoples' Union for Democratic Rights (PUDR) and the Peoples' Union for Civil Liberties (PUCL) jointly conducted a first rate social forensic study and brought out a report entitled *Who are the Guilty?*

Police inaction in Gujarat, as Justice Verma, when he was Chairman of the National Human Rights Commission pointed out soon after the killings, was tantamount to police complicity.

The police do not need orders from anywhere to stop lawlessness. This is like saying every time somebody jumps a traffic light the policeman on duty must have the matter cleared by his Commissioner before taking any action. On straight law and order cases, the police should be able to act on their own. The fact that they did not do so in Gujarat is clearly because they were told not to. In other words, police inaction in such instances is not an innocent case of neglect, oversight, or the usual inefficiency. It is motivated malice.

The Citizens' Tribunal that held hearings on the Gujarat killings strongly indicted the government for its complicity in the massacre of Muslims and also named certain people who were obviously guilty of perpetrating the violence and indulging in it too.[2] It is obvious that citizens can no longer sit on the sidelines when communal carnages occur in the belief that the machinery of the state will do its job and punish the guilty. Citizens will have to be more vigilant and alert to give strength to the democratic system. As those in government positions no longer see themselves as public servants, the public must have to assert itself in the interest of democracy. It is again because of the pressure from the National Human Rights Commission that the Best Bakery case in Gujarat has been re-opened as the earlier judgment that cleared the accused was based on testimonies of witnesses that had turned hostile. Now we know of the threats that were made which made many star witnesses change their accounts.

In all of this, it is public spiritedness that matters. There is little point in talking in terms of generalities like "majority community" and "minority community". What is needed is that the guilty should be punished regardless of which community they may belong to. This is the only confidence-building measure that has a long-term impact. It also sends out warning signals to those who think that they can do what they will because the political power of the day is either actively or tacitly on their side. It must also be remembered that religious sectarians and virtuosos ultimately need each other. They are not thinking of citizens, they are thinking of their own position as spokespeople of their communities. In India, the Hindu leaders of the Ram Janmabhoomi agitation need the Babri Masjid Action Committee to complement each other. Further, as Mark Juergensmeyer rather perceptively pointed out, that sectarians of different faiths not only need each other to demonize, but that they often admire each other as well.[3]

If the guilty are tried and punished then this will also expose another lie on which communalists thrive. The popular assumption is that these sectarians are as willing to kill for a cause as they are to die for a cause. This is a complete fallacy. None of the hotheads of the RSS, or Bajrang Dal or the Vishwa Hindu Parishad (VHP) will ever die for a cause. In which case then, why are they so willing to kill for a cause? The answer to this is very simple. It is because they know that no harm will come to them as they enjoy protection from the government of the day. Sometimes the protection can be a tacit one as was demonstrated in Orissa in 2002 when the state government did not act sternly against Hindu mobs who raided the Assembly as the party in power at the state was also a member of the BJP-led coalition in the Centre. It is cover of this sort that makes sectarian activists appear so frightening. Take away government support and they will all expose themselves as paper tigers.

This is why a hard, intolerant secularism should replace soft secularism. Jawaharlal Nehru's upholding of secular values was a hard one, and it succeeded. It is time now to remember how Jawaharlal Nehru handled the RSS and the Hindu Mahasabha when he was at his best. The Partition had just happened and Hindu sectarians were having a field day, even in the city of Delhi. Nehru did not reason and plead with the Hindu activists. He locked them up in jail whenever they broke the law, and at the same time continued with the rehabilitation of refugees. When Mahatma Gandhi was assassinated, Nehru again acted swiftly and unambiguously. He banned the RSS and other allied organizations and exposed their shallow bravado. The leaders of the RSS made several overtures to Nehru (and Patel) to lift the ban against them. Golwalkar even tried to curry favour with the government by promising to fight communism. In a letter to

Nehru, he said that the ban on the RSS should be lifted so that *swayamsevaks* could help the government in ridding the country of the Red menace. No mention now of the Muslims, nor of any other religious minority. When that did not work, the RSS tried *satyagraha,* which was again a flop. Eventually, the RSS leadership had no option but to agree to a written constitution as demanded by the government. This constitution had to clearly state that the organization would treat all faiths with equal respect and would refrain from entering politics and resorting to violence.[4]

Nehru was not intimidated by the rhetoric of the Hindu activists and simply called their bluff. It was Nehru's uncompromising stand against communalists that allowed the Congress to win election after election, from the perfervid post-Partition days right up to 1967. It was also in the mid-1950s that Nehru steered important legislations through parliament such as the Hindu Marriage Act (1955), the Hindu Succession Act (1956), and the Adoption and Maintenance Act (1956), even though Hindu activists opposed each of these moves. But there was no compromise on fundamentals. This is the best way of fighting ethnicists. Not by engaging in endless debates with them, nor by tip-toeing around them in the hope of letting sleeping dogmas lie, but by taking them on frontally every time they break the law.[5]

III

The electoral victory of the Congress in the years after Independence when one expected that Hindu chauvinists would do well can only be explained by the fact that most Hindus are not professional sectarians. They have jobs to do, they have families to look after, and they have career goals and ambitions. Nehru made these communalists look inept because Nehru promised an economic alternative; he did Bhakra Nangal, Bokaro and Bhilai Steel, he had a land reform programme, he had the Five Year Plans, and it was the Congress government that actually helped refugees with their housing needs. In all these departments, the Hindu communalists were useless. They had no idea as to how the country would handle poverty and disease. All they could talk about was "Hinduism is in peril".

It is futile to hope that elections can be won on a negative platform, and even more foolhardy to believe that the masses can be swayed to your side by asking them to give up their religious or community identities. Secularism can never win on this kind of an abnegationist platform. Secularism thrives best when it makes religious and sectarian passions irrelevant to the political debate. Unfortunately, most of our secularists do not quite realize that *pure anti-communalism is not effective secularism.*

Jawaharlal Nehru was a hard secularist. He succeeded in getting a secular India off the ground by promising a resurgent India resplendent with large dams and steel factories—accomplishments his fellow citizens could be proud of. This was accompanied by land reforms, zamindari abolition, resettlement of refugees, import substitution and non-alignment. On none of these issues did the entire saffron spectrum have any expertise. Their illiteracy was so obviously manifest that they lost election after election for twenty years after the Partition, even in a city like Delhi which was swarming with refugees from Pakistan.

Why is it that secularists are scared of dreaming big things again? True, the Nehruvian vision where dams and smoking chimneys would be temples of modern India now lies in a heap of ruin. But what have we done to replace this vision of secularism with another one that is equally powerful and can light an ideological fire in the country? Free education has meant inferior education, free health has degenerated to unhygenic and deplorable public hospitals, and cheap transport is generally translatable into cattle cars and trains leaping out of tracks. It is not surprising that such empty socialist ruses have been exposed and can no longer enthuse the public imagination.

In the meanwhile, expectations have gone up. Villagers have now realized that given the conditions of agriculture and the structure of land holdings no real development is possible in rural areas. Rural non-farm employment is over 25 per cent according to current estimates. Villagers want to leave agriculture and the countryside for the cities as fast as the urban world will absorb them. But this absorption so far has not been quality absorption. Is it not possible for secularists to put forward a bold plan that will take care of this rural exodus and promise a dignified city life?

Oscar Wilde once said that socialism in his country was only good for keeping the poor alive. Developmental programmes in our country too, whether initiated by the government or by NGOs, are primarily aimed at keeping the poor alive on a day-to-day, hand-to-mouth basis. Such exercises are repeated year after year with some ancillary economic regeneration programmes that alleviate desperate poverty at the cottage level.

Over the past two decades, there has been a perceptible ideological shift in the country. Most Indians are tired of low-level equilibrium; they want a breakthrough. They don't only have needs, they have aspirations too. The paradigm of being poor but pure in the village has no takers, least of all in the villages. A true secular vision for India would be one that promises high levels of urban life, that provides facilities for quality education and health, as well as for technological developments in the countryside such that non-farm employments are not just distress measures of the abject poor. This is how secularists can help India make the grade into the twenty-first century. An alternative political agenda of this sort would also render the saffron brigade completely helpless as they have no intellectual expertise on any of these issues. They are good for Akhand Bharat and Ram Mandirs, but can they handle a thousand Metros?

IV

It must have been noticed by now, but I will say it any way: there is a great difference between killing for a cause and dying for one. Religious sectarians in India are always prepared to kill for a cause, but will never die for one. It should also be remembered that though many Hindus died for the cause of nationalism, independence and for glory of their land, there is not a worthwhile example of a Hindu who became a martyr for the cause of Hinduism. In every other world religion, there are martyrs and these martyrs are remembered by the faithful for giving substance and body to their respective religions. There is no such tradition in Hinduism. Rana Pratap, Rani Jhansi and Lala Lajpat Rai did not die for Hinduism, though they were all Hindus, after a fashion.

When the leader of the Ram Janmabhoomi Nyas, the late Ramchandra Paramhans, said that he would rather die than not start building the temple on the dispute site many in the government and elsewhere got really worried. They should not have been so deeply agitated for the recent record of Hindu chauvinists does not give any reason to believe that any one of them would die for a cause. And this is exactly what happened (or did not happen) on 15 March 2002—the deadline set by Hindu activists for permission to build the temple. The deadline passed peacefully and nothing untoward happened. These Hindu chauvinists are paper tigers and only excel at hitting out at minorities, and that too with government support. Take that away and they stand exposed. Wherever they have had unfriendly governments, for example in West Bengal, these sectarians, not withstanding their hell fire and brimstone rhetoric, have behaved themselves.

The appropriate response then to ethnicists and sectarians of all stripes is simply to implement the law and to hold them responsible every time they break it. To discuss, at such times, historical veracity or the fine points of cultural interpretation only encourages sectarians. They then begin to feel self-righteous and also come through as bearers of intellectual capital. To talk to sectarians about culture, religion, art, etc., is, therefore, very counter productive. When anyone breaks the law, the person should be brought to book. Where is the need to discuss? If the government feels there is an overwhelming reason to hold protracted talks with these people, and not book them under very grievous charges, then please change the law, and along with that our Constitution.

It can be proved beyond doubt, by taking instance after instance of rioting, to show that in all cases the culprits had active or tacit government support.[6] In these riots again, the number of people killed show a hugely disproportionate number of people belonging to the minority communities. This was true in Ahmedabad in 1969 when Muslims died in large numbers. This is true equally of the Sikh killings in Delhi when around 2,000 Sikhs died in Delhi and its environs. This is true of Bhiwandi when the Shiv Sainiks went on a rampage. This is now equally true of Ahmedabad after the Godhra incident on 26 February 2002. Even in this last instance, it is not generally known that before Godhra happened and *kar sewaks* were killed in the Sabarmati Express headed for Ahmedabad, Bajrang Dal activists had harassed and beaten Muslims on 24th February in the same train but going to Faizabad. Muslim women had the veils of their burqas ripped off, some children were also hurt, and many Muslims escaped being brutally assaulted by pretending to be Muslims. This news item appeared on 25th February in *Jan Morcha*, which is a little known daily published from Faizabad.

Tough secularism is hard work. It is not enough to find fault with the communalists and sectarians. It is important to have a full-blown alternative that makes religion irrelevant to politics. The official inheritors of Nehru's legacy undermined all the known pillars of secularism in practice. Instead of attending to poverty, hunger and disease with better and more effective policies, they indulged in the most thoughtless political manoeuvres for short-term advantage. This is what has given these religious chauvinists so much credibility. If ethnicists are stronger today than before it is because the official secular parties abdicated their responsibilities and cleared the road for sectarians to emerge as viable political alternatives. What has also changed is that there is nobody like Nehru who can call the bluff of these paper tigers. Indira Gandhi played the communal card, and sadly, so did her son.

V

Soft secularism which banks heavily on education removing ill will between communities strengthens the popular proposition that communities left to themselves naturally turn against one another. This point of view, sadly, has quite an academic pedigree behind it. There are well known scholars such as Clifford Geertz who argues that in new states cultural primordialism is almost like the law of nature.[7] Though there exist excellent critiques of this position[8], yet there are intellectuals at home in India who argue that the Indian genius is ill suited to secularism.[9]

Secularism is therefore against the grain of Hindus and Muslims in the subcontinent, and if one still persists in this task then they have to be educated in tolerance. In other words, good education is equal to counter indoctrination that will cultivate the right values of fraternity. But the truth is that cultural differences do not lead to cultural conflict. For this to happen there must be the sanction of the state and of the administrative machinery.

Of course, sectarians will justify their hate campaigns in terms of avenging age-old humiliations or in the language of popular grievance offended by generosity unfairly reciprocated. Or in terms of schoolboy physics (action-reaction) as Narendra Modi did after Godhra. In such cases, the root justification is that Hindus have taken many injustices and suffered from their generosity. But recourse to schoolboy science, including Social Science, more often than not, misses the main points of a riot completely. The killings of Sikhs in 1984 and the Bombay carnage of 1993 have proved, if proof indeed was necessary, that riots do not happen because social sentiments overflow normal bounds and move otherwise reasonable people to indulge in murder and mayhem. Instead of a social science analysis, we rather need an *autopsy* of a riot. If such an autopsy were to be conducted, it would become abundantly clear that riots are created by interested organizations that have the tacit, or active, support of the government in power.

A social science analysis of a riot can go off on a tangent. It might suggest that there are certain classes that are situationally more predisposed towards violence. It might also make the claim that there is an inherent and irreconcilable animosity between cow worshippers and beef-eaters. To be anti-Muslim or anti-Sikh, or anti-Hindu is one thing, but to actually seek the hated other with blunt and sharp objects or with petrol bombs is quite another. There is a qualitative difference between the two. Riots do not occur because of structural imperatives, or social compulsions. Nor do they happen because mass sentiments just cannot take humiliations any more.

Take the instance of Gujarat. No social science explanation readily works to explain how and why the riot happened. Godhra, Ahmedabad and Vadodara form a triangle of dense conurbation, and it is here that the riots were at their bloodiest. Though a larger proportion of Muslims live in urban areas in Gujarat than in most other places in India, yet Mehesana district which has only 6.6 per cent Muslims, of which only 34.5 per cent of them can be classified as urban was badly hit this time. Muslims constitute a low 2.9 per cent of Gandhinagar district's population[10] and yet villages in this area were not spared. Por village, in Gandhinagar taluka, even had a Muslim sarpanch but was attacked by mobs from at least nine neighbouring villages.[11] Nor can we ignore the fact that a district like Kacchh, which has a high Muslim population of almost 20 per cent, faced no violence in these riots. All this should make us re-examine: (1) the urban thesis behind riots, and (2) that a high Muslim presence is necessary to provoke riots. Both these positions need to be finessed a great deal more.

That ethnic activists do not take economic considerations into account should not mean that in the actual process of rioting economic scores and rivalries are not settled. Of course they are! Economic jealousies, including real estate speculations, can help fund the coffers of ethnic parties, but the rhetoric that sponsors ethnic riots, and the justification that most rioters use to satisfy themselves that they are killing for a cause, are not significantly informed by economic calculations. Khalistani activists were surely not being energized by economic motives when they went about capturing *gurudwaras* and threatening everyday life in Punjab. That there are economic problems everywhere does not always mean that they are significant factors in all forms of social mobilizations.

While it is true that behind many ethnic disturbances there are clear economic motivations of political elites and real estate mafias, the masses that lend support to these movements are not motivated by economic concerns. They do not want the jobs of the minorities, nor are they motivated by the belief that by displacing these minorities they will be economically better off. Such calculations are paramount in communal movements such as in the various sons of the soil agitations in different parts of the country, from Assam to Mumbai; in various caste mobilizations; as well as in language disputes. Ethnicity functions on a different principle. If ethnic mobs band together to kill, maim and loot, it is because they believe that by hurting minorities they can reassert their national identity. It is status not wealth that they are striving for.

What also comes through loud and clear is that religion has little to do with ethnic strife. This may sound contradictory, but some attention to the details of rioting will demonstrate that most of the activists are not religious people themselves, and neither are their leaders. It is not as if religious faith is the primary mover, regardless of what the activists may say of their own convictions. Very few of them have anything more than a working knowledge of their respective sacerdotal texts. They are not the type that would go to religious classes, to religious services, or attend rituals with any degree of regularity. While a few *swayamsewaks* may have some familiarity with Sanskrit *shlokas*, ethnic activists are in the main religiously unmusical.

Gujarat also forces us to accept that the poor are not necessarily pure. The urban rootless, the jobless, the ill fed and the underpaid, have been the foot soldiers and the torch bearers of many a riot. But in Gujarat, this time around it was not just Scheduled Castes or some backward communities (many of whom have often been labelled as members of criminal communities) who were involved in the killing and looting, but so too were the Scheduled Tribes in a large number of cases. The last shred of romantic make-believe according to which the people of the forests who are far away from the depraved ways of life of class and caste stratified societies are somehow better endowed with humane properties has also been laid to rest. Romantic or realist, everyone was saddened by the fact that now the tribals too can become like the worst among us.

Quite obviously, riots need, as a necessary condition, organizations that plot mass killings with governmental support. The job of Social Forensic is to uncover such conspiracies and to expose the accused and not find extenuating circumstances in the social structure. Only a determined and dogged Social Forensic investigation can tell us about the most interesting and pertinent facts of a riot. The analysis of class structure, or occupational profile, or even historical memory, can hardly enlighten us as to who were the actual perpetrators of a riot. We have no option but to rely on Social Forensics if we want to know who paid money to whom for doing what, and which government officials and representatives protected the rioters, who actually pulled back the police, and who delayed calling in the army? Instance after instance can be cited in this regard to demonstrate the relevance of Social Forensics. Apart from the Sikh killings and the Bombay blasts, one can think of the Bhiwandi riots, the Meerut massacres, the killings of Christians, the Ayodhya blood lettings, and the list can go on.[12] Why should the recent Gujarat carnage be any different?

When Shiv Sainiks went to make the Bhiwandi riots, everybody knew what was going to happen. They boarded trucks in Mumbai, armed with rods and cycle chains, openly announcing their intentions. They all looked like a happy bunch out for a Sunday picnic. They knew very well, each and every one of them, that the government of the day was solidly behind their leader, Bal Thackeray. This is the all-important fact behind a riot and it is only Social Forensics that can help us to grasp it. To bring in concepts of social science at a time like this can act as a smokescreen and provide an escape route for those who are guilty. We might even be tempted to believe that the fault is not that of the rioters and the conspirators, but of the society itself.

There are then three theses of Social Forensics. The first, and the most obvious, one is that riots do not just happen, they are created. There are organizations that have a definite interest in fomenting riots but they need the active support of the government. Without this support a riot would never graduate beyond a skirmish. The second thesis of Social Forensics is that sectarians on one side desperately need sectarians on the other side. A sectarian can do without a friend but is helpless and inarticulate without a good enemy.

Bal Thackeray began his political career by targeting South Indians in Mumbai. Unfortunately, South Indians in this metropolis did not oblige the Sainiks by being good enemies. They learnt Marathi, identified with local festivals, and had no hesitation in putting up Shivaji's portrait and lacing it with incense fumes. This is what pressured Thackeray to cast the communists and Muslims as Shiv Sena's prime targets.[13] The communists lived up to their billing for roughly two-and-a-half decades. But with trade unions in shambles and Russia a distant memory, they lost their good enemy status. Only the Muslims were left, and after 1984 Bal Thackeray has concentrated almost exclusively on them.

The third thesis of Social Forensics is that there is a great difference between those who die for a cause and those who kill for a cause. Social sciences are useful to understand factors that lead people to sacrifice their lives for a larger common good. This is why we have some excellent sociological treatises on mobilizations spurred by the ideals of nationalism, communism, and cultural identity. But when people are ready to kill for a cause, as in a riot, it is plain skullduggery at the highest quarters that is responsible. The interests in this case are very narrow, as any autopsy of a riot will show. When a riot happens it is because the killers know that no harm is going to come to them. If they had the slightest inclination that they might not come home, that they might be in jail, even killed, they would never have ventured out. This is why only Social Forensics is relevant for conducting the autopsy of a riot.

VI

Soft secularism also puts the minority communities, particularly Muslims, in a tight corner. As the onus is on demonstrating goodwill and not the observance of the law, in times of sectarian crises, Muslims are expected to stand up and display their commitment as citizens of India. When the Shahi Imam rants, liberal Muslims are seen as wanting if they do not come out with immediate rebuttals. When Pakistan gets unusually belligerent, Muslims are again supposed to openly reaffirm their partisanship with India. Now even in the case of the Taliban, Muslims are being forced to perform and demonstrate their hostility, from whichever podium, to Bin Laden and to his brand of Islamic politics.

Why are Hindus, even secular Hindus not pressured in the same way every time the Bajrang Dal or the Shiv Sena commit their usual excesses? The same standard should apply to all communities, why only to the Muslims? Surprisingly, it is not just the professional Hindus who apply this pressure, but Muslim liberals too feel the need to stand up and be counted among the ranks of Indian patriots whenever their community spokesmen and religious virtuosos do something stupid.

It must indeed be humiliating for a Muslim citizen to have to performatively demonstrate his or her allegiance with this country every now and again. But, on the other hand, if Muslim liberals do not take on the Shahi Imam and other backward looking religious virtuosos, who will? In the case of Hindu fanatics, the matter is different. Hindu militants are roundly criticized by a host of other secular and political organizations in the country. The Samajwadi Party, the Congress Party, the Left parties, the Janata Party, among others, come out in opposition to Hindu sectarians. The need to criticize and be counted among the ranks of liberals and secular patriots is thus not felt as strongly among ordinary Hindus. As there are several mass organizations doing this job, they can concentrate on their identities as lawyers, doctors, professors, etc., and not be obsessed about being Hindus. As Hindus then, they are not forced to perform.

Muslim liberals do not have this luxury, because even their

friends see them as Muslims first, and secular next. When the Shahi Imam is all hell fire and brimstone, a majority of secular parties with a national presence keep quiet. They suddenly lose their voice. This becomes solely a Muslim matter and not something that implicates the nation-state as a whole. They do not want to even mildly reprimand Muslim virtuosos for fear that they might alienate their Muslim voters. Neither the Congress nor the Socialists would like to make a hue and cry about what the Shahi Imam, or any other Muslim bigot, may say or do. They are extremely uncomfortable if pressured to openly flout such Islamic extremists. If examined closely, the underlying rationale for this abstinence from taking a political position is not neutrality, but a certain stereotyped image of the Muslim that these secular parties also harbour. V.P. Singh even went to the ridiculous extent of having some of his policies vetted by the Shahi Imam of Jama Masjid. The only explanation for why these parties do not take on, for instance, the Shahi Imam, is their perception that the majority of Muslims actually think the way he does, so why lose out on a good vote bank?

Secular parties may remain quiet and non-committal in such situations, but this is just the time when Hindu communal organizations swing into action with another round of hate mongering. All the known stereotypes of Muslims get a fresh lease of life on occasions such as these. If there were no Muslim bigots, the Hindu right would have to invent them just for the sake of their survival. They long for some Muslim preacher or local hoodlum to step out of line so that they can get into overdrive. This state of affairs also suits the secular parties for they can then make political capital safely by criticizing the Hindu right for its bigotry.

But where does that leave the Muslim liberal? High and dry! The basic issue still remains unanswered. As there is no secular forum from where attacks can be launched against Muslim bigots, the popular Islamic stereotype lives on. This is why Muslim liberals cannot afford to be just liberals, like their Hindu counterparts can, and are, on occasions, are forced to perform as Muslims. If no one else will contribute to undermining the Muslim stereotype, not Congress, not

Samajwadi, not Janata, then Muslim liberals have no alternative but to seek forums everywhere just to make the point that there are Muslims and Muslims. Even politics abhors a vacuum.

One of the reasons why Sikhs could not be stereotyped in a similar fashion as secessionists and Hindu baiters for too long was because secular parties were in the fray contesting Bhindranwale and his brand of politics. This gave many Sikhs an opportunity to work through established secular and non-denominational organizations in order to distance themselves from the Khalistanis of various stripes. When I.K. Gujral won a resounding victory in Punjab, it was his opposition to Sikh militants that provided everyday Sikhs with a political platform to act as moderates and committed citizens of India. When V.P. Singh went to Punjab, after becoming Prime Minister, to apply the healing balm, he was perceived as being both anti-Congress and against Sikh extremists too. Even the BJP came out in opposition to the militants and later sponsored many moderate Sikhs for elected positions.

Though there was a great deal of disinformation doing the rounds in those days about the Sikhs, and though a large number of secular intellectuals did not come out in too good a light, the relevant point is that major, national parties had not wiped their hands off the Bhindranwale factor. They were willing to engage themselves against religious extremism in Punjab. This allowed Gujral to win, and this is also why an overwhelming number of Sikhs went against the call for an election boycott in 1984 issued by Sikh militants.

If Muslim liberals feel that they are being painted into a corner, then it is largely the fault of secular parties that have not been consistent in advocating secularism. It is not that the Hindu right alone has stereotyped Muslims, many secular parties also seem to work on that presumption. How else can one explain their inaction when it comes to taking on Muslim bigots and fanatics who pretend to speak for the entire community? Out of this stereotyping, the left and centrist parties may derive different political strategies from the right, but that does not absolve them of their larger secular responsibilities. This is what puts pressure on liberal intellectuals to perform solo in talk shows, seminars, and public gatherings. Naturally, given the circumstances, Muslim liberals stand out alone in professing their secularism and the whole nation watches as if they were members of a passive audience.

It is only when secular parties shake off their stereotyped image of the Muslim voter, and politically engage against Muslim virtuosos, that liberal Muslims will be spared of the humiliation of having to demonstrate their secularism and patriotism time and again. It should be citizenship that counts and not one's religious denomination.

VII

What good is a democracy if a large number of minorities feel that it does not belong to them? While these communities can be kept terrified by majoritarianism for a period of time we must realize that this damages the polity irrevocably over the medium term. Terrorism breeds when minority aspirations are thwarted by undemocratic means. In fact, one should go further and say, terrorism breeds when a community is continuously humiliated. In the past, such humiliations were localized at the village or the qasbah level. Dacoits and highway-men were the products of humiliations against which the only redress they could find was to strike out against the affluent classes, and all those who came in their way.

Humiliation today is supra-local in character. The oppressor is not the village landlord, or the local feudal official. Now the victimizer is the majority community, the government, the state, and sometimes even the international order. Consequently, issues that are much larger in scope must be addressed. These issues are primarily constitutional and it is faith in the constitution and in established legal procedures that has to be established if grievances suffered by those who are positioned as minorities are to feel a commitment towards citizenship. In Punjab, if truth be told, secessionism did not happen for economic reasons, but because ethnic power calculations were steadily displacing democratic politics. This is also true of Kashmir—in fact Kashmir is perhaps the most obvious case one can make in this connection today.

While I was trying to puzzle over why Sikh extremists had the kind of credibility they enjoyed, I realized that to a large extent the voice of terrorism resonated with those who felt that the State was no longer the fount of the law and an impartial arbiter. While to the rest of us what certain secessionists said was largely incomprehensible, there was a section of Sikhs, not quite moved by the Khalistan demand, and yet with a soft spot towards the extremists. I had then used Jacques Lacan's notion of the triad to explain this phenomenon. Simply put, according to Lacan,the relationship between two parties is controlled by the presence of the third. This third node is what Lacan termed as the name of the Father, or the fount of law, or the origin of language. But when the dyadic relationship is not reined in by this triadic node then a state of affairs takes over where no rules hold and limitless dyadic jouissance takes over. In the Punjab case, many Sikhs felt that the Indian state had ceased to be the fount of law, the impartial triadic node, and hence the dyadic relationship between Hindus and Sikhs was without a shared language. Pure dyads are always dangerous, which is why when the state collapses in the minds of some as an impartial triad and joins in, or merges with, the other community, in this case the Hindus, then the language of democracy is no longer possible. From then on you only have the inarticulate "cry" of the terrorist.[14] According to Lacan, a self-image comes into being in a healthy fashion only when there is a triadic setting for it. In a pure dyadic situation one has instead an *imago* that is restlessly in *jouissance* with its constructed primordial "other". Today, we see this quite vividly in Kashmir. And if Gujarat tends to get repeated, it will happen elsewhere too.

Against this background, it is only hard and intolerant secularism that stands a chance against sectarian hordes that depend on unthinking and unreflected loyalties. Citizenship and secularism are not easy to practice. They have to be deliberately crafted without giving any quarter to communal and sectarian sentiments. In the ultimate analysis, only that secularism will work which makes religious passions irrelevant to the political discourse. This can happen when the citizen is at the centre.

NOTES

1. John Locke, *Treatise of Civil Government and a Letter Concerning Toleration*, ed., Charles L. Sherman (New York: Appleton-Century-Crofts, Meredith Corporation, 1965).
2. See also *Communalism Combat* 2002, Nos. 77-8; People's Union for Democratic Rights, *Maaro, Kaapo, Baalo: State, Society and Communalism* (New Delhi: PUDR, 2002).
3. Mark Juergensmeyer, *Religious Nationalism Confronts the Secular State* (Delhi: Oxford University Press, 1994), pp. 63-72.
4. D.R. Goyal, *Rashtriya Swayamsewak Sangh* (New Delhi: Radha Krishna Prakashan, 1979), pp. 101-102; see also Article 4 of RSS Constitution.
5. Dipankar Gupta and Romila Thapar, "Who are the Guilty?" *The Hindu*, 2 April 2002.
6. See also Donald I. Horowitz, *The Deadly Ethnic Riot* (Delhi: Oxford University Press, 2002).
7. Clifford Geertz, "The Integrative Revolution: Primordial Sentiments and Civil Politics in the New States", in Clifford Geertz, *The Interpretation of Cultures* (New York: Basic Books, 1973).
8. See, for example, Judith A. Nagata, "Defence of Ethnic Boundaries: The Changing Myths and Charters of Malay Identity," in Charles F. Keyes ed., *Ethnic Change* (Seattle: Washington University Press, 1981); also Malcolm Yapp, "Language, Religion and Political Identity: A General Framework," in David Taylor and Malcolm Yapp, eds., *Political Identity in South Asia* (London: Curzon Press, 1979) for a review.
9. A. Nandy, "The Politics of Secularism", *Alternatives*, Vol. 13, No. 3, 1988.
10. Census of India, Gujarat Atlas, District Wise Religious Census, 1991.
11. People's Union for Democratic Rights, *Maaro, Kaapo, Baalo: State, Society and Communalism* (New Delhi: PUDR, 2002), p. 20.
12. See Horowitz, n. 6; Aswini K. Ray and Suhash Chakravarti, *Meerut Riots: A Case Study* (New Delhi: Sampradayikta Virodhi Committee, 1968).
13. See Dipankar Gupta, *Nativism in a Metropolis: The Shiv Sena in Bombay* (Delhi: Manohar Books, 1982).
14. See Dipankar Gupta, *The Context of Ethnicity: Sikh Identity in a Comparative Perspective* (Delhi: Oxford University Press, 1997), pp. 92ff.

7

Indian Migration on the European Continent

Idesbald Goddeeris and Sara Cosemans

Over the last few decades, migration to Europe has proliferated. In the nineteenth century, many European regions were sources of emigration rather than pools of immigration: the numbers of Europeans leaving for the New World were far higher than the ones of newly arrived people who settled in industrial areas or booming cities across Europe. After the First World War, Europe turned into an immigration region. Coal mines and factories urgently required labour force and imperial metropoles increasingly became interconnected with their colonies. However, this immigration was heavily organized. Labour migrants were recruited in particular countries, first in Europe (e.g. Poland and Italy) and later also in other countries (e.g. Morocco and Turkey). Colonial migration was subject to restrictions that only opened doors for particular groups, such as students before and certain ethnicities after decolonization. In the wake of the 1973 oil crisis, many European countries closed their borders and only allowed for asylum and family reunification. Importantly, all of this only applied to a limited part of Europe and many countries in Southern Europe and the Communist Bloc remained emigration countries for the bulk of the twentieth century.[1]

It is only at the end of the twentieth century that immigration to Europe really rocketed. The fall of the Iron Curtain started new and massive migration waves from Eastern Europe to Western Europe, both economic migrants looking for a better life and political refugees, for instance fleeing wars in Yugoslavia and Chechnya. The end of the Cold War also shook the world order and brought an end to many dictatorial regimes that had been supported by Washington (e.g. Mobutu's Congo) or Moscow (e.g. Mengistu's Ethiopia). These crises, too, led to new migration waves. The same applies to the new conflicts that arose, for instance in Iraq and Afghanistan.

India was part of this global phenomenon. Many European countries have seen an influx of Indian immigrants over the last few decades. Truly, Indians were not among the largest groups and Europeans had already been put in touch with Indians earlier, for instance with Sikh soldiers of the British army during the First World War.[2] However, Indians have settled in many European countries since the 1980s and have continued to do so during the last years. We may therefore expect that their presence will be permanent.

From an Indian perspective, too, this migration is new. Indian emigration obviously stretches back much further in time, but has neglected the European continent until recently. Concerning Europe, it was mainly directed to Great Britain, which still in the 1970s saw substantial migration from Bangladesh that sidelined the European continent.[3] This is of course explained by the colonial factor: the Indian diaspora was also directed to other parts of the Empire, such as Canada, South Africa, Eastern Africa, Australia, Singapore, etc. However, Indian migration has also headed to the European continent. This chapter aims at discussing this more closely. Rather than giving a comprehensive overview or approaching the issue from a quantitative angle, it will question the key concepts of Indian migration, and Europe. There is much diversity indeed, in the fields of ethnic and religious groups, migration and settlement processes, and European governments' attitudes and policies. The chapter will therefore argue that the diversity of Indian migration to the European continent is so vast that one should wonder if one can talk about Indian migration to the European continent as such.

The chapter is based on a vast range of secondary

literature, next to source research among Indian migrants in Belgium. Indian migration to the European continent is increasingly receiving scholarly attention, both among Indian scholars and European ones. Meenakshi Thapan (University of Delhi) has worked on gender and class identities among Punjabi migrants in Italy and Shakti Prasad Srichandan (JNU) has analyzed migration movements from an economic point of view.[4] The European Union also funds the project "Developing a Knowledge Base for Policymaking on India-EU Migration," which was officially launched on 4 March 2011 and is carried out by the European University Institute (Florence), the Indian Council of Overseas Employment (ICOE), the Indian Institute of Management Bangalore (IIMB), and Maastricht University (Faculty of Law). It has already yielded several publications and a High Level Stakeholder Consultation Workshop, which took place at the ICOE in Delhi on 22 November 2011. On top of that, European researchers have elaborated on particular cases of migrant groups or host countries. Regarding Sikh migration, an in-depth comparison has been conducted under the direction of Knut A. Jacobson and Kristina Myrvold.

Diversity of Ethnic and Religious Groups

Just as in Great Britain and the Commonwealth, the European continent hosted its first groups of Indian immigrants in the postcolonial context. Sometimes, this happened via a detour. The so-called 'Hindustani' migrants in the Netherlands, for instance, came through Suriname. They were descendants of Indian indentured workers that were hired in British India by officials from the Dutch West Indies in order to match the labour demand following the abolition of slavery in 1863. Between 1873 and 1916, 34,000 Indians moved from Calcutta to Paramaribo. About one-third of them returned to Bengal, but the rest would permanently settle in Dutch Guiana.[5] Many of their descendants travelled to the Netherlands in the early 1970s, on the eve of Suriname's independence in November 1975. They were part of the dozens of thousands of Surinamese who profited from the last chance to travel to the Netherlands without a visa—according to some estimates one-third of the approximate 350,000 Surinamese left the homeland in these years.[6] Today, about 160,000 Hindustani Surinamese are living in the Netherlands.[7]

In the Netherlands, these Hindustanis developed their own identity and established their own structures and organizations. Indeed, whereas Suriname immigrants before 1970 had a common Creole identity, the settlement process after 1975 followed ethnic and religious lines and emphasized the differences between African, Hindustani, and (Muslim) Javanese Surinamese. The Hindustanis increasingly identify with India and with fellow South Asian migrant communities, distinguishing themselves from their former Surinamese compatriots. They organize their own annual Milan Festival in The Hague (attended by ca. 70,000 people), established Hindu temples, watch and perform Bollywood movies, integrate with other South Asian migrants across the world, and are in search of their roots among Bhojpuri-speaking communities in Uttar Pradesh and Bihar. Treating the stay in Suriname as an intermezzo and their arrival in the Netherlands as a coincidence, they maintain their distance from the other Surinamese by highlighting cultural values and alleged qualities that could be linked with the Dutch national culture, such as family, discipline, study, and labour. As a consequence, they are seen as a successful group. Both the first city council or (Tara Oedayraj Singh Varma, elected in Amsterdam in 1983) and the first MP of Surinamese descent (Dowlatram Ramlal) were Hindustanis.[8]

Another example of Indians having migrated to the European continent in a postcolonial context is the Tamils in France. Just like the Hindustanis in the Netherlands, they constitute the dominant component of the French-Indian community. With an estimated population of 125,000 Tamil speakers, France holds the largest Tamil community in Continental Europe.[9] Starting in the 1950s, it is also one of the oldest Tamil communities in the West. The first permanent settlers in the metropolis were French citizens from the Southern *Établissements français de l'Inde*: Pondichéry and

Karikal. Established by the French in 1674 and handed over to India in 1956, Pondichéry had been a laboratory for assimilation. Even after India's independence, Pondicherrians had the option to keep French nationality. After migrating, they established networks of mutual aid and laid the foundation of a commercial South Asian infrastructure in Paris.[10] Today the number of Pondicherrians living in France is estimated between 50,000 and 75,000 people.[11]

A second group of postcolonial migrants consisted of descendants of *coolies* from the French Overseas Departments, mainly the French Antilles and Réunion. Just as the Dutch and the British, the French recruited indentured labourers from their Indian colonies to work on plantations after they abolished slavery in 1848. These workers were almost exclusively Tamils who were dispersed from Malaysia and East Africa to the Caribbean and even the Fiji Islands. Next to indentured labourers, free passengers—merchants and traders—also crossed the ocean, paying their own passage and not bound by any contract. In contrast to the indentured workers who were mainly outcasts, the free passengers were farmers and artisans from the middle caste.[12]

There are still other examples of Indian migration to the European continent in the postcolonial context. The Sindhi migration in Spain, for instance, numbering between 10,000 and 30,000 people and accounting for one of the largest migrations outside India, may also be put in this perspective. On the one hand, these Sindhis emigrated following decolonization: their motherland was arbitrated to Muslim Pakistan in the Partition of 1947. On the other hand, they settled in Gibraltar, next to the Canary Islands and Catalonia. Although Sindhis have scattered around the world, their presence on the European continent is exceptional and must be explained by the proximity of the British crown colony.[13]

In Portugal as well, the colonial history partly explains the Indian presence. On the one hand, a significant group of 20,000 Indian Catholic Christians reached the Iberian Peninsula directly via Goa, which was under Portuguese mandate till 1961.[14] On the other hand, many Gujaratis and Punjabis travelled via other Portuguese settlements (Diu and Daman, Dadra and Nagar Haveli) to Mozambique and other Portuguese colonies at the beginning of the twentieth century to improve their job opportunities and living conditions. Most migrated not as indentured workers but as traders, following established trade routes between India and Southeast Africa. Mozambique became the permanent home of these settlers, whose descendants still live there today. However, after the independence of the African colony in 1975, a large part of the Indian community left the country due to a policy of Africanization.

These postcolonial settlers in Portugal were predominantly Muslim—up to 30,000 people—and to a lesser extent Hindu (their number increased from 4,000-5,000 in the 1970s to 8,000 in the 1990s).[15] Despite their Portuguese passports, these 'twice migrants' (ethnic Indians that had settled in Africa and later moved to Europe[16]) remained a marginalized group, overrepresented in low skilled and low paid occupations and settled in the poor districts of Lisbon. This contrasts with the East African Indians who relocated to the United Kingdom in the same era and were rather successful.[17]

The decolonization of Africa and the subsequent Africanization policy in the 1970s played a particular role in the establishment of many Indian communities in Continental Europe indeed. The first Indian immigrants in other European countries did not arrive from India, but from Uganda. Their ancestors had settled there in the imperial era, but were expelled in August 1972 when the new dictator Idi Amin ordered all Asians to leave the country within a ninety-day period. Great Britain received only about half of the more than 50,000 refugees, and the others had to find refuge in the rest of Europe. This is how the Nordic countries first came in contact with South Asian migrants, mainly Gujarati Hindus. In France, where the Indian presence was much older, 10,000 Gujaratis joined the community.

Apart from Gujaratis, a smaller number of Punjabi refugees left Uganda. As a result, the European continent hosted its first Sikh migrants. They may be considered as a footnote within this Asian emigration from Uganda: 'a few' Sikhs in Sweden and not more than eight of them in Belgium.[18] However, these individuals were key in the expansion of Sikh communities in Western Europe in the following decades.

The Sikh emigration rocketed indeed in the 1970s and 1980s. On the one hand, there was a continuous flow of Sikhs leaving India in search of better opportunities. After Great Britain had closed its doors for large groups of Commonwealth immigrants, immigration was redirected to other parts of the world. On the other hand, many Sikhs left their country following the violent clashes related to the Khalistan movement: Operation Blue Star, the assassination of Indira Gandhi, the subsequent pogrom on Sikhs, terrorist attacks, etc. In some countries, such as Sweden and Belgium, there was a link between these new immigrants and their fellow believers who had arrived there from Uganda. In other countries, there was no such connection. The first Sikhs in Norway ended up there by complete coincidence and without much prior knowledge of the country. One example is two Sikhs who were biking around the world, arrived in Norway in 1973, missed their boat to England, were offered a job, decided to stay for some more months, and eventually settled there.[19]

In the 1990s and 2000s, the Sikh diaspora gradually dispersed to a few more European countries. Especially in Southern Europe, new and large communities appeared. This was a response to the growing demand of labour following the economic rise, which created a huge number of job vacancies at the bottom of the social ladder. Moreover, these countries' migration policy was considered less restricted—rightly so, as we will discuss later on.

As of 2010, there are thousands of Sikhs in many countries on the European continent: 3,000 to 4,000 in Sweden; 5,000 in Norway; 10,000 in Belgium and Spain; 15,000 in the Netherlands and France; 10,000 to 20,000 in Greece; 25,000 in Germany; and 25,000 to 70,000 in Italy. Sikhs are less represented in Eastern Europe, which generally has a smaller appeal to immigrants and has a stronger tradition of emigration. In Poland, for instance, there are only a couple of hundred Sikhs, who mainly consider their stay there as temporary. Some West European countries also have small populations, for instance 250 to 4,000 in Denmark and about 600 in Finland.[20] As a matter of fact, Sikhs first and foremost tend to concentrate in particular regions, such as Catalonia in Spain, Hesbaye (and recently also Brussels) in Belgium, and Lombardia (and to a smaller extent also Emilia Romagna and Veneto) in Italy.

On a global scale, these are small communities. The Sikh diaspora amounts to 1.5 million individuals (of the 25 million Sikhs) and Great Britain, for instance, has a population larger than 300,000 Sikhs.[21] Yet, the Sikhs are a very visible South Asian migrants group in view of their turbans and beards. In some countries, they account for the majority of the Indians. In Italy, there are 90,000 Indians (of whom 25,000 to 70,000 are Sikh), and in Greece, 90 per cent of the Indian immigrants are Sikh. In France, by contrast, the 15,000 Sikhs constitute a less substantial part of the total number of 100,000 Indians. In Germany, the Sikh community is the most marginalized Indian group, due to the refusal of their asylum claims while other Indians entered Germany as skilled labourers with appropriate legal statuses.[22]

The majority of these Sikhs no longer arrived in a postcolonial context. This goes for many other Indian groups who have recently emigrated to the European continent. For instance, medical students of West Bengal began migrating to Germany in the 1950s and were followed by other individual professionals and academics in the 1960s and 1970s. They became well-established German citizens and half of the nearly 4,000 men married German women.[23] Other examples will be given in the next subchapter.

There are still more South Asian immigrants who claim to belong to the Indian diaspora. An obvious example is the descendants of indentured labourers and traders whose ancestors originated from parts of British India that is in present day Pakistan or Bangladesh.[24] Another more striking case is the Hindus and Sikhs who dissociate themselves from Afghan Muslims by adopting an 'Indian' identity. This phenomenon is described by anthropologist Urmilla Goel in Germany, but is probably also applicable in other European countries as well. A similar identification is for instance visible in the collaboration between Afghan and Indian Sikhs in Belgium.[25]

The concept of 'Indianness' is indeed under constant debate in the diaspora. This becomes clear when looking at the position of the Sri Lankan Tamil refugees in France. Tamil refugees started to arrive in Western Europe in the late 1970s but their number rose substantially after the anti-Tamil riots of June 1983.[26] The Black July Pogrom first affected the Sri Lankan Tamils in the northeast and the east, the Jaffna region, who had lived there before European colonization, contrary to the Tamils in the centre, who descended from indentured labourers of Indian origin recruited by the British in the 1830s and 1840s. The proliferation of the conflict convinced many "hill country" Tamils to leave the island as well. A large group ended up in France again—the total number of Sri Lankan Tamils in France approaches 60,000 (making France the fourth largest recipient of Sri Lankan refugees after Canada, the UK and Australia).[27]

These refugees were predominantly Hindus, whereas Pondicherrian Tamils were converted Catholics.[28] They found a connection with Gujaratis who arrived in France after their expulsion from Uganda in 1972.[29] Both Hindu groups celebrate the annual Ganesh festival together. This shows that the lines between the Indian and the Tamil diaspora are fluid; Sri Lankan Tamils can be housed in both categories depending on the occasion. Goreau-Ponceaud therefore launches the hypothesis that it was indeed the Sri Lankan refugees that played a crucial role in the definition of the identity for other Tamils and Indians in France.[30] According to Goel, "the multitude of belongingness is not restricted to two". The ethnic identity is the result of various negotiations in which the country of origin, the former and the actual host societies and the social interactions between different South Asian groups play an important role.[31]

Diversity of Migration Processes

The ethnic and religious background of Indian immigrants on the European continent was extremely diverse. This also applies to the migration process. There was indeed much variety in the reasons for migration, the settlement process, and the spread across Europe. Even within one group, such as the Sikhs, there was a vast array of push and pull factors bringing them to Europe.

Some of them have already been discussed in the previous section. Sikhs left their country because of the depressing social-economic perspectives as well as the political violence. Pioneers with positive experiences set the example for other migrants to follow—a phenomenon that is mostly labelled as 'chain migration' or the 'drop-in model'. However, reality was much more complicated, and includes aspects such as illegality, family reunification, and mobility.

After 1974, there were still several ways of travelling to Europe, such as tourism, education, family visits, special programmes set up to import skilled migrants, etc. Yet, many immigrants illegally enter the Schengen Zone. According to the UN Office on Drugs and Crime report from 2009, almost 20,000 Punjabi youngsters try to migrate to Europe illegally.[32] Once in a while, police detect human smuggling of Indians. In Sweden, for instance, three men were arrested in 2008 for having trafficked more than fifty Punjabis.[33] Illegal immigration should therefore not be underestimated. In a survey of 2009, more than half of the interviewed Sikhs in Poland admitted that they had come without official documents.[34]

Most of them apply for a refugee status soon after their arrival. Asylum is indeed one of the main doors that was left open to immigrants after the restrictions of the mid-1970s. However, India has seldom been acknowledged as a hotbed of conflict or discrimination and Sikhs were only in the second half of the 1980s more systematically recognized as political refugees. Many asylum seekers therefore fell into illegal status after their application had been rejected. Their presence was sometimes tolerated, whether for humanitarian, practical or economic reasons. Illegal people were rarely detected and often employed in sectors with an urgent need of labour. Once in a while, their status was made legal in general regularization campaigns of people staying in the country for a certain period of time and being able to prove attempts to integrate.

Marriage was the second main option for legal migration. On the one hand, it was a strategy of illegal immigrants to obtain a residence permit. Already in the 1980s, many Sikh men married local women. Sometimes, these marriages were based on love and produced children, but in other cases, marriages were fake. It is very complicated to quantify this, since sincere marriages also often ended in divorce in view of the cultural differences. On the other hand, family reunification led to more immigration. Once obtaining a regular status, many men travelled to their home country in order to marry. One-third of the Sikhs in Sweden moved to the country because of their marriage.[35] This especially applies to women. According to some scholars, migration has even largely been a gendered process.[36]

Another way of dealing with an illegal status was to travel around. When an application is rejected or a legal status expires in one country, many immigrants, especially younger ones, travel to another country and try their luck over there. Sometimes, they are successful and then return to the country they had initially immigrated to, where they now were allowed to stay legally. However, the opposite also occurs and many immigrants treat their first country of arrival as a transit. Many of them dream of leaving the European continent and going to the UK, the US, or Canada. Even members of the second generation or the 'in-between' one, who were born in India, but grew up in Europe, hope to migrate further west.[37]

Apart from illegal migrants, asylum-seekers, spouses, and families, there are still other groups of Indian immigrants. For over a century, the European continent and Germany in particular has attracted Indian (male) students and scholars, especially in the engineering and sciences departments. Interestingly, during the World Wars—when the Indian army fought at the side of the allies—Germany remained a destination for Indian 'freedom fighters' since it was the enemy of the colonial powers. During the First World War, many of them were socialists; in the Second World War, Subhas Chandra Bose became an advocate of Indian collaboration with the Nazis, which resulted in the formation of an Indian Legion within the German SS.[38] Despite the minimal impact—on the Indian independence movement as well as on the Indian community in Germany—the link between India and Germany was perpetuated and the migration of individual students and interns from all over India to both the Federal Republic of Germany and the German Democratic Republic restarted soon after the wars.

The *Wirtschaftswunder* in West Germany urged the government in the 1960s to set up labour recruitment programmes. Germany is renowned for the presence of Turkish guest workers, but Indians were also recruited. In the 1960s, German hospitals tried to fill the shortage of staff with Catholic nurses from Kerala, but due to the economic recession in the 1970s their work permits were not extended. Many of them returned to India while others relocated to less restrictive federal states such as Nordrhine-Westphalia or to other European countries. In the 1990s, the German government again appealed to Indian nurses, allowing those women whose work permits were not extended in the 1970s, to return to Germany. As a consequence, the actual community of Keralan Christians in Germany numbers about 10,000 members.[39] In the year 2000, Germany adopted a Green Card policy for Indian IT specialists. However, the initiative provoked a racist reaction, known as *"Kinder statt Inder"* (children instead of Indians). This latent racism, along with the fact that the Green Card was restricted to five years, may have deterred Indian professionals from migrating to Germany. Nevertheless, a significant number of young IT specialists responded to the call, bringing their families along, altogether totalling about 8,000 people.[40]

The higher proportion of highly skilled Indian immigrants in Germany is reflected in the remittances from EU countries to India. The EU accounts for about a fifth of the total NRI (Non-Resident Indian) deposits held by Indian immigrants;

about 70 per cent of them are held by Indians in the UK and about 20 per cent by Indian immigrants in Germany.[41]

The settlement process of all these migrants was also characterized by diversity. This can be illustrated by looking at the professions of the Indians. Migration is often marked by ethnic entrepreneurship; migrants of the same community often practise the same profession. This somehow also goes for Indian migration. Some occupations are very typical of this group. But a closer look also reveals that reality is again more complicated and diversity is the rule rather than the exception.

A profession often associated with Indian migrants is the IT specialist. Although Indian IT migration was traditionally directed towards North America and the United Kingdom, the European continent has tried to catch up with these developments by creating attractive migration conditions for Indian highly skilled workers. Indeed, not only did Germany recruit IT professionals during the last decades, but also countries such as Denmark introduced transparent Green Card systems.[42] Indian IT specialists seem not to originate from one region in India or one religious community, since technological education institutes are spread all over India.[43]

Less known is the Indian involvement in the diamond sector. The modern Indian diamond trade is dominated by Gujarati Jains. Till the 1960s, the Jains built up a diamond empire in India, with Surat as the main site of diamond grinding. During the 1960s and 1970s, they started migrating, following diamond trade routes and ending up in one of the major hubs of the diamond trade: Antwerp, Belgium. According to estimations, 60 per cent of rough diamonds and 80 per cent of grinded diamonds are in the hands of Indian Jain traders today. Along with the traders came the Indian bankers supporting the Indian diamond industry in Antwerp. Of the approximately 2,000 Jains living in Antwerp, 90 per cent are active in the diamond sector. It is a very prosperous community, which is especially visible in the grandeur of the local Jain temple, the largest outside India.[44]

Sikhs, by contrast, are often affiliated with agriculture. In a number of countries, many of them have indeed worked in the farming industry. In the 1980s and 1990s, Sikhs in Belgium worked in the fruit-picking sector concentrated in Hesbaye (the region around Sint-Truiden), which still has a large Sikh population today. Sikhs in Greece have done similar jobs during the last decades, cultivating the land, picking vegetables, and raising livestock. Given their farming experience in rural Punjab and the diligence considered as peculiar to their culture, Sikhs are perceived as highly suitable for agriculture. However, their flexibility seems to be a more important explanation for this ethnic entrepreneurship. Agriculture often produced seasonal work, and young and single Sikh males were eager to take these vacancies. Their share in the Belgian fruit industry fell in the 2000s, after they had set up families and searched for more stability, and their jobs were taken over by Eastern European immigrants.

Accordingly, ethnic entrepreneurship is a concept one should treat with caution. It depends on the circumstances and may be subject to quick change. In some other European countries, the majority of the male Sikhs work in sectors completely different from agriculture. In Finland, for instance, most of them are employed in the catering sector, which includes restaurants, pubs, and nightclubs. They usually start as a dishwasher, a kitchen helper or a cleaner: jobs that require neither advanced language skills nor prior work experience. Some of them later set up their own bar. Interestingly, they sell alcohol rather than offering Punjabi food.[45]

In other countries, there is no clear ethnic entrepreneurship. In France, Sikhs are not only concentrated in catering, but also in clothing and construction sectors—two other sectors in great demand of cheap workforce hired informally.[46] In Sweden, Sikhs work in a vast array of sectors, including trade, education, industry, transport, medicine, and the public sector, and practise both low and high-skilled jobs.[47] In Denmark, too, there are Sikh bus drivers, nurses, marketing assistants, mechanics, IT engineers, shopkeepers, restaurant owners, and so forth.[48]

Sometimes, there is a certain specialization within this diversity. In France, the caste an Indian belongs to has an impact on his profession. Jats and Chamars tend to work mostly in catering and building sites, whereas Lohanas are almost exclusively engaged in small trade and street markets. This is not systematic though, and the possession of legal residence documents is the main marker of status among Sikhs. In Italy, specialization follows geographical lines. Sikhs work as farmers in Lombardy, as milkmaids and milkmen in Emilia Romagna, and as tanners in Veneto. This is not related to their ethnicity, but to the local industry; Parma is renowned for its cheese, Venice for its leather industry and shoe manufacturing.[49]

On a more general level, one also notices the huge variety of all these professions. IT, diamond trade, the catering industry, agriculture, and so forth: as a matter of fact, there is a wide range of professions where we find Indian immigrants. This, too, makes them an extremely diverse group.

From a broader perspective, ethnic entrepreneurship may also have a South Asian rather than an Indian label. People with several (South Asian) ethnic backgrounds are often employed in the same ethnic niche. Sometimes, there is no social stratification between the ethnicities, as is the case for the Indian, Pakistani and Nepalese night shop owners in Belgium, or for the Nepalese running Indian restaurants.[50] In other cases, there is a kind of hierarchy, as is seen at building sites in France where Indian Sikhs work under contract for a Pakistani boss.[51]

Diversity of Policies

Europe is characterized by 'unity in diversity'. This also goes for European migration policy. Making laws regulating migration and asylum policies has long been considered a fundamental right of the sovereign states. This is not limited to entrance and regularization, but also includes aspects of integration and acceptance by the host society. European policy makers have adopted a variety of strategies to deal with migrants, though the differences may be less pronounced in reality than they seem on paper. Moreover, next to the policy of the host societies, the life of an Indian migrant is influenced by diaspora policy and sometimes directly linked to political decisions made in the country of origin.

A good example of this diversity is the way national European governments have dealt with undocumented immigration. Regularization programmes were frequently introduced from the 1980s onwards, but there are large differences in application between states. Unlike in the UK, where permanent residency is automatically granted to all migrants who have been living on British soil for 14 continuous years (*de facto* regularization), most programmes in the rest of Europe are "one-shot" regularizations, which target a specific group of illegal migrants and have deadlines for applications. These programmes have been implemented in France, Belgium, Luxembourg, Greece, Italy, Spain and Portugal.

There is a notable divergence between the approaches to legalize undocumented migrants. The Northern countries have been rather cautious and only use regularization as a tool to grant permanent residency in periods of major asylum crises; regularization campaigns were largely set up in response to sustained protest by both migrant groups and local social lobbies. In Southern Europe, regularization programmes are implemented once every few years and usually do not promise permanent naturalization, but temporary work permits.[52]

The lack of European legal uniformity and the free movement of people in the Schengen zone have created a perverse situation in which migrants obtain a temporary residence permit in a Southern country, but 'disappear' into other countries of the European Union right before their permits expire. At the end of the day, this leads to a very inefficient migration policy that provokes not only fervent debates but also real threats to human rights. For instance, Belgium has to cope with an enormous shortage of shelters for asylum seekers, which leads to undocumented people residing in open air—2012 marked the fourth winter in a row. This affects even the Sikh communities of Hesbaye that receive an increasing amount of demands for help from illegal compatriots.

Migration policy has also substantially differed between

West European countries regarding integration strategies. On the one hand, there is the multiculturalist model, which leaves a large amount of freedom to define one's own identity and was considered to be dominant in the UK and in the Netherlands until recently. On the other hand, there is the assimilationist model, where minorities are expected to assimilate to a single culture. France is the prime example, but in Belgium a form of assimilation was also adopted.[53] France banned the headscarf in public spaces and schools, which directly influenced Indian Muslim women and Sikh men.[54] Also, in Belgium and the Netherlands there is an ongoing debate, uncovering sometimes very intolerant stances of the society towards Indians and migrants in general.[55] However, the juxtaposition between assimilation and multiculturalism should not be overestimated. Recent events such as the riots in the Parisian *banlieu* (November 2005) show that assimilation has not happened in practice.

Next to the obvious influence from the host society, Indian migrants are also affected by India's diaspora policy. The country's growing interest in its diaspora is explicable by the economic progress made by Indian migrants. This is visible in many ways, for instance in India's position as the largest recipient of remittances worldwide. To generate profits (economic as well as political) the Indian government launched various initiatives. Already in the 1970s, Delhi created special deposit schemes for non-resident Indians (NRIs) to increase its foreign exchange reserves. Diaspora bonds were sold as a debt instrument three times: in 1991 after a balance of payment crisis, in 1998 after India was sanctioned because of its nuclear tests, and in 2000 after a period of negative economic growth. These measures were popular among Indians in the diaspora and they yielded billions of dollars.[56]

Since the 1990s, India established a number of specific diaspora policies. The reasons are threefold. First and foremost, after the liberalization of the Indian economy in 1991, the Indian government saw the diaspora as a pool of potential traders, investors and technological renovators who could boost the country's economy. Secondly, the government understood the possibilities of the Indians in the diaspora for public diplomacy. Thirdly, the 1990s were the first time Indians became high-level executives of multinational corporations, which has a positive effect on the image of Indian leadership.

To channel the opportunities coming from the diaspora, an annual diaspora conference, the Pravasi Bharatiya Divas, has been held since 2003. In 2004, the Government of India created the new Ministry of Overseas Indian Affairs that coordinated actions involving the diaspora. It was followed by the Overseas Indian Facilitation Centre in 2007, which eased the procedures for foreign Indian investors. In 2009 the Prime Minister Manmohan Singh set up the Global Advisory Council that consisted of diasporic intellectuals and businessmen.

In order to strengthen its ties with Indians abroad, the Government added two new categories of overseas Indian identities to the already existing NRI status. In 1999, India issued the Person of Indian Origin (PIO) Card for all former Indian citizens of any nationality and their non-Indian born descendants (up to four generations). In 2005, it introduced the Overseas Citizenship of India for all those whose parents or grandparents were eligible for Indian citizenship on January 26, 1950—the date on which the Constitution of India came into force. Both imply parity with Indian citizens, but do not grant voting rights. However, due to their financially favourable status, investment in India became easier for PIO's and OCI's.[57]

From the beginning of the twenty-first century onwards, Indian diaspora policies have increasingly influenced the Indians worldwide. Nevertheless, it is important to note that despite the efforts to unite all overseas Indians, there are still large groups who are excluded. The measures taken by the Government are especially beneficial for the wealthier part of the Indian diaspora, whereas in Europe some Indian groups remain rather marginalized.

Conclusions: Challenges for the Future

This chapter has argued that Indian migration to Europe is extremely diverse; the South Asian presence on the European continent has varied origins, consists of diverse groups executing a wide range of professions, is unequally spread, and is hosted with different policies. Yet, this does not mean that is does not make sense to approach them as a single group. Particularly regarding the future, there are a number of challenges, both for the European and for the Indian side.

Europe is facing some massive changes. The outcome of its financial crisis is unpredictable, but it is certain that its demographical structure is shifting dramatically. Given its low fertility rate and low mortality, the European population is greying. The number of retired people is increasing while the amount of working people is declining. This leads to labour demand and skill shortages. Asia could offer a solution. Countries such as India dispose of a very young population, ready to emigrate and increasingly highly skilled. They could supply labour in sectors short of working forces, such as technicians and health professionals.

However, there are still large hurdles that need to be overcome. Foreign nationals eager to work in Europe complain about the restrictive EU immigration policy, which discourages immigration by means of strict visa and certification rules. In 2007, the EU Commission developed a Blue Card programme to attract highly skilled workers from non-EU countries. Foreigners with a job offering at least 1.5 times the average gross annual salary in a EU Member State are subject to a simplified admission procedure, also for their families. Individual countries go further. Germany, for instance, launched a new immigration law in 2005, following its Green Card Programme of 2000-2005. It did not put any limitation on the number of investing foreigners, scientists, and well-paid professionals. However, this did not result in massive immigration. Only 629 highly skilled foreigners immigrated to the country between 2005 and 2009, far less than the number of qualified Germans leaving the country. It appears that English-speaking countries are still much more appealing and that immigrants also have other problems. The German recognition of credentials from foreign universities is not easy. The country has many regulated professions, including in the medical and engineering sectors, where guilds control entry.[58]

It is not only about regulations, but also about attitudes. Indians are aware of European suspicion of non-European migration. Not only the previously mentioned *Kinder statt Inder* campaign following the introduction of the Green Card, but, for instance, also the French reaction to the Mittal Steel bid for Arcelor, are emblematic illustrations of what Indians perceive as an 'outdated and inward-looking' Europe.[59] They often juxtapose this to a tolerant and multicultural India, which has managed to accommodate diversity due to its willingness to adapt, accept, and recognize diversity. Obviously, the truth is more complex. Europe does not only stand for homogeneous nations and India's multiple cultures have not always co-existed peacefully.

This complexity also goes for Indian migration to Europe. This is not only about highly skilled professionals, but also includes irregular migrants. Europe remains an El Dorado for many Indians, who even sell their land to finance their children's travel to Europe. There, however, they often end up in '3D-jobs' (dirty, difficult and dangerous) or in criminal networks. Europe blames India of doing too little to control illegal migration, but has no clear response either and for instance tolerates asylum shopping.

Huge challenges await Brussels and Delhi as well as Europeans and Indians. It is clear though that migration will not be stopped and that both sides are due to entangle in a globalized world. The diversity characterizing India as well as Indian migration will expand across the European continent.

NOTES

1. Leslie P. Moch, *Moving Europeans. Migration in Western Europe since 1650* (Bloomington: Indiana University Press, 1992); Gert Oostindie, *Postcolonial Netherlands. Sixty-five Years of Forgetting, Commemorating, Silencing* (Amsterdam: Amsterdam University Press, 2011).
2. Johan Meire, *De Stilte van de Salient. De Herinnering aan de Eerste Wereldoorlog rond Ieper* (Tielt: Lannoo, 2003), pp. 353-72; Bhupinder Singh Holland, *How Europe is Indebted to the Sikhs?* (n.p.: Sikh University Press, 2005).
3. Claire E. Alexander, Joya Chatterji, Shahzad Firoz and Annu

Jalais, *Bangla Stories* (London: Project of London School of Economics and Runnymede Trust, 2009-2011, accessed on 20 November 2011 (www.banglastories.org)).

4. Meenakshi Thapan and Maitrayee Deka, *South Asian Migrants in Europe: Heterogeneity, Multiplicity and the Overcoming of Difference* (European Studies Programme—Department of Sociology, University of Delhi: Working Paper Series 2010/1).
5. Susan Legêne, *Spiegelreflex. Culturele sporen van de koloniale ervaring* (Amsterdam: Bert Bakker, 2010), p. 90.
6. Gert Oostindie, *Postkoloniaal Nederland. Vijfenzestig jaar vergeten, herdenken, verdringen* (Amsterdam: Bert Bakker, 2010), pp. 32-35.
7. Anja Wiesbroeck, "Indian Migrants in the Netherlands," unpublished paper presented at the High Level Stakeholder Consultation Workshop, organized by the Indian Council of Overseas Employment (ICOE), New Delhi, 22 November 2011.
8. Legêne, n. 5, pp. 84-85 and Oostindie, n. 6, pp. 65-7, 71, 73, 131, and 205.
9. Appasamy Murugaiyan, "Le tamoul, langue classique et langue de diaspora", in Catherine Servan-Schreiber and Vasoodeven Vuddamalay, eds., *Diasporas indiennes dans la ville, Hommes et migrations*, no.1268-1269, 2007, pp. 92-95.
10. Christine Moliner, *Invisible et modèle? Première approche de l'immigration sud-asiatique en France. Rapport d'étude pour la Direction de l'Accueil, de l'Intégration et de la Citoyenneté* (Paris: Ministère de l'Immigration, de l'Intégration, de l'Identité nationale et du Développement solidaire, 2009), pp. 24-25.
11. Anthony Goreau-Ponceaud, "La diaspora tamoule: Trajectoires spatio-temporelles et inscriptions territoriales en Île-de-France" (Bordeau: Université de Bordeau, unpublished dissertation, 2008), p. 104.
12. Ibid., pp. 50-69.
13. Kathryn Lum, "Caste, Religion, and Community Assertion: A Case Study of the Ravidasias in Spain," in Knut A. Jacobson and Kristina Myrvold, eds., *Sikhs in Europe. Migration, Identities and Representations* (Farnham: Ashgate Publishing Limited, 2011), pp. 160-161.
14. Helena M.M.C. Santana, "Goans and Damaninans in Portugal: An Overview of a Singular Diaspora," in Knut A. Jacobsen and Selva J. Raj, eds., *South Asian Christian Diaspora: Invisible Diaspora in Europe and North America* (Farnham: Ashgate Publising Limited, 2008), pp. 133-154.
15. Catarina Valdigem Pereira, *Remembering with and through "Media*

Objects among Portuguese Muslims of Indian and Mozambican Origins: A Family Case Study (www.bocc.ubi.pt, 2010, accessed on 8 January 2012), pp. 4-7; Martin Baumann, "Sustaining 'Little Indias'. Hindu diasporas in Europe", in Gerrie ter Haar, ed., *Strangers and Sojourners. Religious Communities in the Diaspora* (Leuven: Peeters, 1998), p. 115.
16. Parminder Bhachu, *Twice Migrants: East African Sikh Settlers in Britain* (London and New York: Tavistock Publications, 1985).
17. Valdigem Pereira, *Remembering with and through "media objects"*, pp. 4-7; Martin B. Baumann, "The Hindu Presence in Europe and Implications of Interfaith Dialogue: The Hindu Presence in Europe and Implications of Interfaith Dialogue", *Hindu-Christian Studies Bulletin*, Vol. 11, 1998, p. 27.
18. Kristina Myrvold, "The Swedish Sikhs: Community Building, Representation and Generational Change", in Jacobson and Myrvold, n. 13, p. 68; Sara Cosemans, Quincy Cloet and Idesbald Goddeeris, "Migratie en interne breuklijnen: sikhs in België", in Michèle Morel and Cedric Ryngaert, eds., *Migratie: winnaars en verliezers* (Leuven: Acco, 2011), pp. 97-110.
19. Knut A. Jacobson, "Institutionalization of Sikhism in Norway: Community Growth and Generational Transfer," in Jacobson and Myrvold, n. 13, p. 22.
20. Knut A. Jacobson and Kristina Myrvold, "Introduction: Sikhs in Europe," in Jacobson and Myrvold, n. 13, pp. 9-12.
21. Ibid., p. 1.
22. Urmilla Goel, "On people marked as South Asians in Germany," *South Asians in Germany and Europe*, URL: http://www.urmila.de/english/englishindex.html (accessed on 20 November 2011).
23. Baumann, n. 15, p. 113.
24. Pereira, n. 17, p. 6.
25. Urmila Goel, "'Half Indians', Adopted 'Germans' and 'Afghan Indians'. On claims of 'Indianness' and their contestations in Germany", *Transforming Cultures eJournal*, Vol. 3, 2008, pp. 108-111.
26. Manohari Velamati, "Sri Lankan Tamil migration and settlement: time for reconsideration", *India Quarterly*, Vol. 65, 2010, pp. 271-272.
27. Goreau-Ponceaud, n. 11, pp. 123-127.
28. Ibid., pp. 50-69.
29. Baumann, n. 15, p. 116.
30. Goreau-Ponceaud, n. 11, pp. 31-33.

31. Urmilla Goel, "'Indians in Germany' The Imagination of a Community," *Journal of the UNE Asia Centre*, Vol. 20, 2007, pp. 1-2.
32. Jacobson and Myrvold, n. 20, p. 1.
33. Myrvold, n. 18, p. 69.
34. Zbigniew Igielski, "The Sikhs in Poland: A Short History of Migration and Settlement," Jacobson and Myrvold, n. 13, p. 122.
35. Myrvold, n. 18, p. 67.
36. Thapan and Deka, n. 4, p. 18.
37. Quincy Cloet, Sara Cosemans and Idesbald Goddeeris, "Mobility as a transnational strategy: Sikhs moving to and from Belgium," in Kristina Myrvold and Knut Jacobsen, eds., *Sikh across Borders: Transnational Practices of European Sikhs* (London: Continuum, forthcoming).
38. Joachim Oesterheld, "Indians in Berlin: Past and Present," in Klaus Voll and Doreen Beierlein, eds., *Rising India—Europe's Partner?* (Berlin: Weißensee Verlag, 2006), pp. 901-909.
39. Urmilla Goel, "The 70th anniversary of John Matthew—On Indian Christians in Germany," in Knut A. Jacobsen and Selva J. Raj, eds. *South Asian Christian Diaspora: Invisible Diaspora in Europe and North America*, (Farnham: Ashgate Publishing Limited, 2008), pp. 57-74.
40. Louise Meijering and Bettina Van Hoven, "Imagining difference: the experiences of in Germany 'transnational' Indian IT professionals," *Area*, Vol. 35, 2003, pp. 174-82. See also Urmilla Goel, "On people marked as South Asians in Germany," *South Asians in Germany and Europe* (http://www.urmila.de/english/englishindex.html, accessed on 20 November 2011).
41. Chinmay Tumbe, "EU-India Bilateral Remittances," unpublished paper presented at the High Level Stakeholder Consultation Workshop, organized by the Indian Council of Overseas Employment (ICOE), Delhi, 22 November 2011.
42. "Recruitment of IT specialists from India. An investigation of the market, experiences of Danish companies, the attitude of the Indian authorities towards overseas recruitment along with the practices of other countries in this field," *Report from the fact finding mission to New Delhi and Bangalore, India*, 4-14 May 2008, p. 6.
43. Ibid., pp. 9-10.
44. Hannelore Roos and Stephanie Vervaet, "Diamantsteden: knooppunten van transnationale vertrouwensnetwerken", *Agora. Magazine voor sociaalruimtelijke vraagstukken*, Vol. 26, 2010,

pp. 25-27; Hannelore Roos, "Jainisme. Een van de oudste Indische religies bouwt tempel in Antwerpen", *Verrekijkers. Magazine voor intercultureel contact en mondiale bewustwording*, Vol. 11, 2008, pp. 18-19.

45. Laura Hirvi, "Sikhs in Finland: Migration Histories and Work in the Restaurant Sector," in Jacobson and Myrvold, n. 13, pp. 95 and 101-105.
46. Christine Moliner, "'Did You Get Papers?' Sikh Migrants in France," in Jacobson and Myrvold, n. 13, p. 169.
47. Myrvold, n. 18, p. 70.
48. Helene Ilkjær, "The Sikh Community in Denmark: Balancing between Cooperation and Conflict," in Jacobson and Myrvold, n. 13, p. 40.
49. Barbara Bertolani, Federica Ferraris and Fabio Perocco, "Mirror Games: A Fresco of Sikh Settlements among Italian Local Societies," in Jacobson and Myrvold, n. 13, pp. 137, 143 and 152.
50. Nele Bossens, "Hoe later de avond, hoe schoner volk. Zuid-Aziatische nachtwinkeluitbaters in Leuven" (Leuven: unpublished MA thesis, History KU Leuven), pp. 41-42.
51. Moliner, n. 46, p. 169.
52. Amanda Levinson, "Migration fundamentals: why countries continue to consider regularization," *Migration Information Source* (Available at: http://www.migrationinformation.org/Feature/display.cfm?ID=330, 2006, accessed on 6 October 2011).
53. Erik Bleich, "The Legacies of History? Colonization and Immigrant Integration in Britain and France," *Theory & Society*, Vol. 34, 2005, pp. 171-195; Thom Duyvene de Wit and Ruud Koopmans, "Integration of Ethnic Minorities into Political Culture: The Netherlands, Germany and Great Britain Compared", *Acta Politica*, vol. 40, 2005, pp. 50-73; Oostindie, *Postcolonial Netherlands*, pp. 181-201.
54. Sam Scott and Kim H. Cartledge, "Migrant Assimilation in Europe: A Transnational Family Affair", *International Migration Review*, Vol. 43, 2009, p. 62.
55. Gily Coene and Chia Longman, *Ceci n'est pas une voile? De Belgische hijab ter discussie* (Leuven: paper presented at 'Dag van de Sociologie 2008', 2008), pp. 4-6.
56. Daniel Naujoks, "Country Profiles. Emigration, Immigration, and Diaspora Relations in India," *Migration Information Source* (Available at: http://www.migrationinformation.org/Profiles/display.cfm?ID=745#8, accessed on 15 February 2012).
57. Ibid.

58. Philip Martin, *Attracting Highly Skilled Migrants: US Experience and Lessons for the EU. CARIM-India Research Report 2012/1* (Robert Schuman Centre for Advanced Studies, San Domenico di Fiesole (FI): European University Institute, 2012).
59. Karine Lisbonne-de Vergeron, *Contemporary Indian Views of Europe* (London: Chatham House, 2006).

8

Multiculturalism as a Policy of Integration in Britain

Divya Balan

Introduction

Contemporary Europe is diverse in ample ways with a variety of constituting nation-states, religions, cultures, languages and national and minority identities. This diversity is partly the contribution of the historical aspects that shaped the Europe, array of those who populated the continent at various times including Greeks, Romans, Germans, Huns, Slavic, Celts, to name a few and the existence of different belief systems of Christianity (with Catholicism, Orthodox and Protestantism as well as a number of minor denominations like Methodism, Evangelicalism, Pentecostalism etc.), Judaism and Islam; and partly because of the international migration flows to the continent at all times. In Europe, multiculturalism[1] has been the general strategy to manage this diversity. Its manifestations differ from society to society and in the European context the debate on multiculturalism concerns predominantly the identity and culture of ethnic immigrant communities who were largely perceived as 'welfare stealers'.

Even after the Lisbon Treaty (2009), the European Union (EU) does not have any common policy framework on either multiculturalism or integration of immigrants. It has proposed various legislation and policies to create common frameworks. However, the response from the Member States has not been satisfactory since issues related to migration are considered highly sensitive. Their reluctance to transfer their national law-making competence in this volatile area to the EU has led to extended opt-outs by several Member States, especially Britain. The emergence of *de facto* 27 national level policy approaches to deal with migration is a salient aspect of the broader debate of multiculturalism in Europe. This chapter discusses how multiculturalism seeks to accommodate diverse immigrant identities in the social fabric of Britain, which has a unique position in the world migration history as a former imperial power.[2]

The Changing Demography in Britain

Large scale migrations throughout history, especially since 1945, have led to major changes in the ethnic composition of most European countries, including Britain. Growing apprehensions about immigrants and greater ethnic and religious diversity has led to the questioning of various policies of accommodation and the pattern of the formation and manifestation of ethno-cultural and religious communities. Britain has been experiencing serious problems in accommodating immigrant and ethnic minority populations. This has resulted in "long-term adverse social consequences, including the rise of increasingly assertive and alienated immigrant communities."[3] At the same time, Britain needs immigrants[4] undeniably given demands of the labour market for both skilled and unskilled labourers because of severe problems of a greying population and the decline in birth rates.[5]

As a country of immigration,[6] Britain attracted people from all parts of the world. This led to the creation of a multicultural society with unique multinational and multiethnic characteristics. Immigration to Britain dates back to even before its recorded history. The inflow had increased manifold during the Imperial and post-Imperial era,[7] leading to a growing number of both legal and illegal immigrants of different ethnic origin having entered and settled both temporarily and permanently in the country for a variety of reasons including economic, social, political and religious. As a result, contemporary Britain is culturally plural with people of varied origin including, national ethnicities[8] comprising of the English, the Scots, the Welsh and Northern Irish and immigrant ethnicities of various foreign nationalities, including those which the British colonial history identified as Old and New Commonwealth countries.[9] There are also relatively small, scattered groups of Romanians, Ghanaians, mainland Chinese, Colombians, Afghans, Japanese, Kurds, Zimbabweans, Iraqis, Iranians, Yemenis and numerous others. Britain's entry into the European Economic Community in 1973 and the establishment of a single market and the freedom of movement within the EU, and the accession of East European countries to the EU in 2004 led to more immigrants from EU Member States entering Britain. Another group of people who added to the diversity of Britain were asylum seekers from various countries like Iraq, Somalia, China, Iran, Zimbabwe, etc.

The 2001 Census classified 92.1 per cent (54,154,000) of the British population as white and 7.9 per cent (4,635,000) as non-white minority ethnic groups. This represented an increase by 53 per cent since the previous Census in 1991. Non-white ethnic minority groups, of which about half were born in Britain, constitute a relatively small proportion of the total British population. The net inflow of New Commonwealth citizens was the highest of all the foreign citizenship groups. Nearly 80 per cent of net immigration from the New Commonwealth was citizens from the Indian subcontinent, viz. India, Pakistan, Bangladesh and Sri Lanka. Immigration of A8[10] citizens increased slightly from 76,000 in 2005 to 92,000 in 2006. Almost three quarters of the A8 inflow (68,000) comprised Polish citizens. "Work-related" reasons continued to be the most cited causes for migrating to Britain. Immigration for "formal study" reached a record high of 157,000, of which 80 per cent were citizens from outside the EU. Chinese and Indian citizens together accounted for nearly 30 per cent of migrants arriving in Britain to study. London was again the most common destination for immigrants in 2006. Nevertheless, unlike the past, migration within Britain has tended to become increasingly dispersed.[11] In 2007-2008, net migration to Britain fell sharply after the effects of the new Points-Based System (PBS) for managing migration was felt. Moreover, the recession reduced Britain's attractiveness for economic migrants and a significant proportion of EU migrants, who had arrived after 2004 enlargement, have left the country. However, recent statistics suggest that net migration has risen steadily in the second half of 2009 and the beginning of 2010.[12] The resultant plurality poses serious questions about the very meaning of the notion of *Britishness* and British national culture. It also poses challenges of how national and immigrant ethnic minorities deal with their multiple identities and loyalties as well as how Britain deals with this diversity.[13]

Multiculturalism as an Integration Policy

Growing diversity of migrants has led to a total shift in the focus on integration of immigrants in British society and polity. The question of accommodating an ethnically diverse population arises at two levels: how to accommodate different nationalities like the Welsh, the Scots and the Irish and how to address various immigrant identities like the Asian, the African, the Caribbean, the Hindu, the Muslim, etc. Attempting to accommodate diverse immigrant identities is a rather complicated process. In popular parlance, accommodating diversity is nothing but accommodating "others", i.e. the immigrants. British integration policies have been a highly sensitive issue which has had a far reaching impact on society, politics, culture and the economy. The development of subsequent models of inclusion by Britain has been influenced by its colonial and post-colonial policies, specific economic and political histories, the post-war economic situation, historical racism and restrictive immigration and citizenship practices.[14]

Britain has had a unique mix of inclusion policies ranging from an early assimilationist policy to the current strategy of integration and community cohesion. In the immediate post-war period which witnessed large scale unintended population movements, there was a serious debate for the first time on immigration and integration policies. However, it did not lead to a clear and coherent policy framework. The underlying ideology was explicitly assimilationist generally understood in strongly racialized terms.[15] Apart from its inherently defective assumptions, the failure of the assimilationist model was due to a number of factors including immense cultural diversity, active resistance of ethnic minority groups in the wake of their socio-economic marginalization and the consequent labour market and residential segregation, racial discrimination and hostility which ultimately resulted in race riots like those in 1958.

Growing recognition of the lack of assimilation of immigrants and the formation of distinct social, cultural and political associations by immigrants concentrated in particular occupations and residential areas, led Britain in the 1960s to introduce the policy of integration based on the concept of multiculturalism which entailed an explicit recognition and value of cultural diversity.[16] A series of Race Relations Acts (including 1965, 1968, 1976, 2000, 2006 Racial and Religious Hatred Act, etc.) were enacted to ban racial and ethnic discrimination in public places as well as in employment, education and housing. Various institutions like the Commission for Racial Equality (CRE)—the body to oversee the implementation of Race Relations Acts were established to manage inter-group relations and facilitate social integration of immigrants.[17] Britain, in fact, consistently used the language of race. The policy was embedded in the concept of the "race relations model" as the dominant way to deal with diversity.

After the terrorist attacks of 9/11 and the London bombings of 7/7, the focus of the contemporary integration debate turned towards issues of religion and ethnicity from the long cherished goal towards race and race relations with the promulgation of the Policy of Integration and Community Cohesion. Since 2001, three issues have been at the forefront of the integration debates—the debate on common values often prompted by Labour politicians; the seeming division between diversity and solidarity; and the security concern and the implicit focus on ethnicity and religion of immigrants, especially Muslims in the wake of the 9/11 and 7/7 terrorist attacks.[18] Till then, multiculturalism was presumed to be the ideal policy in dealing with the integration issues and the best way of combating the dangers of the marginalization of minorities from the mainstream. Even after more than forty-five years of experiencing multiculturalism, the persistence of socio-economic deprivation among some ethnic minority communities, recurring race riots, instances of "home-grown terrorism", religious fundamentalism, and extreme ethnic identity assertion posed serious questions about the success and viability of multiculturalism and the allied Race Relations Acts.

In his *Multicultural Odysseys: Navigating the New International Politics of Diversity*,[19] Will Kymlicka argues that multiculturalist policies are the best hope for building just and inclusive societies around the world. Indeed, they have helped to pacify ethnic politics, encouraged the minorities to be more vocal in their claim makings, and deepened and strengthened democracy and human rights. However their success largely depended on the commitment to and the effectiveness of their implementation. The lack of any legal or constitutional commitment to multiculturalism, reluctance to make it a matter of official public policy coupled with the existence of institutional racism have resulted in a complex, confusing and arbitrary system which fails to respect the cultural and individual rights of members of the resident ethnic minority populations.[20] From the outset, multiculturalism was blamed for the perpetuation of segregation and ethnic enclaves, violent youth gangs, disunity among the working class, inadequate manifestations of patriotism, and divisions between ethnic communities. It was criticized for welfare dependency, preventing immigrants from integrating into the language, culture and traditions of the dominant culture and national identity, undermining Western democratic values, allowing an inflated "tolerance" to cultural and religious difference, and ultimately, focusing on cultural rights of groups rather than those of the individual. Moreover, multicultural policy and practice have been unsuccessful since it encouraged Muslims to maintain their identity without becoming part of the larger community. This, in turn, led to separatism, the propagation of extremist views, and contempt for the British nation and its "core" values.

In response to the summer disturbances in Northern Milltowns of Oldham, Bradford, Leeds and Burnley in 2001, the Policy of Community Cohesion was introduced, while retaining Race Relations, on the argument that the disturbances were a signal of the failure of multiculturalism. Concerns about "community cohesion" have been further heightened by violence between other ethnic groups. These have included clashes between Pakistanis and Kurdish asylum-seekers in Peterborough in 2004, in clashes between Blacks and Asians in Birmingham during 2005,[21] the rise of ethnic extremism, and the growing popularity of the British National Party (BNP), on the other. A Community Cohesion Unit in the Home Office was created to mainstream community cohesion. This was later renamed as the Cohesion and Faith Unit, thereby, broadening its scope by including religious as well as cultural differences.

Debates over religious education, the veil, and "parallel lives" suggested that the period of self-satisfaction over British multiculturalism ended.[22] In April 2004, Trevor Phillips, the head of the Commission for Racial Equality, commented that multiculturalism was "dead". In the wake of the 7 July 2005 London bombings, the then opposition Conservative Shadow Home Secretary David Davis called on the government to scrap its "outdated" policy of multiculturalism. In August 2006, the Community and Local Government (CLG) Secretary Ruth Kelly made a speech perceived as signalling the end of multiculturalism as official policy. In response to such calls, the Home Office functions concerned with race, equality and faith were moved in 2006 to the Department of the Community and Local Government, which became the secretariat of an independent Commission on Integration and Cohesion.[23] Moreover, the Commission for Racial Equality was merged with other equality bodies to form the Commission for Equality and Human Rights (CEHR). Despite these renewed efforts, the 2007 Report of the Commission on Integration and Cohesion acknowledged that integration of new migrants under the policy of community cohesion has lacked a strong departmental lead within the British Government. In official terms, "community cohesion" was conceptualized as social cohesion at the neighbourhood level and the community began to be regarded as the domain through which common social values could be asserted and a sense of belonging and citizenship nurtured.[24] However, the policy was largely perceived by many as a partial return to the early assimilationist and monoculturalist perspective. It reflected a tendency towards the creation of new citizenship practices as well as the promotion of the English language, "core" values and a national identity based on *Britishness*. As a result, the focus of the integration debate shifted from institutional racism, economic and structural inequalities towards cultural values and traditions of ethnic immigrant minorities.[25] The community cohesion policy seeking to overstretch to an assimilationist character would be extremely damaging for immigrants since it urges the homogenization of identity and culture as well as a definite merging into the larger *Britishness* by giving away their otherwise eternal characteristics and virtues of ethno-cultural identity. Multiculturalism is imperative in such situations, as a response of a democratic polity to the "melting pot" tendencies of the host country and to ensure that human rights, socio-economic equality, social justice and cultural plurality are preserved for the society at large.

Conclusion

Migration is certain to increase cultural pluralism and ethnic diversity. It creates new dimensions to the way in which nation-states respond to the key issues of immigrants' integration to their socio-political structures in a successful manner. Globalization has led to national borders becoming increasingly porous. Population movements have increased with the ageing of population and a decline of the population making a productive contribution. In spite of these trends, the issues of immigrants' incorporation have growing significance, especially after the incidents of 9/11 and 7/7 stirred by the tendencies of religious fundamentalism and home-grown terrorism.

Integration of immigrants is perhaps the greatest challenge for Britain. It is a critical question because of the recurring tensions between the host and the immigrant community due to problems of integration which are further magnified by many factors including imperial legacy and the perceived white superiority of a forever colonial master. Similarly, the structuralist model of the nation-state presumes that the immigrant is a) a consumer of the benefits of the nation-state and competitors for jobs, b) has ceased to contribute to the production of the nation-state, and c) has set up its own isolated structure of being within the national landscape and hence they are "others" and, as such, is separate, separable, and isolable from a national people[26] and a major threat to majority national culture. Such concerns raised disquiet among British policy-makers, service providers, politicians across the broad spectrums including anti-immigrant lobbies and the media bringing the issue to the socio-political forefront. The manipulated and unreliable immigration statistics and the subsequent "number game" by stakeholders, especially policy-makers and the media, in turn stirred up the negative public opinion against the integration of immigrants in British society. Popular notions of "illiberal and inferior" cultural practices such as forced or arranged marriages, wearing of veils by women, genital circumcision, etc. coupled with multiple loyalties and community affiliations of immigrant groups fostered the construction of prejudiced racial, religious and ethnic identities by the host society. These apprehensions were reinforced by the increasing assertiveness of the immigrant communities, the persistence of race riots and, above all, by the perceived fear of the "clash of civilizations" and growing evidences of home-grown terrorism. This led to the formulation of a more coherent government policy facilitating the integration of immigrants and the evolution of policies like assimilation, multiculturalism, and the current policies of integration and community cohesion.

The failure to fully integrate immigrants challenged the

viability of the multiculturalism as a policy of managing diversity in British society. The implementation of multiculturalism so far has not been very successful in fully accommodating the ethnic minorities in British society by paying adequate respect to their cultural and individual rights. Multiculturalism in practice has not eliminated elements of xenophobia, racism, and anti-Islamism in mainstream society. But the defect is not of the multiculturalist policy as such and hence it could not be considered a failure too. The faulty manner in which the multiculturalism was implemented in Britain is one of the main reasons for the failure of comprehensive integration of immigrants in British society. The lack of a legal and constitutional commitment to multiculturalism and the reluctance to make it a matter of official public policy coupled with the British colonial past and implicitly exclusionary and racially biased immigration policy, and the complicated and burdensome citizenship procedures all played a role for the relative failure of multiculturalism in Britain.

Mainstream arguments against the British policy of multiculturalism are mainly concerned with cultural recognition and ethnic identities of immigrants. They rarely concentrate on the issues of inequality and racial discrimination experienced by many immigrant groups throughout various societal institutions and structures in Britain. A frequent criticism of multiculturalism is that the strict adherence of ethnic and cultural identities by immigrant communities acts as a barrier to integration rather than inequality and systemic institutional racism (with implications of current Islamophobia and anti-Muslim racism). Social identity theorists claim that in circumstances where groups feel devalued, they have a need to boost their self-esteem by distinguishing themselves from the natives and hence use their distinctive identity as a self-defensive mechanism against the inequality and discrimination they faced in British society. Migrants sometimes find it beneficial to retain their ethnic and cultural links since ascriptive aspects like colour, race, etc. cannot be entirely done away with. Migrants thereby seek to recapture or compensate for the loss of their social position in their home country by acting as community leaders in Britain. Ethnic identification and religion often become the strategies with which immigrants and ethnic minorities struggle against racism and marginalization. They are often labelled with negative connotations such as "identity politics" or "segregation". Perceptions of immigrants as social disintegrative forces broadly act as barriers to integration in British society. Even though multiculturalism has considerable potential to deal with excesses, it still needs to be revamped. To that end, Britain needs to secure a strong public consensus and commitment on multiculturalism and such other immigration related issues at large since public confidence is crucial to the successful management of issues relating to immigration and multiculturalism. Intercultural dialogue also serves as a confidence-building measure where all parties have equal room for expression. This could be an important step towards promotion of cultural diversity and the evolution of a thriving multicultural polity. At the same time, measures to guarantee a just share of social, economic and political power to the minority ethnic communities and provide equal access to employment, education, housing and public facilities should also be ensured.

NOTES

1. Rosado defines multiculturalism as "a system of beliefs and behaviors that recognizes and respects the presence of all diverse groups in an organization or society, acknowledges and values their socio-cultural differences, and encourages and enables their continued contribution within an inclusive cultural context which empowers all within the organization or society." Caleb Rosado, "Toward a Definition of Multiculturalism" (1996), URL: http://rosado.net/pdf/Def_of_Multiculturalism.pdf., p. 2.
2. Migrants entered Britain through the doors of the Empire, the colonial capitalist penetration played a significant role in the initiation of large scale labour migration from the increasingly subordinate economic periphery or developing countries to the 'core' or the British imperial metropolis, thereby making Britain the metropolitan centre of immigration and this largely resulted

in the presence of a substantial diversity of immigrant population there. Alejandro Portes, "Immigration Theory for a New Century: Some Problems and Opportunities", *International Migration Review*, 31 (4), 1997, p. 810.

3. Rajendra K. Jain, "Fortifying the 'Fortress': Immigration and Politics in the European Union", *International Studies*, 34 (2), 1997, p. 187.
4. See Nissa Finney and Ludi Simpson, *'Sleepwalking to Segregation'?: Challenging Myths about Race and Migration* (London: Polity Press, 2009) and Philippe Legrain, *Immigrants: Your Country Needs Them* (London: Little Brown, 2006). By making sense of race statistics, Finney and Simpson reject many of the popular myths relating to British immigration. Those myths are "Britain takes too many immigrants", "So many minorities cannot be integrated", "Minorities do not want to integrate", "Britain is becoming a country of ghettos" and also of "Whites are becoming a minority in British cities". The authors argue that the myths of race and migration are the real threat to an integrated society, which misguides policy and promotes racial disharmony. They recommend that the policy focus should return to problems of rising inequality and racist prejudice from these misleading myths about migration. Claims by the Head of the Commission for Racial Equality Trevor Phillips that Britain is 'sleepwalking' into racial and religious segregation are also dismissed in the book; in turn argues that no race ghettos existed whereas ethnic mixing is at an increase in Britain. Finney and Simpson also argue that numbers have become central to fears and forecasts of ethnic relations in Britain and figures are often manipulated. By linking social problems to segregated areas, they say, politicians have stigmatized the areas and the residents. The authors also provide evidence that areas with large populations of Muslims do not act as a breeding ground for terrorism. For them, the truth is that Britain's 'so-called' ghettos are diverse areas both ethnically and socially with no one ethnic group dominates.

   Philippe Legrain in *Immigrants: Your Country Needs Them* (2006) strongly argues that open borders with transparent, fair and effective immigration and integration policy offers huge benefits for both migrants' country of origin and the host country economy. He discusses the most common stereotypic attitudes that immigrants steal the native jobs, abuse the welfare system, destroy the native culture and way of life, abuse the asylum system with bogus claims and also immigrants' perceived connections with the terrorists outfits. He says that immigrants instead of stealing the native job opportunities undertake those jobs which the natives no longer wanted to do or they cannot do. Again, their diversity enriches the native culture and society. He offers a number of real accounts to expose the ill-informed prejudices from the part of native public, political elites and parties. Through the book the author asserts the undeniable fact that immigrants' needs US and we need THEM too.

5. Ian Diamond, "Mosaic Society: Complex Changes in the UK Society Bring with Them Policy Challenges," *Britain Today*, Vol. 1, 2007, pp. 91-3.
6. For a detailed account of the early history of immigration to Britain see, John Oakland, *British Civilization: An Introduction* (London: Routledge, 2006); F.W. Tickner, *Outlines of British History: Part I The Beginnings to 1603* (London: University of London Press Ltd., 1925); and David Miles, *The Tribes of Britain* (London: Weidenfeld and Nicolson, 2005).
7. Zig Layton-Henry, *The Politics of Race in Britain* (London: George Allen & Unwin, 1984), p. 8.
8. The national ethnicities themselves were derived from mixed genesis and internal migration overtime within and between those four individual nations.
9. The Old Commonwealth includes Australia, Canada, New Zealand and South Africa. The New Commonwealth includes all other Commonwealth countries of South Asia, East and West Africa and the Caribbean. From 2004, the New Commonwealth excludes Malta and Cyprus. Other foreign nationalities include all countries that are not covered by former groupings, excluding citizens of the eight central and east European countries since they joined the EU in May 2004 (National Statistics (2007), "News Release: Emigration from UK Reaches 400,000 in 2006," URL: http://gianlucasalvatori.nova100.ilsole24ore.com/files/emig1107.pdf, p. 7.
10. Accession 8 countries are popularly expressed in the EU terminology as A8 countries. The A8 countries include the Czech Republic, Estonia, Hungary, Latvia, Lithuania, Poland, Slovakia and Slovenia. They joined the EU15 after the 2004 enlargement. The EU15 includes Austria, Belgium, Denmark, Finland, France, Germany, Greece, the Irish Republic, Italy, Luxembourg, Netherlands, Portugal, Spain, Sweden and United Kingdom. Since then, the EU25 includes the EU15 plus the A8 group and

Cyprus and Malta. Net immigration by citizens of the A8 countries fell dramatically after 2007, as the initial surge in demand to migrate passed, and many of the first waves of migrants returned home or moved elsewhere. Britain actually experienced net emigration by this group in the year to September 2009. The net immigration by A8 nationals was estimated at 12,000 for the year 2010 that led to a new and substantial A8-born population in Britain—estimates from the Annual Population Survey suggest that Britain now has around 750,000 residents born in A8 countries of whom over 500,000 were born in Poland. Institute for Public Policy Research, "Migration Review: 2010/2011", URL: http://ec.europa.eu/ewsi/UDRW/images/items/docl_17689_255157698.pdf, p. 2.

11. National Statistics, "News Release: Emigration from UK Reaches 400,000 in 2006," 15 November 2007, URL: http://gianlucasalvatori.nova100.ilsole24ore.com/files/emig1107.pdf, pp. 2-3.
12. Institute for Public Policy Research, "Migration Review: 2010/2011", URL: http://ec.europa.eu/ewsi/UDRW/images/items/docl_17689_255157698.pdf, p. 1.
13. John Oakland, *British Civilization: An Introduction* (London: Routledge, 2006), p. 52.
14. P. Weil and J. Crowley, "Integration in Theory and in Practice: A Comparison of France and Britain," in Martin Baldwin-Edwards and Martin Schain, eds., *The Politics of Immigration in Western Europe* (Ilford: Frank Cass, 1994), p. 113.
15. P. Weil and J. Crowley, "Integration in Theory and in Practice: A Comparison of France and Britain," in Martin Baldwin-Edwards and Martin Schain, eds., *The Politics of Immigration in Western Europe* (Ilford: Frank Cass, 1994), p. 116.
16. Stephen Castles, "Democracy and Multiculturalism in Western Europe," in L. Holmes and P. Murray, eds., *Citizenship and Identity in Europe* (England: Ashgate, 1999), p. 298.
17. Andrew Geddes, *The Politics of Migration and Immigration in Europe* (New Delhi: Sage Publications, 2003), p. 44.
18. Will Somerville, *Immigration under New Labour* (UK: Polity Press, 2007), p. 51.
19. Will Kymlicka, *Multicultural Odysseys: Navigating the New International Politics of Diversity* (New York: Oxford University Press, 2007).
20. Will Kymlicka, "Immigration, Citizenship, Multiculturalism: Exploring the Links," in Sarah Spencer, ed., *The Politics of*

Migration: Managing Opportunity, Conflict and Change (London: Blackwell Publishing, 2003), p. 203.

21. Roger Eatwell, "Community Cohesion and Cumulative Extremism in Contemporary Britain," *The Political Quarterly*, 2006, 77(2), p. 204.
22. Christopher Hill, "Bringing War Home: Foreign Policy-Making in Multicultural Societies," *International Relations*, 2007, 21(3), p. 269.
23. Will Somerville, *Immigration under New Labour* (London: Polity Press, 2007), p. 78.
24. David Robinson, "The Search for Community Cohesion: Key Themes and Dominant Concepts of the Public Policy Agenda," *Urban Studies*, 2005, 42(8), p. 1417.
25. Pauline Hope Cheong, et al., "Immigration, Social Cohesion and Social Capital: A Critical Review", *Critical Social Policy*, 2007, 27(1), p. 26.
26. Brian Keith Axel, "Diaspora Theory and Multiculturalism in the UK", *Cultural Dynamics*, 2002, 14(3), pp. 235, 249.

9

Cultural Policy of the European Union and India-EU Cultural Cooperation

Imre Lázár

The Role of Culture in the European Union

If we talk about Europe we mean not only a geographical, but also a cultural entity with common cultural values and traditions. However, the founders of the European Union seem to have forgotten about culture. During the process of the European integration, the political, economic and social factors were emphasized and the cultural aspects were almost totally ignored. When the European Community took shape in 1957, the Treaty of Rome did not even mention the notion of culture, and even education was discussed under the heading of vocational training. It was only in the latter half of the 1970s that the EU started to pay greater attention to the questions of culture and education, when it was realized that a European community, which is based on the Europeans' identity, should be understood and handled as a cultural project as well.

The activities supporting culture since 1970 have been shaped by impulses coming primarily from the Council of Europe, the European Parliament and UNESCO. Until then the Community was able to pursue this sort of activity only within the framework of subsidies realized in other fields of politics. Culture gained independence only after the then twelve Member States signed the Maastricht Treaty on 7 February 1992 (entered into force on 1 November 1993). This Treaty placed

European integration on new bases. A series of non-economic policies like education, training and youth policies, health and cultural policy appeared here on EU level for the first time. Acknowledgement of the importance of cultural policy is indicated in Article 3 of the Maastricht Treaty where the list of common aims included the task that the Union should contribute to the flourishing of the culture of the Member States. Article 128 of the Treaty established the legal foundations of those programmes and initiatives of the EU which were called into being specifically for supporting cultural activities on the territory of the Community. This intention was confirmed later by the Amsterdam Treaty (signed in 1997, entered into force in 1999) and the Lisbon Treaty (signed in 2007, entered into force in 2009) where without significant change of its content it was renamed as Article 151.[1]

Article 151 specified the concrete targets of EU cultural policy. According to this regulation, the Union shall contribute to the flowering of the cultures of the Member States, while respecting their national and regional diversity and at the same time bringing the common cultural heritage to the fore. One of the most important intentions of supporting culture is assisting the diverse cultural activities and emphasizing their uniqueness. At the same time, it is also wished to make the people aware of the common heritage affecting all fields of art and to contribute to their preservation. It was this intention from which the motto of the EU "Unity in Diversity" emphasizing the existence of a multicultural, still united EU was born. According to Article 151, action by the Union shall be aimed at encouraging cooperation between Member States and, if necessary, supporting and supplementing their action in the following areas: improvement of the knowledge and dissemination of the culture and history of the European peoples, conservation and safeguarding of cultural heritage of European significance, encouragement of non-commercial cultural exchanges, support of artistic and literary creation, including in the audiovisual sector. Article 151, paragraph 4 requires the Union to take culture into account in all its actions so as to foster intercultural respect and promote diversity. Promotion of culture and cultural diversity should be given due consideration when all regulatory and financial decisions or proposals are made.

Further development in the cultural policy of the EU led to the adoption of the European Agenda for Culture.[2] This new European strategy for culture was proposed by the Commission in May 2007.[3] The Agenda attempts to respond to the challenges of globalization and aims to intensify cultural cooperation in the EU. The document is based on three common sets of objectives: cultural diversity and intercultural dialogue; culture as a catalyst for creativity; and culture as a key component in international relations. The Agenda was approved by the cultural sector during the Lisbon Forum of September 2007 and was also endorsed by the Council in its Resolution of November 2007[4] and then by the European Council in its conclusions of December 2007.[5]

The first set of objectives encourages the Union and all other relevant stakeholders to work together in order to foster intercultural dialogue so that the EU's cultural diversity would be understood, respected and promoted. To realize that aim, they should, for example, seek to enhance the cross-border mobility of artists and workers in the cultural sector and the cross-border dissemination of works of art.

According to the second set of objectives, the promotion of culture could act as a catalyst for creativity in the framework of the Lisbon Strategy for growth and jobs. Cultural industries are important as an asset for Europe's economy and competitiveness. Creativity generates both social and technological innovation and stimulates growth and jobs in the EU.

The third set of objectives defines the promotion of culture as a vital element in the Union's international relations. As a party to the UNESCO Convention on the Protection and the Promotion of the Diversity of Cultural Expressions[6], the EU is committed to developing a new and more active cultural role for Europe in international relations and to integrating the cultural dimension as a vital element in Europe's dealings with partner countries and regions.

In spite of the growing importance of cultural policy in the EU, culture and related fields remain in national competence, as EU institutions can take only encouraging measures on the level of the Community, with no effect on the harmonization of the laws and regulations of the Member States. By excluding any harmonization, cultural policy of the EU—similar to educational policy—is limited to launching community programmes and initiatives. Member States preserve their independence in this field, and the task of the Community is first of all to encourage and promote cooperation of the Member States. Cultural policy of the EU should be implemented in accordance with the principle of subsidiarity.

Cultural Programmes and Actions in the EU

Pilot Programmes

As a result of the Treaty of Maastricht recognizing cultural cooperation as EU action, an initial range of pilot programmes and subsequent sectoral programmes was launched. The background to these had already been prepared when the Commission published the selection criteria and conditions for participation in the Platform Europe, which became the first kaleidoscope programme in support of artistic and cultural events involving at least three Member States. This was reorganized to encourage artistic creation and cooperation, to promote better public access to European heritage and improve artistic and cultural cooperation between professionals. More than 500 cultural projects received Community support, several pilot projects were initiated in the area of translation and the promotion of books, providing support for more than 500 projects or translations.[7]

Kaleidoscope, Ariane, Raphael

These pilot programmes then gave rise to three full cultural programmes, like Kaleidoscope (1996-1999), to encourage artistic and cultural creation and cooperation with a European dimension, Ariane (1997-1999), supporting books and reading, including translation and Raphael (1997-1999), to complement Member States' policies in the area of cultural heritage of European significance.[8]

Culture 2000

With this experience to build on, preparatory actions were undertaken in 1999 to bring Culture 2000 into play. This was an EU programme established for seven years (2000-2006). It differed from earlier financial instruments in that it provided grants to cultural cooperation projects in all artistic and cultural fields. The objective of Culture 2000 was to promote cultural diversity and a shared cultural heritage. The programme had three actions to support artistic and cultural projects with a European dimension. Activities supported included festivals, master classes, exhibitions, new productions, tours, translations and conferences.[9]

Culture 2007-2013

The EU's new Culture Programme (2007-2013) has a budget of •400 million for projects and initiatives to celebrate Europe's cultural diversity and enhance shared cultural heritage through the development of cross-border cooperation between cultural operators and institutions. The Culture Programme aims to achieve three main objectives: to promote cross-border mobility of those working in the cultural sector; to encourage the transnational circulation of cultural and artistic output; and to foster intercultural dialogue. For the achievement of these objectives, the Programme supports three strands of activities: cultural actions; European-level cultural bodies; and analysis and dissemination activities.

Cultural actions strand enables a wide range of cultural organizations coming from various countries to cooperate on cultural and artistic projects. This strand supports multi-annual cooperation projects, running over a period of three to five years, cooperation measures, running over a maximum period of two years and special measures, which relate to high-profile actions of considerable scale and scope.[10]

Media

Media is a programme of the European Union to strengthen the competitiveness of the European film, TV and new media industries and to increase international circulation of European audiovisual works. The aim is to enhance the level of competence, strengthen the pre-production phase, stimulate the marketing and distribution of European films, television programmes and multimedia productions, and to build up new networks and industrial infrastructures. The Media 2007 started on 1 January 2007 with a seven year programme lasting until 31 December 2013. With a budget of •755 million, Media 2007 supports professional training: screenwriting, management and new technologies, production companies in project development for single projects and slate funding, access to finance and TV-distribution. It also supports cinema distribution, promotion of European audiovisual works, festivals and new technologies.[11]

Besides cultural support, the EU realizes several symbolical initiatives that transcend individual initiatives. We briefly review the most important ones.

European Capital of Culture

The first European Capital of Culture was Athens, in 1985. Since then, the event has been a highly popular and successful annual feature. The event is so attractive that Europe's cities vie with each other fiercely for the honour of bearing the title. In 2010, Pécs, a town in Hungary, was selected (together with Essen and Istanbul) for the title of the European Capital of Culture.[12]

Cultural Prizes

The Culture Programme supports the awarding of prizes in cultural heritage, architecture, literature and music. The objective of these EU prizes is to highlight the excellent quality and success of European activities in these sectors. The prizes put the spotlight on artists, music groups, architects, authors and those working in the field of cultural heritage and on their work. In doing so they showcase Europe's rich cultural diversity and the importance of intercultural dialogue and cross-border cultural activities in Europe and beyond.[13]

Thematic European Years, European Month of Culture, Europe Day

The EU selects every year a leading theme for its cultural activities. One of the most successful among these labelled years was the European Year of Intercultural Dialogue in 2008. The project helped to raise the awareness of all those living in the EU, especially young people, of the importance of engaging in intercultural dialogue in their daily lives and of becoming active European citizens. With a budget of •10 million, the European Year of Intercultural Dialogue aided this process of communication between cultures and subcultures. It fostered dialogue in education, training, and in the workplace but also in leisure, cultural, sports centres and civil society organizations.[14]

By a resolution adopted in 1990, the Culture Ministers meeting at the Council of the European Union set up a new cultural event, the European Month of Culture, taking place each year in a city "of a European country based on democracy, pluralism and State law principles". Actually, this event was for the benefit of countries of Central-East Europe after the changes had taken place in their political and economic systems. Countries were selected by the ministers. Hungary organized the European Month of Culture in 1994.[15]

Europe Day is celebrated on 9 May, remembering that Robert Schuman presented his proposal known as the "Schuman Declaration" on this day in 1950. This proposal on the creation of an organized Europe, indispensable to the maintenance of peaceful relations is considered to be the beginning of the creation of what is now the European Union. Today, 9 May has become a European symbol, the Europe Day, which, along with the flag, the anthem, the motto and the single currency (the Euro), identifies the political entity of the European Union. Europe Day is the occasion for activities and festivities that bring Europe closer to its citizens and peoples of the Union closer to one another.[16]

The European Union Youth Orchestra and the European Union Baroque Orchestra

The European Union Youth Orchestra (EUYO) and the European Union Baroque Orchestra (EUBO) were created with a view to represent the European ideal of a community working together to achieve peace and social understanding. The aim of these orchestras is also to give pre-professional orchestral experience and training to Europe's most talented young musicians, acting as a bridge between their post-graduate studies and entry into the professional music world.

The EUYO is a training orchestra for young people in the European Union. It was founded in 1978 and is funded centrally by the European Union and by a number of EU Member States. It brings together young and talented musicians from the EU and internationally proclaimed professors to form an internationally renowned orchestra.[17] The EUBO was originally conceived as a one-year project to celebrate European Music Year in 1985. Such was the success of the original project that the Orchestra's work has been continued permanently on the initiative of the European Parliament. The EUBO is an official training programme of the European Union, and is granted annual funding by the European Parliament.[18]

Culture in the External Relations of the European Union

The European Community, alongside the EU Member States, is committed to making cultural diversity an essential element of its external action and to developing a new and more active cultural role for Europe in international relations. Article 151 of the Treaty, in accordance with the Convention, requires the EC and its Member States to promote cultural aspects in its international relations with partner countries and regions within the EU enlargement, as well as in the context of development and trade policies, as a contribution to a world order based on sustainable development, peaceful coexistence and dialogue between cultures.

After the adoption of the European Agenda for Culture—

providing strategic guidelines for EU policy development also in external relations—a number of positive developments have taken place in the external dimension. In the first half of 2008, the Slovenian Presidency made the external dimension of culture a priority. On 13-14 May 2008, a conference "New Paradigms, New Models—Culture in the EU External Relations" was organized in Ljubljana[19], also involving civil society participants. The event provided a good opportunity for foreign policy makers to exchange views with the cultural sector and deepen their understanding of the potential of cultural cooperation with regard to external relations objectives. The Presidency issued a Declaration[20] containing the main messages emerged from the Conference, which was politically followed-up both in the Culture and General Affairs and External Relations Councils. The European Council of June 2008[21] also confirmed the importance of culture in the EU's external relations. The French Presidency—in order to follow up these positive developments—had submitted draft Council Conclusions on the promotion of cultural diversity and intercultural dialogue[22] in the external relations of the Union and its Member States to the Cultural Affairs Committee, which were adopted by the Education, Youth and Culture Council on 20-21 November 2008.[23]

India-EU Cultural Cooperation

The European Union finds it important to focus on the presence of cultural provisions in international agreements, e.g. in Partnership and Cooperation Agreements (PCAs), Free Trade Agreements (FTAs) and long-term strategic programming tools (e.g. Country Strategic Papers or Action Plans). It also finds it necessary to establish sustainable policy dialogues on culture with emerging partners of the EU (e.g. on the legal and regulatory environment for the emergence of creative industries in those countries).[24]

The EU maintains an ever closer relationship with emerging global partners like India. India-EU cooperation is usually dominated by political, economic and trade dialogues. However, besides these, there is a strong supporting cultural interrelationship encompassing many sectors and levels of both societies. The strategic bilateral partnership involves a growing number of cultural aspects, too.

A constant flow of cultural exchanges are carried out in different forms and on different levels, organized by the EC Delegation and Member States' embassies in New Delhi: European Union cultural weeks; film festivals; seminars and informative visits for Indian journalists to the EU; and academic programmes, such as the Erasmus Mundus scholarship programme, which enables Indian scholars to study in EU universities and centres of excellence.[25]

It was also encouraged to use the existing cooperation mechanisms for the benefit of culture, via e.g. the setting up of the Indian Culture for Development Fund, which would support cultural projects.

Some Major EU-India Projects in Education, Science and Culture

Erasmus Mundus

On 22 March 2005 the European Commission and the Indian Government signed an agreement in the frame of which the EC provided •33 million to finance approximately 1,000 scholarships for Indian graduate students to study at Europe's best universities. This agreement is part of the EC's flagship Erasmus Mundus programme which supports top-quality European Masters Degrees and provides scholarships for the best graduate students from third countries to follow these. A •33 million budget was allocated for the Erasmus Mundus India Window programme to provide new opportunities, thus enabling more than one thousand Indian graduates to study in Europe between 2004 and 2007.[26]

Both sides are undertaking promotional actions to raise further awareness about this programme. In order to further stimulate research on contemporary Indian issues in the EU, the European Commission has supported the establishment of an Academic Network of European Research related to India (ANERI).[27]

India-EU Study Centres

The India-EU Study Centres Programme (IESCP) was launched with the objective of promoting a better understanding between the EU and India through stronger higher education inter-institutional links and an increased academic cooperation. It was also the aim of the programme to provide support to existing, and for the creation of new study centres. The programme provides technical assistance and grants for joint research on topics of common interest and for curricula development on contemporary political, economic and social studies on India and Europe.

The main beneficiaries of the India-EU Study Centres Programme are, on the one hand, Indian higher education institutions and their relevant departments dealing with EU studies and interested in establishing or develop European Study Centres. On the other, European Higher Education Institutions and their relevant departments dealing with Indian Contemporary Studies and interested in establishing or develop Indian Contemporary Study Centres are also involved in the programme.[28]

EU-India Joint Declaration on Education

During his visit to India in November 2008, Ján Figel, Member of the European Commission responsible for Education, Training, Culture and Youth signed a Joint Declaration on Education[29] with the Minister for Human Resource Development Arjun Singh. This agreement established, for the first time, a wide-ranging dialogue on education and training between the EU and India. The Declaration will be implemented from 2009 based on a rolling work plan. Among the subjects included in this dialogue are the reform agenda for higher education in response to changes in the nature of work and society, the challenge of establishing quality assurance mechanisms in educational programmes, vocational education and training, ways of addressing the objectives of equity and inclusiveness in education, teacher training and lifelong learning mechanisms, including the creative use of information technology for teaching.[30]

Higher Education Fairs

The first European Higher Education Fair (EHEF) in India, was held at New Delhi from 25-26 November 2006 as a follow-up of the India-EU Joint Action Plan (JAP) where higher education cooperation and academic exchanges have been identified as a priority of mutual interest. The EHEF was organized under the theme "Innovation and Culture" and aimed to contribute to bringing peoples and cultures together through the promotion of the EU as a study and research destination. At the same time, it also intended to introduce the EU policies and programmes in higher education and research. Indian graduate students wishing to pursue higher education opportunities abroad had the opportunity to meet representatives of more than 100 recognized European Higher Education Institutions from more than 25 European countries who had come to New Delhi to participate in the Fair. The event was a big success with a turnout of more than 4,000 students at the Fair.[31]

The second European Higher Educational Fair was held in New Delhi on 13-14 November 2008 and was inaugurated by Commissioner Ján Figel. There were 69 universities from 26 EU Member States, and 21 national higher education bodies participating at this Fair. In the course of the Fair students were provided information on EU education systems, universities and courses. A major success was the question and answer sessions between 17 Ambassadors of the EU countries represented in India and the visitors to the Fair. During its two days the event drew over 6,000 visitors.[32]

Asia-Link Symposium

On 24 November 2006, an Asia-Link Symposium focusing on the theme "Academic cooperation and student mobility between India and Europe" was held. This event was a platform for high-level dialogue between government officials, key senior managers and policy-makers from India and Europe and representatives from higher education institutions and academic networks. The main idea of the Symposium was to exchange knowledge on different cooperation and mobility programmes, as well as to deepen understanding in India about Bologna reform processes in Europe. The discussions centred on sharing experiences on the relevance of the Bologna Process to India, on strengthening the India-EU academic and institutional collaboration including Joint Study Programmes. The Symposium also intended to develop awareness of EU mechanisms and programmes. A matchmaking activity provided representatives from European and Indian higher education institutions with the possibility to discuss future cooperation projects.[33]

India-EU Higher Education Symposium

The India-EU Higher Education Cooperation Symposium organized by the European Commission under the new EU-Asia Higher Education Platform, was held in New Delhi on 12 November, 2008. Commissioner Ján Figel, addressing the audience of policy-makers, officials, academicians, and members of the business community, participating at the symposium noted the great success of the academic and cultural institutes of the European Union Member States in India and observed that "relatively new initiatives at the European level comprising university collaboration projects under the Asia Link programme and student and researcher mobility under the External Cooperation Window of the Erasmus Mundus programme had also been a resounding success. Indian students obtained 1,103 out of 6,181 scholarships to study in Europe, and its researchers numbered 90 out of the total of 1,125 so far."[34]

Science and Technology

The EU, at its Heads of Government meeting in Lisbon in the year 2000, set out as one of its key strategic goals for Europe to become the most advanced knowledge-based economy in the world by the year 2010. The Common Minimum Programme of the Government of India also sees advances in research and development as a means of achieving its societal goals of poverty alleviation and rural development and in becoming an advanced knowledge economy. While India has had fairly long-standing Science and Technology (S&T) cooperation with a number of EU Member States including Hungary, S&T cooperation between India and the EU as a whole, is relatively new. It began with the signature of a S&T Cooperation Agreement in 2001.[35]

Several EU-India workshops have been organized since the signing of the Agreement. Themes discussed during these workshops include IT, climate change and natural disasters; road transport, nanotechnology and functional materials, genomics and biotechnology for health and computational materials science. Further workshops are planned in the domains of genetics, genomics of diseases linked to development, infectious diseases with focus on TB, HIV and malaria, information security and language computing.

Following the fourth Meeting of the EU-India Scientific and Technology Cooperation Agreement Steering Committee on 8 November 2007, the EU and India took a few significant steps forward by renewing their S&T Cooperation Agreement on 30 November 2007.[36]

India is an important partner for Europe in its Research Framework Programme (FP). There are more than 100 Indian research institutions have participated in over 80 research projects funded in FP6 (2002-06). These projects received more than 250 million in funding, the share of the Indian partners being more than 11 million. Indian organizations have also been active in FP7, which started on 1 January 2007, with more than 400 research institutions involved in proposals submitted in response to the first set of Calls for Proposals. Based on submitted proposals, India was the fourth largest international partner of the EU, after Russia, China and the USA.[37]

Protection of Historical Monuments

On 17 March 2005, the project Protection of Historical Monuments organized a state-of-the-art conference at the Indian Institute of Technology, Delhi that included the presentation of a series of technical papers addressing restoration issues specific to heritage. In collaboration with the Archaeological Survey of India (ASI), Humayun's Tomb was identified as the monument where measurements will be carried out to investigate climatic effects and possible solutions. The project is carried out by the Technical University of Dresden, IIT Delhi, the Indian Council of Architecture, the Catholic University of Leuven and the Malaviya National Institute of Technology in Jaipur.[38]

Cross-Cultural Programme

Under the EU-India Economic Cross-Cultural Programme (ECCP) the "Europe-India Maritime History Project" was initiated and co-financed by the European Commission. The aim of the project was an appreciation of the historical relationship between the two continents, and its impact on our daily lives, leading to a greater support for increased economic and cultural ties. It was also the goal of the project to document, profile and promote interest in the history of maritime contacts and exchanges between Europe and India, and evaluate their impact on varied fields such as ecology, cartography, optics and navigation, architecture and urban planning, medicine, art, economy, religion, cuisine, clothing, warfare and political history, highlighting the necessities, which gave rise to the maritime contacts, the forces which shaped them, and the vast—although often unknown—linkages that have ensued from them.

During the course of the "Maritime History Project", a series of video documentaries were produced that summarised these relations. The five films produced depicted contacts between the European and Indian continents from the Roman to the British Empire. The project resulted from a research partnership between universities, museums, cultural foundations and archive centres. The purpose was to evaluate the economic, cultural and political impact of these exchanges in areas such as cartography, urban planning, medicine, religion and warfare.

Another interesting film-series that was produced by the project was "Built Environment and Sustainable Habitat

Architecture Partnership". This project pooled and mobilized capacities and know-how in the academic, professional and entrepreneurial sectors in the field of sustainable built environment. Partnerships between small and medium enterprises, a resource centre, a network for universities and associations and a media and communication unit producing short films and pedagogic material have been set up within the framework of the project.[39]

Multiculturalism

From 25 to 27 March 2005, a Symposium and Film Festival was organized in Mumbai on multiculturalism by the project "IMPORT/EXPORT". The project addressed the concerns of multiculturalism in contemporary academic discourse and representations in various art forms. The central themes of Import/Export addressed interactions were:

Moving People: dealing with individual, incidental uncontrollable ways of cultural transfer, which can also be called Migration and Travelling;

Moving Concepts: examining the circulation of ideas of Modernity and anti-modernity, health issues and multiculturalism (among others) between India and the German-speaking Europe;

Moving Goods: involving the research of strategic forms of export of material culture.[40]

Multilingualism

On 11 and 12 December 2008, a conference on "Multilingualism and Intercultural Dialogue in Globalization" was held at the University of Delhi. The conference was organized by the European Commission in collaboration with the French Embassy, the National Knowledge Commission, the European Union National Institutes for Culture (EUNIC) India Cluster and the University of Delhi. Over 130 academic participants gathered to debate the question of multilingualism and its implications in the fields of business, politics, identity, intercultural dialogue and education.

2008 being the European Year of Intercultural Dialogue, the

aim of the conference was to further "exchanges of best practices and expertise, the review of policy developments and challenges and the promotion of knowledge building and sharing in relation to common identified issues". These goals have been identified as the main topics for the dialogue on the EU-India Joint Declaration on Multilingualism that was signed later in Brussels on 6 March 2009.[41]

The seminars analysed the issue of language and multilingualism from all possible angles—ranging from policy to action, from poetry to economics—and compared and confronted European and Indian perspectives and views.[42]

Cultural Activities of the EU in India

Cultural initiatives have been organized, such as the *EU Cultural Weeks* in India (in September 2005), the 11th European Film Festival in India (in March-April 2006), as well as the India Festival in Brussels (from October 2006 to January 2007), organized by 'Bozar' in association with ICCR.[43]

As a part of the EU-India strategic partnership established at the sixth EU-India Summit in September 2005, the European Commission organized the 12th European Union Film Festival in India from 27 April to 24 May 2007. Intending to be an annual event from this year onwards, the Festival screened over 20 widely acclaimed films during these four weeks in New Delhi, Pune, Kozhikode and Kolkata.[44]

Exhibitions, music and dance performances and cinema screenings as EU Member States staged the third EU Cultural Weeks in Delhi in November, 2007 in the run-up to the eighth EU-India Summit. To mark the start of the events, eight different exhibitions were opened at the Mati Ghar gallery at the Indira Gandhi National Centre for the Arts (IGNCA) on 21 November 2007. In all, there were 35 different events including 12 exhibitions, 10 musical events, 11 film screenings and two talks organized as a part of the Cultural Weeks. Almost all the Member States of the EU present in India participated in the Cultural Weeks.

Cooperation in the area of culture was also on the agenda of Commissioner Ján Figel, during his visit to India in

November 2008. Following the successful conclusion of the European Cross Cultural Cooperation Programme with India, which featured over 60 projects on inter-cultural understanding for representatives of academic institutions, the media and business, there will shortly be a new cooperation initiative called "Building Culture Heritage Capacities". This will contribute to the Indian government's own evolving plans to manage the country's rich cultural assets to improve capacities in the sustainable management and marketing of heritage sites.[45]

Conclusions

Nowadays culture has become an important factor of the European integration, too. Culture is playing an increasing role in the life of the European Union and developing a cultural policy and a cultural strategy for the EU has become of vital importance. The growing importance of culture within the EU and in its relations with third countries is coinciding with the general international trends of the expanding role of culture in international relations all over the world. The EU has realized that the fulfilment of this task that was neglected for such a long time cannot be delayed any longer.

With the advancement of integration, and especially with the enlargement of the EU, the accession of the Central-East European countries, a greater demand appeared for strengthening a common European identity, for which culture —the awareness of a common European culture—would play a decisive role. This would demand further integration in the field of culture and further harmonization of cultural policies as well. However, culture is a very sensitive field where the Member States vehemently oppose any integration and protect their cultural identities. This tendency, as a counter-effect of globalization can also be observed in the broader international scene. Strengthening of local identities and cultural fragmentation tendencies are developing parallel with globalizing trends. In the European Union we can also observe these to two simultaneous and contrasting trends.

For the time being, in spite of the growing importance of

cultural policy, in the field of culture the EU sticks to the principle of subsidiarity, and culture and related fields remain in national competency. Time will show how long and how far Member States will preserve their independence in this field.

Strengthening of a common European cultural identity on the one hand and insisting on national identities and sustaining the differences on the other are only apparent contradictions. Paradoxically, preserving Europe's cultural diversity also means the strengthening of the common European identity at the same time. A new common cultural identity should not any way influence or diminish national cultural identities. Defining national cultural identity remains of great importance, because this could form the base for elaborating the common identity. It is true, that differences of local cultures can lead to conflicts, but it is also true that differences can lead to a useful competition. Different cultures can mutually influence and enrich each other. Diversity is of great importance, as it should be considered as the most important characteristic feature of a common European identity.

NOTES

1. *The Lisbon Treaty Article 151*, [Online: web] (accessed 19 April 2009), URL: http://www.lisbon-treaty.org/wcm/the-lisbon-treaty/treaty-on-the-functioning-of-the-european-union-and-comments/part-3-union-policies-and-internal-actions/title-xii-culture/455-article-151.html.
2. *The European Agenda for Culture*, [Online: web] (accessed 5 October 2008), URL: http://ec.europa.eu/culture/our-policy-development/doc399_en.htm.
3. *Communication from the Commission to the European Parliament, the Council, the European Economic and Social Committee and the Committee of the Regions on a European Agenda for Culture in a Globalizing World*, {SEC(2007) 570} /* COM/2007/0242 final */, [Online: web] (accessed 19 April 2009), URL: http://eur-lex.europa.eu/LexUriServ/LexUriServ.do?uri= COM:2007:0242:FIN:EN:HTML.
4. *Resolution of the Council of 16 November 2007 on a European Agenda for Culture*, Official Journal C 287 , 29/11/2007 P. 0001 – 0004,

[Online: web] (accessed 19 April 2009), URL: http://eur-lex.europa.eu/LexUriServ/LexUriServ.do?uri=OJ:C:2007:287:0001:01:EN:HTML.

5. *Brussels European Council, 14 December 2007, Presidency Conclusions*, Council of the European Union, Brussels, 14 February 2008, 16616//1/07, REV 1, CONCL 3, [Online: web] Accessed 19.04.2009, URL: http://www.consilium.europa.eu/ueDocs/cms_Data/docs/pressData/en/ec/97669.pdf
6. UNESCO (2005), *Convention on the Protection and Promotion of the Diversity of Cultural Expressions* 2005, Paris, 20 October 2005, [Online: web] (accessed 5 October 2008), URL: http://portal.unesco.org/en/ev.php-URL_ID=31038&URL_DO=DO_TOPIC&URL_SECTION=201.html
7. *Former Programmes and Actions.* European Commission – Culture, [Online: web] (accessed 15 May 2009), URL: http://ec.europa.eu/culture/our-programmes-and-actions/doc419_en.htm
8. Ibid.
9. Ibid.
10. *Culture Programme: A Serious Cultural Investment.* European Commission – Culture, [Online: web] (accessed 15 May 2009), URL: http://ec.europa.eu/culture/our-programmes-and-actions/doc411_en.htm
11. *Overview: Media 2007*, [Online: web] Accessed 15 May 2009, URL: http://ec.europa.eu/information_society/media/overview/2007/index_en.htm
12. *European Capital of Culture.* European Commission – Culture, [Online: web] (accessed 15 May 2009), URL: http://ec.europa.eu/culture/our-programmes-and-actions/doc413_en.htm
13. *The Prizes.* European Commission – Culture, [Online: web] (accessed 15 May 2009), URL: http://ec.europa.eu/culture/our-programmes-and-actions/doc511_en.htm
14. *European Year of Intercultural Dialogue: Overview.* European Commission – Culture, [Online: web] Accessed 15 May 2009, URL: http://ec.europa.eu/culture/our-programmes-and-actions/doc415_en.htm
15. *History.* European Commission – Culture, [Online: web] (accessed 15 May 2009), URL: http://ec.europa.eu/culture/our-programmes-and-actions/doc443_en.htm
16. *Europe Day, 9 May*, [Online: web] (accessed 15 May 2009), URL: http://europa.eu/abc/symbols/9-may/index_en.htm

17. *European Union Youth Orchestra,* [Online: web] (accessed 16 April 2009), URL: http://www.euyo.org.uk/index.htm
18. *European Union Baroque Orchestra,* [Online: web] (accessed 16 April 2009), URL: http://www.eubo.org.uk/
19. *New Paradigms, New Models – Culture in the EU External Relations,* Ljubljana, 13-14 May, 2008, [Online: web] (accessed 6 October 2008), URL: http://www.mzz.gov.si/si/zunanja_politika/kulturno_sodelovanje/nove_paradigme_novi_modeli_kultura_v_zunanjih_odnosih_eu/
20. Slovenian Presidency Declaration based on the recommendations of the conference "New Paradigms, New Models – Culture in the EU External Relations" (Ljubljana, 13–14 May 2008).
21. *Brussels European Council 19/20 June 2008, Presidency Conclusions,* 20/06/2008 Nr. 11018/1/08 REV 1, [Online: web] (accessed 6 October 2008), URL: http://www.consilium.europa.eu/uedocs/cms_data/docs/pressdata/en/ec/101346.pdf
22. *Council of the European Union. Council Conclusions on the Promotion of Cultural Diversity and Intercultural Dialogue in the External Relations of the Union and its Member States.* 2905th Education, Youth and Culture Council Meeting, Brussels 20 November 2008, [Online: web] (accessed 16 April 2009), URL: http://ec.europa.eu/culture/our-policy-development/doc/ICD_external_ relations_en.doc.pdf
23. *Culture in External Relations,* [Online: web] (accessed 16 April 2009), URL: http://ec.europa.eu/culture/our-policy-development/doc1567_en.htm
24. *Strategic Bilateral Partnership,* [Online: web] (accessed 16 April 2009), URL: http://ec.europa.eu/culture/our-policy-development/doc1747_en.htm
25. "A dialogue between two old yet modern, dynamic countries", in *The European Union and India: A Strategic Partnership for the 21st Century,* New Delhi: Delegation of the European Commission in India, 2005, p. 2.
26. *EU-India Summit in Marseille: Strategic Partnership to Tackle the Major Global Challenges,* Press Release, Brussels, 26 September 2008, [Online: web] (accessed 17 April 2009), URL: http://europa.eu/rapid/pressReleasesAction.do?reference=IP/08/1413&guiLanguage=de
27. *EU-India Update* (New Delhi: Newsletter of the Delegation of the European Commission in India), 6(5), September-October

2006, p. 5.

28. Ibid., 8(3), May-June 2008, p. 11.
29. *Joint Declaration of Mr. Ján Figel' Commissioner for Education, Training, Culture and Youth, European Commission and Shri Arjun Singh, Minister for Human Resource Development, Government of India on Education*, New Delhi, 12 November 2008, [Online: web] (accessed 16 March 2009), URL: http://ec.europa.eu/education/external-relation-programmes/doc/jdindia_en.pdf
30. *EU-India Update*, 8(6), November-December 2008, pp. 8-9.
31. Ibid., 6(6), November-December 2006, pp. 8-9.
32. Ibid., 8(6), November-December 2008, p. 10.
33. Ibid., 6(6), November-December 2006, pp. 8-9.
34. Ibid., 8(6), November-December 2008, pp. 9-10.
35. *European Union and India to Cooperate on Science and Technology*. Press Release, Brussels, 23 November 2001, [Online: web] (accessed 16 March 2009), URL: http://ec.europa.eu/research/press/2001/pr2311en.html
36. *Agreement Renewing the Agreement for Scientific and Technological Cooperation Between the European Community and the Government of the Republic of India*, New Delhi, 30 November 2007, [Online: web] (accessed 15 April 2009), URL: http://www.delind.ec.europa.eu/pdfs/EU-India-Science-and-Technology-Agreement-EN.pdf
37. *EU-India Update*. 7(6), November-December 2007, p. 5.
38. Ibid., 5(2), March-April 2007, p. 11.
39. Ibid., 7(4), July-August 2007, pp. 10-11.
40. Ibid., 5(2), March-April 2005, p. 11.
41. *Joint Declaration by Mr. Leonard Orban, Commissioner for Multilingualism, European Commission and Smt. Daggubati Purandeswari, Minister of State for Human Resource Development (Higher Education) Government of India*, 6 March, 2009, [Online: web] (accessed 15 April 2009), URL: http://ec.europa.eu/commission_barroso/orban/docs/CAB27_0402123101_001.pdf
42. *EU-India Update*, 8(6), November-December 2008, p. 10.
43. Ibid., 6(5), September-October, 2006, p. 5.
44. Ibid., 7(2), March-April, 2007, p. 12.
45. Ibid., 7(4), July-August, 2007, p. 10.

10

Can Multiculturalism Promote Gender Equality?

Anuradha M. Chenoy

Confronted by an ideology of 'cultural nationalism', i.e. constructing a homogeneous cultural paradigm on the basis of a Hindu majoritarianism, multiculturalism appears as an alternative that can provide the spaces for the co-existence of multiple groups that make up Indian society. This is because multiculturalism claims that even in liberal democracies, minority cultures are not sufficiently protected since minority group rights that differ from that of the majority group are not ensured. This is because individual rights guaranteed by liberalism are 'difference-blind' and can erode minority groups' cultural rights. Thus minorities should be protected by being given special group rights and privileges, since distinctiveness must be affirmed and sustained by the political order.[1] Most cultures have practices that endorse the control of men over women and norms of inequality and rights subsume such controls and gender hierarchies. Such group rights simultaneously involve practices that are considered oppressive for women like the right of polygamy; the right to wear the hijab for young girls at school, personal laws that are unequal for men and women. At the same time, these practices are part of the cultural identity of these groups. Before we accept the multicultural alternative, we first examine why feminists and democrats reject cultural essentialism that in our country comes in the form of cultural nationalism and its implications for women. And then construct the kind of model of multiculturalism that would allow a feminist culture.

The Feminist Argument on Culture

The core feminist argument is that women should not be disadvantaged because of their sex and should have opportunities and options that are equal to men. Most cultures in history have denied this equality to women and women's value has historically been lower than that of men. The reason for this devaluation is centred on women's role as reproducers and primarily responsible for upbringing of children. Stemming from this is women's confinement to the private and domestic sphere, where culture and norms dominate and often remain outside the domain of public law. Women's reproductive and sexual role has been the cause of a collective male anxiety that led to the control of women's autonomy and became part of patriarchal ideology common to all traditional ideological frameworks like religion and culture. Since patriarchal ideology has been presented and accepted as universal and natural and one that provides the basis for family, kinship, community, nation and state, it remains an integral part of culture long after laws attempt to change gender power relations.

At the same time, feminists like other democrats are faced with the problem of identity as 'embedded in culture' and how cultural norms and symbols that oppress women are accepted by women and men as part of their identity, especially when identity is threatened, is in question or at times of conflict. This is especially so in the case of India, where community ties prevail over individual rights and debate about community rights initiated in the constituent assembly and guaranteed by the Constitution remain unresolved. It was the issue of community versus individual rights that rocked this country in the Shah Bano case in which the court's award of a small alimony was rejected by representatives of the Muslim community since it was seen as threatening community rights. In such circumstances should group rights or individual rights prevail?

Hindu women are also embedded in cultural practices that curb their autonomy and devalue their roles. This valuation is based on traditional Hindu practice where women are both empowered and subjugated. They are empowered when they are identified with the nation/community as mothers, reproducers and signifiers of culture; upper caste women can be empowered when sanctioned by upper caste men; women can gain empowerment when they are needed for caste and national duties. Women are simultaneously subjugated even if they can 'perform rituals' because there are complex sanctions against women. Even with empowerment, women are lower in the hierarchy as compared to men and their reproductive role privileged over any other identity. Women's identity and empowerment is outlined in traditional texts, to quote one: "In childhood a female must be subject to her father, in her youth to her husband, when her lord is dead to her sons; a woman is never independent." (Manu V.148) Thus, her empowerment is sanctioned and dependent on men under Hindu tradition since she guarantees the purity of the race.

As upholders of culture, women are to wear cultural symbols on their bodies, for example *bindi* and toe rings (that are removed when widowed, since the widow has a lower status) and don the traditional dress for example the *chunni*. Those who do not do so are seen to be violating culture and 'honour' unlike men who have the option and freedom to choose whether they wish to display cultural symbols or not. Since women are seen as the 'honour' of the community and the nation, norms to control her are imposed by society through various ways ranging from social stigmatization; isolation, even rape and killing. That is why even newspapers report the killing of women if they marry outside their caste. Every once in a while a community panchayat orders that a couple that violated community codes, be paraded naked, lynched or dishonoured in a variety of ways. Is it surprising then, that while raping a Swedish diplomat in central Delhi (October 2002) the rapist is stated to have said to her, that she was not 'dressed properly'. In other words she invited rape. Such words have come from different levels of society including the judiciary that have evicted rapists because the victim might have invited attention because of her manner of dress or behaviour did not conform to accepted codes.

As transmitters of culture, women in Hinduism are to accept this subjugation and transmit it to their children, especially daughters. For example, women fast for their husbands/sons on *Karva Chauth*, but do not do so for their daughters.[2] This example of valourizing the male leads not only to pejorative gender stereo-typing but to the devaluation of women and their sexual roles are stereotyped and confined to the private sphere. The devaluation of women lead to the widespread practices of gender-based discrimination from female foeticide to favouring boys and violence against women.

This cultural burden on women is a result of the long patriarchal militarist cultures that have dominated our society and have been presented as a universal culture that is part of one's identity and tradition. Concepts such as the secondary role of women are presented as universal truths that harm the community and the nation if they are challenged. Thus besieged communities are especially harsh on individual rights and women give up their demands for individual rights at such times.

Cultural Norms and Public Institutions

Cultural norms for women in India, like the necessity of 'purity' of women; the focus on virginity; the confinement to the private sphere, signified by the chunni, etc, gets translated into institutional pratice and laws. Rape, marriage and laws governing inheritance thus remain unequal and biased in favour of men. To give an instance. In case of rape, the woman victim has to prove that she did not consent (Article 375 of the Indian Penal Code). This has meant that most rape victims have not only not got justice, but they have been implicated as inviting sexual abuse. That is why so many rape cases go unreported.

Why We Reject Cultural Nationalism?

The danger of cultural nationalism appears self-evident, yet large sections of our middle class are prone to accept it. Cultural nationalism is based on the idea of an Indian nation identified primarily with the majority Hindu religious community. The Hindu nationalist organization (the RSS) and their political affiliates like the BJP use selective aspects of the multiple traditions of Hinduism to allow religion and culture to collapse as the core aspect of a Hindu identity and nation. The Sangh wants to carry out this homogenization by using the cultural front by 'liberating our brethren' from their cultural enslavement.

The Hindu cultural nationalists of the Sangh Parivar identify the Indian Muslims and the Christians as the 'other' linked to a 'foreign religion' and characterized with foreign cultures that are alien to the majority Hindu culture and thus incapable of patriotism and nationalism.[3] By doing this they consider all other religious groups as 'outsiders' or foreigners that came into India to 'rob and plunder'.[4] They argue that forcible conversions were carried out as 'they' settled here, but 'they' remained loyal to foreign religions and thus nations. The Sangh especially targets the Indian Muslims because of the long standing dispute with Pakistan that is identified as India's main 'enemy' in public consciousness. The Sangh is engaged in a constant vilification campaign of Muslims as responsible for the past excesses of Mughal feudal rulers who are seen as destroyers of Hindu temples, who violated Hindu women in order to violate Hindu culture.

The mobilization of communities along the lines of homogenized cultures in opposition and contradiction to each other has led to communal genocide of the minority community, like we witnessed in Gujarat where besides the 2,000 killed and thousands of properties of the minority community destroyed, women were special targets of gendered violence. The violence against women was an attempt to humiliate and dishonour the entire minority community since women signify the 'honour' or *izzat* of the community as a whole. Thus, cultural essentialism as evident in cultural nationalism severely impacts women.

Cultural essentialism not only targets the 'other' but

homogenizes the 'majority' community itself. For example, the Sangh believes that it can homogenize a Hindu nationalist culture in various ways that include clubbing distinct but indigenous religions like Jainism, Budhism and Sikhism as mere offshoots of Hinduism; propagating the difference of other religions as alien and evil; proselytizing tribals through Hindu ceremonies and 'converting' them into Hinduism; constructing the idea of a Hindu 'race and original culture.' The Sangh keeps such tensions rife, especially as an electoral strategy to mobilize and 'unify' the caste and class divided Hindu community, which they believe can become cohesive only when confronted by an enemy nation with internal linkages. In constructing a homogenized enemy other, the Sangh Parivar attempts to homogenize the divided and highly plural Hindu traditions, swallowing or marginalizing the minor and multiple traditions into a false version called Hindutava that never existed at any time in history at all.

Underlying these tasks is the message of a re-assertion of Hindu manhood, that is articulated in different ways in Sangh literature, speeches and practices. For instance, RSS writers argue that the dormant Hindu man needs to be awakened: "The lion of a man who has been caged for centuries has become oblivious of his own manhood."[5] The concept of a pure manhood is contrasted with 'womanhood' that valorizes virginity, purity, subservience and other patriarchal norms meant strictly for women.

The gender policies and implications of the Hindutava construction are evident. Since selected aspects of traditional Hinduism are integrated with modernized and political needs, the Sangh ideology actively re-enforces patriarchal Hindu practices. For instance, according to the Sangh Parivar, Hindu women were 'pure' but 'evil practices' came into Hinduism when the 'foreign invaders' came to India. With this Hindu women were forced to go into 'purdah' (veil), etc. It is in this context that the Sangh Parivar constantly warns against 'Muslim virility' against Hindu cowardice.

Cultural codes and gender stereotypes are sharpened during periods of conflict or nationalism. For instance, the concept of motherland that was popularized by nationalists like Bankim Chandra during India's freedom struggle was adopted by Sangh leaders as a core principle of their ideology. Veer Savarkar wrote a series of poems and essays describing India as 'the super strong Aryan motherland' who is guarded by Hindu God Shanker with his trident. Thus, Savarkar "exhorted young patriots to develop their manliness and keep their fervour at the highest pitch."[6] The mother cult is now repeated in BJP pamphlets and statement of their leader like L.K. Advani who argue that by advancing this mother-cult based nationalism is the only way to 'advance' the Indian nation.[7] The Sangh argues that it 'honours' women and gives them equality. But by homogenizing women and portraying them as the primary carriers of a particular kind of culture that valorizes militarist Hindu nationalism both genders get stereotyped in traditional roles, where men are the protectors and women need to stick to their role as reproducers and nurturers for the family and the nation. She will be honoured for this role. It is no wonder then that the BJP minister M.M. Joshi has ordered that Women's Studies in all Indian Universities that are State supported be re-named 'Women and Family Studies'. The gendered implication of such Hindu nationalism will mean a structural stereotyping of women and gender power relations where women will always be secondary especially if they do not conform to these stereotypes.

Feminist theory, on the other hand, is arguing for a feminization of culture, where women and men are not portrayed unequally by any culture and everyone has the option to accept or opt out of their given community culture. The issue is does multiculturalism guarantee this cultural freedom? Will a policy of multiculturalism provide an alternate framework?

Multiculturalism or Pluralism?

Clearly, political systems and states are multi-ethnic, have distinct religious minorities, are divided by classes, have multiple ideologies and groups that adhere to them, and so on. Does multiculturalism have the strength to accept all these differences while ensuring group rights to minorities? Multiculturalism can have opposing contents, i.e. egalitarian but also hierarchical, liberal but also authoritarian. It can essentialize and harden identities that generate radical exclusions of people, lead to communal expulsions.[8] Multiculturalism by granting group rights can at one level respect difference but it can also homogenize groups to the extent that they can enforce oppressive rules to enforce their difference. Thus, for example, it can insist that women continue to wear cultural and identity symbols, and at the same time give men the option to dress like the 'majority' since their roles are in the public domain.

Further, do we as individuals have only one identity? Can minority or majority ethnic/religious identities be satisfied by group rights? On the contrary, I might choose that my cultural identity is the least of my identities. I might want to assert my gender, my class, or my ideological identity, rather than my ethnic or religious identity. Does multiculturalism give me these rights? Do group rights override individuals? Further culture may be autonomous of identity, i.e. high culture that can be shared internationally.

Feminist analysts like Susan Okin, argue that from a feminist point of view, that the granting of minority rights, are far from the solution.[9] These issues have been debated by political theorists like Charles Taylor, J. Cohen, Dornboos. Here, I believe there is strength in Rajeev Bhargava's argument that the value of the groups are not reducible to its value for individuals and the moral worth of groups needs just as much protection as the moral worth of individuals. This creates conflicts between group values and individual rights. But clearly, certain basic individual rights are more basic than group rights and groups that violate individual rights are morally guilty.[10] Bhargava argues that democratic multiculturalism is a better option than liberal individualism that denies the importance of practices and cultural traditions. Liberal multiculturalism makes large areas of public life immune from political intervention. Democratic multiculturalism tackles tensions between identity and belonging and requirements of individual autonomy and brings both issues into the political domain.[11]

Within this domain, however, since patriarchal remnants survive and assert in all cultures whether in liberal and democratic societies or traditional ones, multiculturalism can only work if it is democratic, allows dissent and pluralism internally and externally, and is engaged with feminist culture that radically alters gender roles. This would be possible if women are supported not discriminated because of their reproductive roles. This involves giving value to domestic labour and equal sharing of family/domestic responsibility. It involves equal rights in the public and private spheres. It means that women (and others) have the option of adopting and adapting to group cultural rights that are part of their identity and yet having the option of opting out of those aspects of culture that restrict their individual rights. If multiculturalism accepts these, it can be a viable and necessary alternative.

NOTES

1. Charles Taylor, "The Politics of Recognition," in David Theo Goldberg, ed., *Multiculturalism: A Critical Reader* (Oxford: Blackwell, 1994), pp. 75-106.
2. The national channel of Doordarshan in 2002-2003 showed this festivity with one of the BJP women ministers leading the fasting women.
3. Besides the ideologues of the Sangh Parivar, almost every issue of their official journal carries articles that repeat this. The argument is: Muslim, but also Christian invaders brought political subjugation and cultural depredation. Those who converted to these religions cut themselves away from Indian culture and "the people one homogeneous nation were divided under sectarian labels." Ramesh Patange, "The Struggle for Akhand Bharat," *Organiser*, 46(2), 1994, Independence Day special, pp. 41-43.
4. The ideas of the RSS were shaped by the writings of Vinayak Damodar Savarkar who argued that everyone who has ancestral roots in India is a Hindu and Hindus collectively make up a nation. This, according to him, was Hindutava. V.D. Savarkar, *Hindutava: Who is a Hindu?* (Bombay: Veer Savarkar Prakashan, 1969).

5. Ramesh Patange, "The Struggle for Akhand Bharat," *Organiser*, 46(2), 1994, Independence Day special, pp. 41-43.
6. V.D. Savarkar, "Hindi sundari' quoted by Harinder Srivatava "Hind Sundarar Ti and Priyakar Hindusthan–Savarkar's hymns to Motherland," *Organiser*, 45(36), 10 April 1994.
7. L.K. Advani's Presidential Address, *BJP Pamphlet no. 66* (New Delhi: Bhartiya Janta Party Office, not dated), p. 6.
8. Rajeev Bhargava, "Introducing Multiculturalism," in Rajeev Bhargava, A.K. Bagchi, R. Sudershan, *Multiculturalism, Liberalism and Democracy* (New Delhi: Oxford University Press, 1999), pp. 1-59; Javeed Alam, "Public Sphere and Democratic Governance in Contemporary India," in Bhargava, n. 8, p. 328.
9. Susan Moller Okin, "Is Multiculturalism Bad for Women?" *Boston Review*, at www.bostonreview.net.
10. Bhargava, n. 8, p. 43.
11. Ibid., p. 49.